THE INVISIBLE GAME

MATHS, MINUTES AND MOVEMENT

KEVIN WALSH

WITH DARAGH Ó CONCHÚIR

www.**HERO**BOOKS.digital

HEROBOOKS

PUBLISHED BY HERO BOOKS
1 WOODVILLE GREEN
LUCAN
CO. DUBLIN
IRELAND

Hero Books is an imprint of Umbrella Publishing
First Published 2020
Copyright © Kevin Walsh and Daragh Ó Conchúir 2020
All rights reserved

ISBN 9781910827246

Cover design and formatting: jessica@viitaladesign.com
Ebook formatting: www.ebooklaunch.com
Photographs: Inpho and the Walsh family collection

Dedication

To my parents, Tom and Ann

My wife, Mary

And Caoimhe, Orlaith, Cathal, Laoise and Dara

Contents

ACKNOWLEDGEMENTS

THE PEOPLE WHO made me the man I am, and who continue to 'make me' a better man I hope, can never be thanked sufficiently. My mother and father, Ann and Tom. My wife, Mary, and our children Caoimhe, Orlaith, Cathal, Laoise and Dara.

I'm not forgetting my brothers and sisters, either, who made up the Walsh family in Doon, the townland in the small parish of Killannin. Tommy, Gerard, Breda, Bosco, Angela and Frank.

These are the people I need to thank first and foremost at the beginning of this book – but, in truth, they are people I thank every day. Mary most of all.

My life as a footballer and manager would not have been possible without her unflinching love and constant support, through the greatest times, the toughest of times, and the times in between when she never once questioned my ambition – or second-guessed the sacrifices she needed to make on my behalf.

Daragh Ó Conchúir did the heavy lifting on this book, and each time he visited my home and helped me walk through my life as a footballer and a manager his care and attention to detail, and total professionalism, made the 'work' much easier, and far more enjoyable, than I ever imagined. I thank him for his company, and his brilliant skills as an interviewer and a writer.

I also must thank Liam Hayes for introducing me to Daragh, and recommending him as my co-author. In addition, Liam and his team at Hero Books have been excellent in guiding me through the whole process of writing my memoir. When I first sat down with Liam, when he visited my home in Doon over 18 months ago, we set out to build a book that would be more than just a memoir – but would be there for players and coaches all over the country to help them in a practical way through their own careers.

This is the book we imagined from the very beginning, so thank you to Liam for being at my side and making it real.

There are others, of course, who have been so important in my life. So many good, kind people to me. Some of them are mentioned in the pages to come, and I hope I have done them justice in recollecting their precious roles in my upbringing as a sportsperson and, later, my life as a county footballer and manager. These are my school teachers, my coaches and, vitally, the people who always afforded me their time and knowledge from my home club, Killannin. It was in the club and also in national school where I found my first love for football.

We are a small club, in a small parish, but we have always boxed above our weight. And that does not happen by accident. It happens, and does so repeatedly, because of the great love the people in the club have for our games and their willingness to volunteer and help others. I was lucky, I guess.

Lucky to be born in the arms of such a club and a parish, and lucky with my schooling too. My secondary school, St Paul's afforded me the opportunity to excel on the basketball court and realise the great honour of representing my country on court. The individual and team honours, down through the years in basketball, were the result of exceptional care and attention I and others received.

With the life I have lived as a basketball player and a footballer, I've been lucky too to develop and sustain so many friendships. These friends made me, too. All of us helped one another to share so many values that we have been able to carry into so many other parts of our lives.

All the help I received, however, did not protect me from a life of pain as a sportsman. The injuries came early for me, but again I found people around me who were there for me, above and beyond. I need to mention one such person, while at risk I know of not mentioning so many others. But there is one person I must thank here and now.

Aofaine Walsh is a remarkable person and a brilliant physiotherapist who was there for me when I was a footballer in the early 1990s, and was still with me on my Galway management team right up to 2019.

Having spent my whole adult life out on the field and working the sideline, I have seen so many good people giving their all in the GAA – and not just in dressing-rooms in which I was housed. I want to say well done to everyone who gives their all as players and coaches, and who are willing to enter the arena of public life.

They do so knowing that only the very few ever achieve the 'success' that comes with medals and trophies. However, they know that success can be measured and shared in so many other ways. They also give of their time bravely, especially at elite level, where their best efforts are left at the mercy of commentators and analysts, some of them fair-minded, many of them unjust and unbalanced in their judgments.

I urge everyone who strives to compete at elite level, as a player and coach, to remain strong in their own convictions, and to continue to do what they know they are good at doing, and never allow the so called 'experts' who are paid good money often for sloppy analysis – and who often fail spectacularly in their lazy efforts – to never make them feel dispirited.

You are bigger than them. What you are doing as an amateur player and coach is of value to whole communities of people who appreciate who you are and what you are doing.

We put in the hard work.

We make the ultimate sacrifice. And it is tough at times, but it is also fun and amazingly enjoyable, which is the reason why we do it in the first place.

I have enjoyed the company of everyone I played with, and everyone I shared a sideline with as we managed teams to the best of our abilities. I thank you all for that company, and that unstinting support as a teammate and a management colleague.

Again, I have to say I was lucky.

I have been lucky to work with people who are brilliant and courageous. When I think of these people, I also think of the oath I made when I joined the Garda Siochána as a young man.

I remember saying that I would live my working life without 'fear, favour, malice or ill will'… and that I attempted to do.

But I have also met and worked on GAA teams with so many people who have upheld this same promise. These people are my heroes.

Thank you all.

Kevin Walsh
February 2021

★★★★★

THANKS TO DARAGH Small, Sharon Murray, Aonghus Ó Maicín and Kieran Shannon, for their invaluable help throughout this process.

There is a reason freelancing suits me and Liam Hayes recognises that. His hands-off approach is greatly appreciated. Even more appreciated is the boundless positivity, as well as the ego massaging when called upon, and needed.

Kevin was so helpfully enthusiastic about this project, flexible with regard to the challenges provided by the coronavirus and committed to making the book as good as it could be. No question was out of bounds and communication was constant. He was all-in, a pleasure for a writer.

The hospitality from Mary – who as readers will deduce, is clearly a saint – Caoimhe, Orlaith, Cathal, Laoise and Dara was very welcome. It's never easy walking into the house of someone you haven't met before and asking him to bear his soul. It must be harder being on the other side of that equation.

There is a huge element of trust there and the family will naturally be protective. You wouldn't have known it. I hope the trust wasn't misplaced.

Finally, in my own house, there is an equally saintly Mary. We are a team and if I am a touch of a gunslinger, she is the warrior who ensures we are consistently competing to win.

Until very recently, Alfie was another veteran warrior on our team.

We will never forget you.

Daragh Ó Conchúir
February 2021

Home Game

CHAPTER 1

79:1

I was part of that group that was in Division 2 and we couldn't get out of it but Kevin came in. When I played football with Kevin Walsh, we used to call him the daddy of the team, he was always organising us, telling us where to go, what to do. He always had that capability of the first (of us) that would be managing Galway.

He has left Galway in a great place. He has a lot of work done. He might have got a little bit of harsh criticism going at the end, but… I'm thankful he's left us in Division 1 and I'm taking over a team that are on the way up and an established Division 1 team. There shouldn't be a bad word said about Kevin Walsh.

– Pádraic Joyce, Galway Bay FM, November 4, 2019

HE COMES AT me, eyes bulging, finger pointing, spitting a venomous tirade. A man on a mission, he shapes like he's going to pop me one.

'Get Lavelle out of goal… the Connemara b*****ks. And all the rest of the Westies. Get them out to f**k.'

No wonder Ruairí has come off the field with tears in his eyes. It's the type of abuse he has been getting from some of his own just a few feet behind him over the course of the entire game, the same bile he got during the semi-final too, when he excelled as we beat Mayo by a point.

At least this beauty is targeting me rather than a young man who has acted completely to instruction.

But we have lost the Connacht final by nine points to Roscommon, so I'm feeling disconsolate. What's more, my 17 year-old son Cathal is with me, bearing witness to the ugliest side of county management.

I know this individual.

He has a club-based agenda, mired in that old north-west divide that has stunted progress through the generations, and militated against any hope of success since my own playing days when we won All-Irelands in 1998 and 2001, and contended at a high level consistently.

That our last great squad contained plenty of 'Westies', including Seán Óg de Paor, Seán Ó Domhnaill, Paul Clancy, Gary Fahey, Richie Fahey and me, has escaped the attention of my not-so-learned 'friend' and his ilk.

I like to deal in facts, but the problem is that oft-repeated perception becomes reality. When you have high profile media figures perpetuating a fallacy without any recourse to truth, whether that be because they have no understanding of what is going on or some other prejudice, the public latch onto it.

And it feeds idiots like the one throwing his inane, ill-informed crap right at me in Pearse Stadium on a July evening in 2017.

I feel like having a go at him, though I know I shouldn't. I was never sent off for club or county as a player, a record I am proud of, but when you played in the engine room in an era when all the kickouts are landing down upon you and you are battling men like Brian McGilligan, Paul McGrane, Pat Fallon, John Newton, Liam McHale and John McDermott, you had to be able to impose yourself. I never backed down.

A manager can't go decking members of the public, but I am not altogether sure there isn't a slap coming my way.

Cathal obviously thinks so. He is only a youngster, laid-back and relaxed by nature, so his response surprises me. He is incensed by the aggression and moves into protective mode. I am proud of that, but that Cathal is there and becoming involved angers me more. Your family and especially your children should not have to be exposed to that type of aggravation.

'You've made a laughing stock of us, you stupid b*****ks... getting hammered by Roscommon. What would you expect with two fellas from the f***ing Aran Islands because you were out there? And another from your own club?

'You're a f***ing disgrace.'

I flip and lunge towards him but the people around us hold me back. I still don't know if I would have hit him or if I just wanted to put the frighteners on him but am thankful that neither of us got to find out.

◆ ◆ ◆ ◆ ◆

THIRTEEN DAYS LATER, we annihilate Donegal in Markievicz Park by 4-17 to 0-14 in the qualifiers, when the consensus was that we were lame ducks waiting to be put out of our misery.

We work really hard as a management to lift the team after Roscommon but it is the players that drive everything. They are outstanding.

Ruairi is brilliant, carries out his role to a tee. Johnny Heaney, the clubmate referred to by my unhinged critic, scores 2-2 and is named Man of the Match. It is the consummate team performance, combining all the attacking and defensive elements required.

As I cross the pitch, who do I see walking towards me as if nothing had ever happened, only this Galwegian – I could never call him a supporter, because a supporter gets behind his team.

He wants to make nice. Suddenly we're great, and footballers and managers from the west are okay again.

'Go away!' I growl.

That wouldn't be the norm for me, especially after such a huge win. But he has crossed a line and I am not pretending everything is okay now by shaking his hand after the threatening, ignorant poison he had spewed at me, with my young son by my side.

The vitriol has become all too common, the reaction from the stands increasingly unstable from one game to the next; from one moment within a game to the next. The Wexford hurling manager, Davy Fitzgerald has spoken about the abuse he gets during matches frequently and did so again at the beginning of January 2021. He pointed to the nameless and faceless cohort that can write whatever they wish online. I thought about it a lot as the world ground to a halt last year (2020) due to Covid-19. People really missed sport at that time and there's a valuable lesson there.

There's a lot of vile diatribe at games now. People are doing their best, in the public eye, to provide some joy and yet you have those assholes that are just constantly negative. They need to re-evaluate their life philosophy, and those commenting in warm television and radio studios need to put more thought into the fuel they are providing such invective.

It is almost as if because they're paying good money at stiles, some people believe they are owed something and that's bullshit. It is good money but it's not near what the players are putting in on time. An ESRI study in 2018 found that the average time put in by a county player is 31 hours a week. Give him his minimum wage of €10 for that and you have €310. That's not €20 on the stile.

As a supporter, you should go through the full gamut of emotions and react instinctively when on a knife edge. That is part of the experience. And sometimes that will manifest itself in an outburst.

That's human. But the negative fool with a bias based on region, or his clubmate not being picked, is no supporter.

Sport is not life or death and should not precipitate persistently toxic vilification. The participants are giving everything to be the best they can be. For everyone else, it should be about enjoyment. The response to the old games shown on RTÉ and TG4 during the first lockdown in 2020 was a reminder of that.

♦ ♦ ♦ ♦ ♦

I WAS SO proud to become Galway manager.

I had played 17 years at senior level (1987-2004), added a pair of senior All-Irelands to the minor championship brought home in 1986, and had been named on three All Star teams, the third in 2003 when just a few weeks shy of turning 34. I had accumulated vast coaching experience by the time I took the job, in football and basketball, from club to county.

I finished with Sligo in 2013 after a very successful five-year period that included two Connacht final appearances, winning National Football League Division 4 and 3 titles in turn and setting a number of historical milestones.

I had only a year off from football management when Alan Mulholland stepped down after three seasons as Galway boss, and I had just opened the Moycullen office of CMCC Financial Solutions. The timing was far from ideal.

But I had been in Salthill as a supporter when Mayo beat Galway by 17 points in 2013. Andy Moran came on at the end, got a goal and raised his fists to the crowd as if it was an injury time winner. It was humiliation, and he was revelling in the humiliation. Mayo were rubbing our faces in it.

To hell with this, I thought to myself.

That got at me and I thought if my opportunity came, they wouldn't be doing that.

The chance to take on Mayo, the Connacht standard-bearers and in the top two in Ireland was a significant incentive. In time we did that, finishing my five seasons with a winning record against them and every team in Connacht, as we did against all bar three teams we played more than once in that term.

If I was coming in and committing to do it, I certainly wasn't going to come in without a plan and it was going to be actioned. I knew there would be a bit of pain. That's the habit curve, it takes time.

I had to be thick-skinned, take a bit of flak, and go after what I believed in.

I wouldn't be a person that's looking for controversy. If I felt I was right, I'd stand the course. What do I value? What's my attitude towards it? If my value isn't high enough, my attitude isn't going to be high enough. If you have a very big 'Why?', you're going to have a massive attitude. Conviction and action follow automatically.

My 'Why?' was to make Galway consistently competitive again, improve them to an extent that they would always be competing to win, not just pulling off the odd good victory here and there. That was what we achieved with Sligo, and we did it too at Galway, as the numbers demonstrate.

We had to shed the soft underbelly, stand up to teams like all the best Tribesmen had done. People talk about the swashbuckling Galway traditions of the three in-a-row team and the best sides I played in, but there was steel in those teams. That had been lost and Galway were easy to get at. They were rolling over.

We had to tear the whole lot down and start from scratch. That's not what you expect to need to do as a senior county manager, but it was necessary. That made it a long-term project. By 2018, Galway were unrecognisable from the team that threw in the towel in 2013. We ended that year as the second-best team in the country.

Not that the players got much credit for that. Many so-called experts were against us by then and we weren't going to get praise, not to mention balanced viewpoints. How Shane Walsh did not get an All Star that year will forever be a mystery to me. There would be little context when it came to Galway, little dealing in fact. Just populist generalisations.

That happened with referees in the last couple of years of my five-year term too. But we'll come to that.

◆ ◆ ◆ ◆ ◆

YOU PLAN FOR 80 minutes in a county game, allowing for injury time. The ratio of that period that a player is out of possession and in possession is *79:1*.

In fact, the average time in possession is under one minute, but we'll round it up. In my opinion, it is ludicrous for a coach to be happy that a player is not attempting to influence the game for 79 out of 80 minutes, or 69 out of 70 if you are discussing club fare.

People would come to interpret that viewpoint as defensive, getting players into a good structure when the opposition are on the ball, but workrate is just as important when you are trying to build an attack as it is attempting to foil one. In the first instance, you are trying to create space. In the second, you must take it away.

You need all your players involved in both scenarios. After all, even when you are making an offensive foray, only one player has the ball. Runs to provide options, decoy runs to draw away cover, V-Cuts and screens are just some of the methods used by players without the ball to create a chance.

The scorer will get the praise, but others have had a crucial influence without ever touching the ball.

And it is the same defensively. Just filling a space early can be the difference between the opposition getting a score or not. The move won't get a player a headline, or an All Star, but it has had a positive bearing on his team's performance.

Having an extra man comfortable in possession in your own half is supremely advantageous when it comes to creating openings, especially when teams are pushing up extremely high on you. In basketball, it's called a full-court press.

BASKETBALL HAS HAD a significant influence on my coaching, in terms of philosophy and application.

I played for Ireland at underage level before concentrating on football and continue to coach the sport to this day. There is much to be learned from it, as there is from other sports such as rugby and hockey. You are foolish if you are insular in that regard.

Good coaches are always looking to evolve. It is customary in the GAA to criticise them for that, and if influential elements of the media are against it, the public soon will be.

I smiled to myself when I heard it described as 'revolutionary' that Jim Gavin was bringing in Mark Ingle, the well-known basketball coach in 2015 to help work on closing off space defensively and creating it against packed defences, after Donegal had picked them off for 3-14 in the 2014 All-Ireland semi-final. I was teaching V-Cuts, leveraging and screens a long time in football by that stage.

Using the goalie as an extra man was part of my expansive thinking. When Sligo beat Galway in the 2012 semi-final at Pearse Stadium, Philip Greene took the ball 23 times. He was a central cog of a game plan that was processed over two and a half years to suck opposition players in all around the field.

It secured a first championship victory on Galway soil for the Yeats County. We used the spare man then to get behind our opponents and create opportunities. Adrian Marren was the primary beneficiary, scoring 2-6, of which 1-4 came from play. The other goal came from a penalty after we had carved Galway open and Paul McGovern was fouled.

Obviously, I was going to look to do the same at Galway and the tactic would work a treat against Mayo, who loved the press. Roscommon picked off a few of Ruairí's kickouts at the stadium in 2017 from which they scored but he was not afraid of the ball and had the skills as well as the mindset to carry out the plan. This was only his second championship game remember and he was 23 years-old.

HE WASN'T ON the radar yet though when I started. Mánus Breathnach was the man in possession but we always tried a lot of players in the league – building depth was going to be a foundation of becoming competitive, along with improving the culture, attitude, process and skillset.

For a fifth round Division 2 tie with Laois, Brian O'Donoghue had the jersey. Brian, a gentleman through and through, came into the squad first in 2003, when I was still playing, and was very experienced, though more accustomed to the traditional way of playing as a goalie.

After winning our first two games, we had lost to Down by a point and then to Cavan by two. We played with a gale in the first-half and led by six points at the break. It should have been more but Donie Kingston got a goal completely against the run of play after dispossessing Brian, who was doing what we asked of him, bringing the ball out to draw in the opposition.

We didn't score into the unforgiving elements in the second-half. Unfortunately for Brian, we turned over another short kickout late on and Tom Shiel lobbed him for the goal that stole Laois' triumph.

The overall performance wasn't bad and I was not down in the dumps about it. No more than we turned things around after winning our first two games, we were not suddenly the dregs after three narrow losses.

We had a bit of a debrief afterwards and when the players left, the management had our own conversation about it. A high-ranking county board official was hanging around, glancing over every now and then. When he was still there an hour and a half later, it was obvious he had a bee in his bonnet about something.

'That wasn't good', he says.

'Who are ya telling? Jaysus, we're sick as a parrot after that.'

'Yeah, but it wasn't good.'

'Oh no… it wasn't.'

I don't want to get into a row but this isn't Jim Gavin stepping into Pat Gilroy's shoes here. This is a complete rebuild. What was he, or anyone else expecting after a few months?

'There were a few lads out there that just weren't happy losing such a big lead and all that short stuff at the back,' he continues.

That riles me a little.

'Do you think I'm happy about it?' I say.

'No,' comes the answer, 'but it's something that has to be addressed.'

This must be nipped in the bud. Right now.

'Did ye put me in as manager?'

'Yeah but…'

'Hold on a sec now,' I tell him. 'Either you back me or you don't back me. I have a vision I want to develop and I'm going to stick with it. Either you get lost, or I'll get lost… or you'll back me. Take your pick.'

The man in question was Galway through and through. He wanted what was best for the county and was responding to a few lads giving him an earache. In fairness, he backed off.

We got plenty of support over the five years but the board maintained its tendency of responding to every little groan and moan, instead of focusing on constructing permanent and long-term building blocks, so as to ensure a more professional coaching structure and player production line.

We went on to win the next two games and only just missed out on promotion but it was for the best. We weren't ready. When we did make the step up, we got to the Division 1 final first time around.

In 2019, we developed so much that despite being shorn of around 10 players with an horrendous catalogue of injuries, we were still a win away from reaching the decider again. That campaign was one of the most satisfying of the five years, given how short we were. The players trusted completely in the process and were mentally strong enough to deal with the multitude of setbacks over which they had no control. And the squad was deep enough to ensure we remained competitive.

Pádraic Joyce acknowledged as much when he took over the reins and declared that winning an All-Ireland was a realistic goal.

I started the job in 2015 and when I passed on the baton, it was with Galway in a much better place, with a strong panel in every sense, and an average age of between 24 and 25. It was a squad capable of being in the mix for all the honours on a consistent basis.

That is success.

You are always learning but my belief system – who I am, what I am and what I believe to be fundamental in life and in sport – came from home.

From the family and the land.

CHAPTER 2

BELONGING

Each blade of grass has its spot on earth whence it draws its life, its strength; and so is man rooted to the land from which he draws his faith together with his life.
— Joseph Conrad, Lord Jim (1900)

Ar scáth a chéile a mhaireann na daoine.
— Irish proverb

DOON IS WHERE I was founded and forged. A townland in the small parish of Killannin overlooking Lough Corrib, it made me who I am. Wherever I went, I could never leave it behind. Nor did I want to.

When it came to building a home to share with my wife Mary and what would conclude at a quintet of children, I did so on a couple of acres I knew every inch of, less than half a mile from the house I grew up in and where my father Tom was brought up before that.

He died of cancer in 2002 but my mother Ann still lives there and it is a tremendous comfort to us that we can look out the window and see one another. To be able to visit during the Covid-19 lockdown was a luxury we did not take for granted.

She is a mother by nature as well as biological actuality, drawn to looking after people. Apart from her own seven children, she was taking elderly neighbours under her wing from my earliest memory and did so until my father was diagnosed in 2000. She is an innately nurturing person.

I like to think some of that caring disposition passed onto me. I believe it is an integral element of leadership, along with courage and consistency. I certainly placed a heavy emphasis on it as a player and manager. I have always taken an interest in players' lives away from the football pitch or basketball court, and offered a helping hand where possible, even if that was just as a sounding board. It is a lot easier to get the best out of someone with a relationship of trust rather than one of fear.

My mother is from Rosscahill, two miles away, and was 20 when she married my then 33 year-old father at Killannin Church in 1961. They became known years later as Mom Mom and Bom Bom, because of how they were initially greeted by their first grandchild, my sister Breda's daughter, Laura Molloy. The names stuck, not just with the rest of the grandchildren, but with their neighbours as well.

I always hankered to be back in this place. In 1989, I went to Boston to play football and with work at a premium in Ireland, had a notion that I might stay and make a go of it. It wasn't long before I realised I was too bound to where I had grown to fly the coop. Ego prevented me from just hopping on the plane, however. I didn't want it to seem like I couldn't hack it. I needed an excuse.

In the end, an evening invitation to a wedding was enough.

Later, when I was a Garda stationed in Blacklion, on the Cavan side of the Northern Ireland border with Belcoo in Fermanagh, I thought of home a lot.

In five years doing the four-hour minimum round trip to Sligo, at either end of meetings and training sessions, not once did I stay overnight. Even as the cumulative nature of it all made it more arduous towards the end, I wanted to lay down in my own bed at night, surrounded by my people, and the sounds and smells of the fields I had played and laboured in. I am not alone in that. Most of my brothers and sisters are still close by.

Apart from working in Dublin for a short while, my father never left. Plenty of his 11 siblings spread their wings and he became the heir to the throne under Doon Mountain. It wasn't a rich inheritance, 10 acres of hilly property, but it was Walsh land from which we wrung every bit of its potential and where I built my own home with a fierce sense of pride and belonging.

My father could never have reared us off such a small holding, so he worked full-time in the forestry. The jobs were done before and after work – before and after school in our case – and on Saturdays. Sunday was the day of rest, or the day to be taken to some sort of sporting event.

I WAS THE fifth child, born on November 5, 1969 in Galway Hospital. There are nine years between the first six of us; Tommy, Gerry, Breda, Bosco (who was christened John), me and Angela. Frank is the baby, 10 years younger than Angela. I ended up minding him because by the time he was two, the first four had moved out.

We weren't loaded but we were happy and never felt like we wanted for anything. The familial cord could not be broken but the bond with the land, our environment and the people was strong also. There is a reason we never wanted to stray far for long.

The work was hard. My father was a quiet man but he knew what sweat and toil meant. He didn't fear it. He embraced it. We were expected to contribute from a young age.

We give Frank a hard time because he had it far easier than us. He had a small tractor. He had a sausage machine for the turf. It was a very different story for us, when we got our hands blistered and cut and dirtied.

My father had to eke everything possible from his 10 acres of mountainside arable land so it was highly intensive farming. You had to manage what was available to you. To me, that is the best sign of managers in any walk of life, that they can maximise their resources.

I take great satisfaction myself as a sports mentor from being successful in a broad spectrum of activities, at different levels. We are still going strong with the teenagers at Corrib Basketball Club and have been doing so for a while now.

In football, I operated in all four divisions of the National League with Sligo and Galway, reaching the finals of each and winning three of them, raising expectations with the former, restoring them with the latter. I managed at senior, intermediate, junior and underage level with Killannin, Aran Islands and Micheál Breathnach's, and coached Galway's senior ladies' footballers. There were significant accomplishments in most of those settings, be it reaching a county senior final with Killannin or winning a *Comórtas Peile na Gaeltachta* championship with The Islands and Michael Breathnachs.

It is one thing prevailing when everything is at your disposal. It is another entirely to do so without the figurative 10,000 acres, 1,000 cows or in horseracing terms, a barn full of Galileo progeny. That is not to say that operating among the elite is easy.

This scenario provides another set of demands.

You must adapt to a particular set of circumstances, which is why doing well at each tier is the ultimate measure of achievement.

♦ ♦ ♦ ♦ ♦

THERE WAS AROUND 625 acres of commonage ground on Doon Mountain. Though unusable in winter because it was covered in heather, it proved invaluable to the families with access to it in the summer, when we could save our own grass for winter fodder.

In the early years we had no running water so one of the first jobs any of us had was to go down to the well about a quarter of a mile away with buckets to get a supply. Potatoes and oats were sown by hand, something you were eligible for as soon as you were of a school-going age. You would dig the potatoes up with spades.

We had three cows. We milked them by hand before school and again in the evening. One of those cows was milked for the house, from which we churned our own butter. I loved homemade butter and it took a long while before I could eat shop butter. My mother baked 'caiscín' (wholemeal brown bread) from the butter milk. We would buy four or five calves as well and the milk from the other two cows would be used to feed them, watered down and mixed with some bits of leftover bread.

Some of my schoolmates might have been watching *Wanderly Wagon* while I was cutting potatoes for the cattle's fodder or hauling out a *beart* (bundle) of hay for them to munch on. This was loose hay we would have packed into the sheds for the winter. You'd pull it out, tie it together with a rope and throw it over your shoulder to carry it out to the field.

I became a dab hand with the slash hook to cut the briars back, and the scythe for the corn. You'd tie the corn then with its wisps and the guy with the threshing machine would come. That was a great community event.

It was the same with the turf. Each sod was cut individually with a *sleán* and you spread it with barrows. The neighbours would congregate at the bog to help and that applied to whoever was harvesting a crop or cutting and bringing in turf.

There were about 25 families around the commonage and the shared circumstances engendered a wonderful spirit. We were all making the best of what we had, looking out for one another. Friendships were moulded and solidified on a *meitheal*, or 'a big day' as it was known, when there was a communal event helping out a farmer haul the turf or harvest a crop.

When you endure difficult and positive times together, uniting and grafting for a mutual purpose, a connection is formed that strengthens you further.

When we were aged between around five and nine, we had the job of going around collecting money on a Saturday for the Church. There were little pockets within the parish that were broken up and ours revolved around this two-mile loop where we lived and where I still live. You knew every single person and would do odd jobs for them too.

The church was another community focal point. It is situated next to Maloney Park, the GAA grounds. We went to mass as a family every Sunday and at that time, most of the parish would be in attendance.

More than 40 years later, we are still regular mass goers. I have always retained that bit of faith, and the hope it provides people, something we all needed in the past year due to the Covid onslaught. Before the bigger matches, I would always have visited graves. I wouldn't be quoting the Bible at you but it is just one more aspect of life passed on by my parents, and when we were children especially, it was a weekly gathering of our friends and neighbours,

That developed to the building of our own community centre in the last 15 years. We are small but we don't think small. It attests to the spirit within Killannin parish that we have a community centre admired by many neighbouring parishes.

The 'big day' was great fun but contained an ultimate goal. The work had to be done and if someone was acting the maggot and being a hindrance to progress, they would be taken to task. There was an old saying… 'Talking never brought home the turf' and it has basis in truth.

I HAVE ALWAYS appreciated the benefits of labour and was never someone who would just clock in the normal daytime hours. When I was in the Guards and building houses at the same time, that was obviously the case, as it is in the financial services sector. The same applies to the coaching of sports teams.

Industry without ego was what I valued most on the pitch as a player, and later as a manager. The value of the collective over the individual. I always admired the hewers of wood and drawers of water, who never hit the headlines but were central to success.

On a practical level, due to the manual work, I developed a core strength that is very hard to get in a gym. This is why good strength and conditioning coaches develop programmes that replicate the jobs in the fields, such as throwing heavy objects across your body.

Being strong around the hips was one of my greatest attributes and when people talked about how good I was at the throw-in, that was why. The same under a kickout. Yeah, I could field a ball but more importantly, particularly as my knees became such a problem, I could outmuscle my opponents and take ownership of the piece of ground I wanted. That was all about the hips, the core. Not grappling or wrestling.

That wasn't all I developed at home, even though I would not have thought about it for a second at the time, or even much when I was playing. Footwork is criminally undercoached in football. In basketball, I start the eight year-olds off with basic movements. I did it with Sligo and Galway in a variety of indoor arenas to good effect. But I was trained in it by nature.

If my father told me to take the three heifers away from the four bullocks and put them in a different field, it had to be done. You could not come home and say you weren't able. It might take three or four turns to get them through the first gate. Eventually you'd get a bit smarter, realise you needed to step back a yard because the heifers were beating you on one side or the other. Every time they beat you, they were gone back up to the top of the field. Your consequence was, 'Go up and get them again'. Meanwhile, they became more agitated, making the job harder.

There were a few things in that.

You became better at understanding space, when to close it down and how; at knowing the difference even half a yard left or right could make, and when the time was to make that move and apply a bit of coaxing pressure rather than physical pressure, which just didn't pay off with a cow.

This was all about having the right body position.

It was just like corralling a player down an alley you wanted them to go, but particularly one who was faster than you – if you over-committed by just a yard, they had you beaten and you were chasing them, having to do a lot more work than you needed to if you had gotten it right first time.

So, you needed to be standing at a 45-degree position, able to react quickly but all the while shepherding your target in a direction that suits you and not them.

There was also the problem-solving aspect to it. You had a set of circumstances, with no option but to achieve a certain result. It is up to you, in real time, to come up with the answers.

Bosco and I were invariably the two who would have to drive the livestock to the mountain in the morning and it was always a race back home. We were competitive, we wanted to win, but it wasn't like a flat 400m track.

So, you had to take in everything around you, make split-second deductions and choose a course based on that.

When you were young, you got it wrong a few times, hit a patch of ground that looked dry but wasn't and went down through it. You learned that you needed to be two steps to the left tomorrow.

I was invariably a thinker on the pitch and as hard as I ran and grappled and fought, my mind was working the most. Playing smart will get the better of a well-meaning headless chicken any day of the week.

◆ ◆ ◆ ◆ ◆

THERE WASN'T A lot of downtime but my father always made space for sport.

He never played himself, probably because he was too busy, but he encouraged us. His brother Michael was a very good footballer who played with Oughterard in a county final in the 1950s. He joined the Guards and was posted around the country, becoming a superintendent in Dublin.

Another of his brothers Pete, was a sergeant in Gort who was heavily involved in Galway Bord Lúthchleas Óganach na hÉireann (BLOE). The was the underage arm of Bord Lúthchleas na hÉireann (BLE), which merged with the National Athletic and Cycling Association of Ireland (NACAI) to form Athletics Ireland in 2000.

We were introduced to athletics young in Oughterard.

My father brought us and a few other children from around the parish. Himself and my mother had been involved for years (when all of us were young) in sporting committees in the parish – like the parish Community Games – to make sure that all local children got a chance to participate in sport and, if good enough, go on to represent Killannin at county level, and if successful there advance to represent Galway in Mosney at the All-Irelands. My brother Tommy represented Galway in the under-14 long jump in Mosney, winning a bronze medal. My parents never got involved beyond that, being the antithesis of the 'pushy parents'. They saw the value in sport and for all the work that had to be done at home, it never got in the way of football, basketball or athletics.

My father didn't say much, win or lose.

You rarely got a sense of what it might have meant to him when I was playing for Ireland or winning All-Irelands in shot put, basketball and football – but even if he did not say much I would see his face light up with pride.

Being already very tall and strong, I was directed towards discus, javelin, shot put, long jump and triple jump. I won an under-11 All-Ireland in shot put in 1980, throwing 9.25 metres. That was only 13 centimetres off the championship record at the time. I won Connacht and county championships in the other disciplines.

It's funny the way genetics work.

Tommy is 5'8".

Gerard is 6'4".

Breda's about 5'8".

Bosco is 5'10".

I'm 6'4".

Angela is about 5'9".

And Frank is 6'4".

I haven't grown an inch since I was 13 and thanks to the physical labour, I wasn't like a newborn foal. I was 14 and a half stone, playing midfield for Killannin footballers and holding my own.

OUR OWN CHILDREN are all tall and they have it on both sides as Mary is close to six feet herself. She contributes significant sporting DNA as well.

Born Mary Dolphin, from Mullagh, she was a dazzling camogie player who won five All-Ireland schools' titles with St Raphael's.

Two of those came at junior and 1985 was particularly momentous, as not only was she captain for the second junior triumph, she played in the senior success the very same day.

She would add two more senior championships to her tally before leaving Raphael's but the Dolphin story didn't finish there, as her sister Tríona captained the five in-a-row unit of 1989. Raphael's would go on to make it eight, which remains a record to this day. Mary's brother Seán was an excellent hurler, who played in the All-Ireland under-21 final for Galway in 1987.

Mullagh was the club and it was a huge occasion when they won their first county title in 1989, following up with a Connacht. They lost the All-Ireland final to an all-conquering St Paul's unit completing a three in-a row. By the time Mullagh returned to Croke Park two years later to scale the summit, Mary had joined the Guards and was based in Dublin, no longer able to commit to club or county.

Later on, she turned her hand to coaching and was heavily involved in the Galway ladies' football development squads, taking charge of the under-12s and involved in the management of the county under-14 and under-16 teams. Some of the players that won the All-Ireland senior championship in 2004 would have gone through her hands at some stage.

Our eldest, Caoimhe (22) is touching six feet. She used to play basketball with Corrib and ladies' football with Killannin. Orlaith (21) is 5'10", which isn't short, but it makes her the shortest in our house. She represented Galway and Connacht in underage basketball. The pair of them were on the St Paul's team that bagged the All-Ireland Post-Primary Schools' under-19B League and Cup double in 2015-2016.

Orlaith was on the Maree panel that won the Division 1 National League title in 2019, with Laoise (18), who is six feet and has been on under-16 and under-18 Ireland development teams.

Cathal (20) stands at 6'6". He emulated Caoimhe and Orlaith when part of a National under-19B League and Cup-winning St Paul's outfit, this time in 2017-18. That was lovely because I was on the school's All-Ireland-winning team of 1986 and contributed to triumphant under-17 and under-15 squads too.

Cathal was also on the St Paul's football team that reached the All-Ireland post-primary schools' senior C decider in 2019 as well, and then the Killannin side that made the county under-20B football final. He is pushing to break through to the club's senior team now.

The youngest of the clan is Dara (16), who is already an inch taller than me at 6'8". He has been called into Galway's minor football development squad and was a member of the Ireland under-16 basketball set-up when Covid brought indoor sport to a halt last year.

♦ ♦ ♦ ♦ ♦

I ACCUMULATED A multitude of Galway and Connacht titles in basketball and athletics through my teens but it is the one I didn't win that stands out. The sting of defeat would always imprint itself on my psyche more than any satisfaction of victory.

Anyway, I was second in the under-14 shot put at the 1983 Community Games All-Ireland finals at Mosney. By then, team sport was more attractive, for a variety of reasons, not least the sociability of it.

That sense of a group striving to achieve something together, sharing triumphs and disappointments, had more appeal than the solitary nature of doing your own thing.

So did the contact and non-stop action. And I always felt that we were representing our place as a group, where despite the singlet, individual competition just felt like me doing it for myself.

Either way, I always wanted to win.

The shot put was in the morning and with each of the 30 participants having three throws, it was a monotonously drawn out process. The top six would get another three attempts to improve their distance.

I was under a bit of pressure for time as Killannin were in the under-16 basketball semi-final, which was scheduled for Gormanston College early in the afternoon and that was my priority. Growing anxious I might miss it, I asked the officials if I could do my throws consecutively. Thankfully, they saw no harm in it.

Clearly there was no advantage to me. In fact it was a disadvantage, having no recovery time and no chance to react to the distances posted by my rivals. But it was all about the basketball so I got in there and let them fly.

Bang... Bang... BANG.

It was two or three miles to Gormanston, I think, and off I ran across the fields.

I arrived just as the lads, led by Bosco, who was captain, were walking onto the court. We played the game and lost but would seal the bronze medal in a play-off with a school in Cavan. The All-Ireland would be ours the following two seasons but being in the future, that was no consolation then.

When it was over, I tore back to Mosney.

The shot put had just concluded when I landed. I was second, beaten a centimetre, without getting to complete the second set of throws. Finishing that close left me gutted and feeling a little cheated.

Incidentally, the winner was a guy called Jarlath Gilroy, who I would come across in subsequent years when he played with Kildare, although he had departed the scene by the time we got the better of the Lilywhites in the 1998 All-Ireland final.

◆ ◆ ◆ ◆ ◆

IT IS REMARKABLE really that such a minute region has produced so much success in a range of different sports. The parish has grown a bit with people moving into the area but even back in the 1990s, there wouldn't have been more than 400 houses. The pride and visceral connection we felt to the region had to be at the heart of it.

Basketball was to play a central role in my life thanks to the passion of a brilliant teacher and coach, Mary Nihill (née Conlon), who revitalised the game at St Paul's Secondary School. Not just did basketball have an inherent influence on how I played football and coached it later, Mary did too as a truly brilliant mentor.

We went all the way from this tiny school and later at Corrib, which was benefiting from the Nihill nursery and where Kevin Blehein was doing a lot of good work too, to numerous successes in county, provincial and national competitions.

I would play for Ireland at under-15, under-17 and under-19 in the same year (1984) and Tony O'Connor, Kevin O'Reilly, Patrick Faherty, Ann Marie Kyne and Mary Kyne also emerged from St Paul's to represent the country. But then that tradition had been there from the school's foundation in 1964, producing future National League players of the calibre of Ita Walsh, but it took Mary to light the fires once more.

Another from the area who represented us internationally was Mick Molloy, who ran the marathon in the green singlet at the 1968 Olympics in Mexico, battling extreme temperatures to finish 41st of 75 competitors.

Niamh Fahey is considered one of the best female soccer players Ireland has ever produced. She was still only 16 when propelling Galway to their only All-Ireland ladies football championship in 2004.

By then, Niamh was already standing out as an elite operator in the no-hands code. Having established herself with Salthill Devon, scoring the definitive penalty in the FAI Women's Cup in 2007, she went on to garner three league titles and five FA Cups with Arsenal. She also played with Chelsea and Bordeaux and is currently captain of Liverpool.

At international level, she is closing in on a century of caps for Ireland and has been named Player of the Year on three occasions. She remains a key contributor as the Girls In Green target an historic first major championship qualification.

♦ ♦ ♦ ♦ ♦

THE CELEBRATIONS WERE long and hard around Killannin when Galway won the All-Ireland in 1998, with Niamh's brother Gary and myself on the team, and another Fahey sibling Richie on the bench.

That came 12 years after the All-Ireland minor, where I mirrored the feat of another Killannin man, Tom O'Connor in playing midfield in a successful Galway under-18 group. Fantastically for our family, Bosco came on as a sub, after picking up an injury in the semi-final.

Galway's senior triumph of 2001 was the standout for Killannin though, with Richie having forced himself into the 15 and Gary becoming the first son of Connemara to be presented with the Sam Maguire Cup. You cannot downplay what that meant and still means, when you're constantly battling for your place in the world, operating out of your weight division against traditional superpowers and even locally, boxed in by the major towns, Moycullen and Oughterard. Killannin, like Killkerrin, had the largest number of starters from any club in the county.

It was a proud time for St Paul's Secondary School also, as the Killannin trio as well as Matthew Clancy and Pádraig Boyce from Oughterard were all past pupils. Only St Jarlath's provided more to those two panels.

We have always flourished in the face of a challenge. From the time we were born, we had not encountered easy.

It made us better.

There are managers in business and sport all over the world who would pay big bucks to replicate and cultivate that sort of culture. You cannot advance without it.

PART TWO

Playing the Game

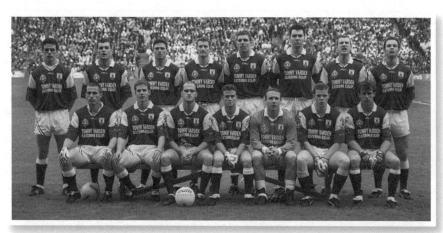

CHAPTER 3

HOOP DREAMS

I challenge you to take me into one of the classrooms across the land and have someone teach me something about teamwork, loyalty, self-discipline, sacrifice, unselfishness, determination, commitment and hard work. There are no such classrooms, but all these things are taught on our basketball courts daily.

– Earl 'Red' Blaik

Basketball gave him the vision he had playing Gaelic football. The awareness, the lightness of the feet for such a big man. There is many a Galway footballer who will tell you he is the best passer of a ball they've played with. He had great soft hands.

– John Tobin, Irish Independent, June 25, 2010

LUCK PLAYS A role in any success. You can have heart, motivation and ability along with a good plan, process and workrate but still not get over the line because of one hop of the ball, not executing at key moments or a couple of refereeing decisions have gone against you.

It was serendipitous that Mary Nihill had just begun teaching at St Paul's when I went into first year of secondary school. She would influence me as much as anyone in my life, both in how I played and coached.

St Paul's did possess a strong basketball tradition but had been struggling for a while by the early 1980s. Mary changed that, but it wasn't plain sailing. For the first six months, I didn't like what she was doing at all but she was forcing a change of habit and that can be difficult to accept. From the coach's perspective, once you believe in what you are doing, you must stay the course in the face of resistance. We came around to Mary's way of thinking because we saw its value as we improved.

Her messaging was so uncomplicated and consistent.

She created a culture, though nobody talked about culture in that context then.

She set high standards when it came to discipline. It wasn't severe, just straightforward things like being on time for training, and not wavering from game plans. Regardless of your proficiency, if you did your own thing on the court, you were warming the bench very quickly.

Before Mary, training consisted of just playing a game. Mary brought structure and commitment. She organised training three times a week, where she worked on establishing her principles, patterns of play and honing our skills. She was particularly good on footwork and movement.

Two of her key principles were having the hands up at all stages in the passing and shooting lanes, meaning you were covering as much space as possible; and being loud, using the mouth. Communication was intrinsic to teamwork.

The dividends this professional approach yielded were rich.

Within two years, we had won the All-Ireland at under-15, a game in which things went well for me and I scored 53 points. We added an under-17 championship and appeared in three consecutive under-19 deciders, annexing the senior A title by overcoming Dublin powerhouse and defending champions Coláiste Caoimhín in 1986, when I was lucky enough to be named MVP after shooting 40 points.

Such a run inevitably caught the attention of the national selectors. Tony O'Connor, Kevin O'Reilly, Patrick Faherty and I played for Ireland around that time, as did Ann Marie and Mary Kyne from the girls' teams. I got my first under-15 nod in 1983 and it was a thrill to represent the country on Galway territory, in a jam-packed Renmore Sports Complex against Scotland.

I was named on the under-15, under-17 and under-19 lists in 1984. Tony joined me on the under-15 squad, having been on the 14s the year before. I remember us losing in Scotland but Tony was selected MVP and I was top scorer.

One of my first under-15 games was against England; I was as tall as most of the team, despite being much younger but was given the job of picking up a guy who was 6'11". He had long, blond hair. It was a tough environment.

You had to find solutions, quickly, or you sank.

Two years later, Kevin, Tony and I were on the Irish under-17 panel after our contributions to a Mary Nihill-coached triumph with Connacht in the Inter-Regional Cup, and of course winning the All-Ireland with St Paul's.

We took all of this for granted. We expected to flourish. We were oblivious to how extraordinary it was for minnows from a three teacher co-ed school in rural west Galway to go toe-to-toe with behemoths of the stature of North Mon in Cork, St Malachy's of Belfast, St Declan's in Dublin, Colaiste Caoimhín or Magherafelt High School in Derry, and to be making such a considerable contribution to the national cause.

We were part of something special and Mary deserves the credit. Yes, she had the players, but she mentored us tremendously.

St Paul's are still enjoying some success but the dynamics have changed. For my generation, it was the teachers driving our cultivation and much of the success with either Corrib Basketball Club or in Community Games was founded on what coaching and training was provided at school, although Kevin Blehein offered good guidance with Corrib.

It would be wrong to say that the volunteer element of teaching has vanished but it is far less prevalent. That is to the detriment of the pupils, particularly given the different types of challenges they are facing compared to people of my age bracket, not least on their mental health with the advent of social media especially.

Now the clubs are doing the hard yards to bring players through and while that is a positive development, this process should always have been taking place in tandem with schools. In terms of whatever sport is involved, kids are missing out when they are not getting high performance training in school and the impact of this fall-off is evident throughout the country.

◆ ◆ ◆ ◆ ◆

WE HAD BECOME so strong as a group it was decided that an amalgamation of players from St Paul's and Mountbellew should try out for the National League in the 1986-87 season. The combination gelled well.

We qualified for Division 3, which was an astonishing accomplishment. Bosco was captain of this historic Team Corrib Hotel unit. Mary was the only female head coach in the entire league, with John Fahy manager, and we were the youngest team to ever participate in the competition.

I was still only 16 when the campaign began and we had a solid season, with the crowds turning out in force for our home games at Westside Community Centre.

I was already experiencing a lot of problems with my knees and groins at this juncture. Playing on so many teams undoubtedly contributed to that. If you're playing adult football at 13, there are under-14, under-16, minor and under-21 commitments as well that same season. You have your junior and senior schools' teams. Add the variety of age groups at school and club basketball and then, representative teams with Galway and Ireland in both codes.

I wanted to play but when you are involved in international basketball at three age groups in one year, when I look back on it now, I realise I was not being looked after. I should have been protected from myself.

I was the perfect example of a schoolboy athlete being overplayed while still developing in a musculoskeletal sense. I was exposed to training and playing loads that were excessive for the body of a developing adolescent, even one as powerful as mine. Moving from the soft ground for football to hard courts for basketball accentuated the problem.

Travelling directly from one game to the next without changing back into my clothes wasn't unusual and of course with the basketball, you might be travelling considerable distances; the lactic acid building up in the legs and the knees stiffening up.

My mother often said I rarely had a pair of trousers on me and she wasn't wrong.

IT WAS A different era, without any of the scientific knowledge and medical support that exists now. Nobody knew what training loads were. I was tall, strong and athletic. Everyone wanted me to play on every team, to push through the pain and worry about an injury after the game. And I was enthusiastic about doing so.

At first, around 1987, I started getting the type of pain you might feel from a dead leg. This could last a couple of months rather than a couple of days.

Patellofemoral syndrome, or jumper's knee as it is better known, developed and I had chronic groin problems from my first groin injury in 1992 playing with the Garda College in the Trench Cup. That lingered for years.

Even after I gave up basketball, this lack of knowledge and care characterised my first decade as a Galway senior footballer, really until John O'Mahony's arrival as manager for the 1998 season.

An inguinal hernia contributed to much of the groin trouble that plagued me. Meanwhile, I had three operations on both of my knees, including when a bit of the patella broke off against Kerry in the All-Ireland final replay in 2000.

Despite the catalogue of injuries even as a young man, it hadn't really dawned on anyone that there might be a root physical cause or at least a major contributory one apart from overuse. Instead, because there was no blood or a cast, you were doubted. The perception that I was soft existed in some circles for much of my Galway career.

I was aware of this train of thought and it was insulting to me, given my upbringing.

It was embarrassing to be missing so much. I did very little in the early 90s. I might play one game and then miss out on three. I was in discomfort most of the time and just wasn't contributing.

I didn't want to let anyone down, particularly the people of Rosscahill, who had supported me and my family all our lives and were so proud that I was representing them in Ireland and Galway jerseys. But I wasn't managed well.

Being thrown into full-forward on one leg, with the other lads told to throw it in high on top of you might have been considered 'minding' you, but it wasn't. And then people criticised that you weren't doing what you did in Croke Park as a 16 year-old, but I was in no condition to.

In an interview with the *Irish Independent* many years later, when I was with Sligo, John Tobin recalled putting me out against Dublin when I was injured and regretting doing so as I suffered another setback. That was just the culture at the time, that you would push through it.

The first thing John O'Mahony did when he came in was put me through a full biomechanics assessment with the Galway physio Aofáine Walshe, to try and get to the bottom of what was going on and then provide me with what I needed to be able to perform at my optimum level. The evaluation lasted three hours and Aofáine knew she was in for a challenge as I listed off the variety of ailments.

After a while she asked me to take off my shoes and socks.

I was mildly perturbed. I never had any problem with my feet. She explained that it was necessary when doing an assessment of this nature. This is all run-of-the-mill stuff now but it meant nothing to me then. Throughout all the treatment I had gotten until then, at 28 years of age, it was my first time undergoing such an evaluation.

It emerged that I had flat feet, low arches and one leg longer than the other. My balance was so bad I could not stand on one leg and there were different parts of my body overcompensating for the various deficiencies. Many of the muscle pulls and strains would have had a basis in this biomechanical flaw which when added to the ridiculous workload of my teens led to many issues.

The entire foundation of my body needed addressing. A combination of intensive physio and orthotics for my shoes and boots meant I played a full season that year and we won the All-Ireland.

◆ ◆ ◆ ◆ ◆

IT WOULD NEVER be a trouble-free run, but I was being looked after much better and placed enormous value on that. In stark contrast, it was a distinct lack of caring that contributed to me giving up playing competitive basketball. The unsustainable workload, creaking body and preference for football were the ultimate reasons I made the decision at 20, but one incident from a few years earlier had diluted my passion for basketball at international level at least.

It was inevitable given all my commitments that there would be the odd fixture clash, even within the one code, and on one occasion an attempt to back me into a corner had the reverse effect.

I was due to play for Ireland under-19s in Wales on the same weekend that Killannin were competing in the under-16 Community Games All-Ireland final in 1985. On paper, it was a difficult choice to make, especially as the senior squad was on the same international trip, which would have been an excellent experience.

But to my mind, the international was a challenge match, with nothing at stake. It was my second year on the 19s but I still had another three. This was my last with the Killannin under-16s and we were defending our title against Newbridge of Kildare.

The Ireland head coach sent a letter which left me thinking that if I did not travel to Wales, I might not wear the green singlet again. The bottom line for me was that I would feel like I had let down not just my teammates had I chosen a meaningless game for Ireland over an All-Ireland final with Killannin. I felt that I would have let down the entire parish! The choice was simple.

There was no choice. The letter served only to copperfasten my resolve; it also soured me on playing basketball for Ireland after that.

Killannin beat Newbridge in a tight enough battle. I felt maybe if I hadn't been there, we would have lost and that would have killed me. The happy ending did not just conclude with another All-Ireland medal, however. The best was yet to come when the parish committee made a special presentation to me, in recognition of my loyalty.

I won countless All-Irelands in both codes, the two with Galway at senior level being obvious standouts. I have three All Stars. But the trophy I was given that night remains among my proudest possessions.

CHAPTER 4

MINOR MATTERS

The young do not know enough to be prudent, and therefore they
attempt the impossible, and achieve it...
– Pearl S Buck

IMAGINE THE GLOW of winning an All-Ireland.

The sights, the sounds… the smells.

You don't realise how fast it all goes. That was something I finally got the hang of by 2001. To slow down. Take it in.

It was a little different 15 years earlier but sharing Galway's minor triumph with Bosco on the same piece of grass that witnessed Stockwell, Purcell, McDermott and Colleran visiting glory on the county was heady indeed.

In 1970, Killannin had Tom O'Connor at midfield and Patsy Kinneavy on the panel as the Tom Markham Cup came west. The little club did it again in 1986, with the Walsh boys from Doon.

I was at midfield though I spent some time in the attack. Bosco played throughout the campaign at corner-back until getting injured during the semi-final. That cost him his place for the decider, but he came off the bench in the second-half and was on the pitch when the final whistle blew, which was special.

This was a real reward for my parents, after carting us all over Galway and beyond to play any sport available to us; my father at the wheel and my mother joining us, having filled the boot with sandwiches and tea in the flask.

MY FATHER WAS bringing us to county games from the time we could walk and he got to see two of us win an All-Ireland in the maroon jersey.

He gave us a fright on the day of the final. Well not Bosco and me, as we were out on the field. He gave my mother a big fright though and it was a shock when we learned the following day that he had gotten a weakness in the stand and was in hospital. It turned out that he had an enlarged heart, but he refused to leave the stadium when it happened.

After the presentation, he came down on to the pitch to shake hands with the two of us. Let me tell you, that was worth any bear hug because it was the first time, for all the games and competitions we'd won. And for all the cattle herded and turf cut either! He can't have been feeling well but he toughed it out through the game to give us that and under no circumstances were we to be told while we were enjoying such a momentous occasion. He was an extraordinary individual.

There was one time when he caught me completely by surprise. It was a month or two before he died in 2002 and I suppose he wanted to impart some wisdom before he left us. So, he called Mary and me into him.

'You've enough done now with the football,' he said. 'Give it up. Now go and get another *laidín* to be friends with Cathal.'

Talk about being stumped! Football and family planning advice in the one go, from a man who was the antithesis of oversharing. It was funny looking back on it, but we didn't know what to do or say.

Clearly, he knew his time was running out and that he had to break the habit of a lifetime to tell me I had put myself through enough to play with Galway over the years, and that it was time to focus on the family. That was the exception though.

Was he proud of Bosco and me climbing the hills of the Hogan Stand? He never said it, but given what he endured to give us that handshake, I think so.

◆ ◆ ◆ ◆ ◆

IT WAS A far cry from winning All-Irelands at Croke Park when I played my first games of football at St Annin's National School. We had such small numbers

I was thrown into the deep end in first class and we got pulverised, 18-1 to 0-1. I'll never forget that scoreline.

We improved and won a final of some sort against Barna when I was in fourth or fifth class. We would go on to have a real rivalry with them at school and underage level with the clubs, and there were some real bruising battles up to minor.

John O'Callaghan was the trainer at St Annin's and he put a lot into us. He had fantastic support from the principal Séamus Ó Cualáin. Seámus was fiercely passionate about our heritage and Gaelic games were the mainstay of that for him. He made the annual All-Ireland final pilgrimage without fail.

Every Monday morning, he would take out the paper and read the reports of whatever matches Galway had played over the weekend. It wasn't difficult to get him talking about the old days and before you knew it, you were whisked back in time to the 1940s, picturing the heroic deeds of Oughterard's Sullivan brothers Tom, Dinny and Charlie in the Galway jersey.

Galway completed the three in-a-row three years before I was born and nobody considered for a second that it would take 32 years before Sam Maguire's memorial would vacation Corribside once more. I was aware of the tradition but there were no real local role models to look up to.

Tom O'Connor had been unlucky with injuries after his minor success and never managed any sort of a sustained run with the seniors.

But thanks to my father, the fires of passion for Galway football were stoked. He brought us to plenty of games in Pearse Stadium. He would park what seemed like miles out and we'd walk in. The excitement of what was to unfold shortened the hike. The result determined what the return trip felt like but the multitude of talking points got us back to the car before we knew it.

The first time I pulled a Galway jersey over my head was for a National Schools' selection. You played one game a year and we took on Cork down in Páirc Uí Chaoimh. I was only nine and slotted into corner-back. Bosco was on the same team.

A real benefit of being so tall was that I got to play on a lot of successful teams with Bosco in both football and basketball over the next few years.

Having attended so many games and listened to commentaries of football, hurling and soccer matches in the parlour at home, I always thought playing for Galway was for special people. Not for a lad out in the mountains of Connemara like me.

But I had gotten a taste. And I liked it.

♦ ♦ ♦ ♦ ♦

I STARTED PLAYING first team adult football for Killannin in 1983.

I was only 13 but already as tall as I would get, weighing 14 and a half stone. So I was thrown into midfield, where I played my last game 32 years later.

We got to the Western final of the intermediate championship in 1985, where Moycullen got the upper hand in a local derby. They had experience of this kind of stage and a more considerable pick of players. We were still only building.

I stood toe-to-toe with Galway's midfield duo of Richie Lee and Pádraig 'Dandy' Kelly in that game. Pádraig died young in 2001 – his son Seán came through to the Galway panel during my tenure as manager.

I was still two months off my 17th birthday when we won the All-Ireland minor title under the management of John Tobin, who was a teammate of Tom O'Connor's in 1970 and had also garnered an under-21 medal. Our captain was John Joyce, another who died prematurely, in 1997.

I could recall far more about 1986 than '98 off the top of my head, without having to delve back into the videos or Google. Maybe it's because it was my first taste of serious success in football. Maybe it was because there were no other aspects to my being.

By the time we won the senior, I was married with kids, had a job, a house built and a mortgage to pay. At minor, it was off you go to play a game and nothing else mattered. I actually missed most of the Connacht League, which we won, because of my international basketball commitments but John wanted me involved in the summer and facilitated that.

I was a little bit intimidated when I went in initially. Apart from the rest of the lads having been together for a while, a lot of them would have been at St Jarlath's, the famed footballing academy in Tuam. And being young, it was a big deal to be getting the call-up. I was playing international basketball and in All-Irelands for school and parish but football always meant that little bit more and therefore, playing for Galway meant more.

I had performed with the county under-14s and under-16s after national school but was a little more in awe of the thing going into minor, because that's the first time the public take any notice. It's just bigger. It didn't take me long to relax into the environment once I sat down with the lads though.

We had a very good team. John Joyce, Tomás Mannion, Alan Mulholland, Tommy Finnerty, Ger Farrell, Brian Silke, Bosco and myself were among those to go on to be seniors, though Bosco gave up the county scene after two years.

We were well prepared and played a good brand of football but central to the success was that we got along, trusted each other and were selfless in working for one another. Friendships were made that have lasted the test of time, even if there might not be a whole pile of communication with some of the lads nowadays.

But when we meet up, there is no awkwardness. We had a lot of fun together.

The consensus at the start of the season was that John would be using the experience to build for the following season, as Mayo would be hard to overcome with a number of the All-Ireland-winning outfit of the previous campaign still eligible. That was probably reflective of the morale among the football fraternity in the county anyway. Optimism was in scant supply.

That changed a bit after the league. Winning that was a considerable boost to everyone's confidence. As a manager, I always believed in trying to win as many games as possible, whatever the competition. We got to the final of the FBD League in each of my five seasons with Galway and left with the spoils three times.

I can't see any downside to winning games and cups, especially with a group unaccustomed to doing so.

We made light work of Sligo in the first round by 1-12 to 1-0 in Tuam on May 10. I was at full-forward and though I had a hand in a couple of scores, I didn't enjoy not being involved in general play. It wasn't my natural environment.

It was seven weeks before we were back at the Stadium to cruise past Leitrim by 4-12 to 1-4. Playing on the edge of the opposition square was more enjoyable on this occasion, as we were well on top and I managed to tack up a goal and two points and contribute to another of the goals.

As expected, Mayo emerged from the other side of the draw to provide the opposition in the Connacht final at Hyde Park. They had five starters from the year before and were heavily fancied. This was the day we showcased the steel necessary to go with our talent, as we dealt with the concession of two early goals to the All-Ireland champions.

Had there been any doubt, it would have risen to the surface, but we rallied and Mayo only scored another point, failing to move the scoreboard in the second-half at all. A goal from Peter Maher drew us level at half-time and with our defence dominant, we gradually drew clear.

I kicked the point to put us ahead early in the second-half but the full-forward experiment wasn't exactly a resounding success and I was taken off with a quarter of an hour or so remaining. That stung a bit, but to be Connacht champions was incredible and with the seniors completing the double later on, it was an unforgettable occasion.

Next up were New York in August, after they had emerged from a battle of the ex-pats with London after extra-time. We gave them due respect and recorded a bloodless victory in Tuam, 4-20 to 1-4. Peter notched up a hat-trick of goals and I provided two points, more comfortable now that I had finally been given a midfield jersey.

The All-Ireland semi-final was just a week later and all I could think about was running out onto Croke Park. It's the dream of everyone who laced a boot, not just wide-eyed children. You think of the history that was created there, the legends that bestrode the Jones' Road venue and created theatre for the masses.

Spectacular feats of skill, vision, strength and endurance were exhibited on this grass and without the benefit of much TV footage, became ever more spectacular in the mind's eye with each passing year.

There was an aura about Croke Park and that two Walsh boys from Doon would be battling for glory there was frankly unbelievable.

AS A RULE, I loved the big stage.

I had always felt comfortable on it and would for the rest of my career, but I became very nervous before this game. I knew what it meant to worship at the High Church of Gaelic games and thought too much about it. Consequently, I did not play well.

Down had the likes of James McCartan, who would be on the team that would annex the minor championship the following season and go on to establish himself as a bona fide hero of the Mourne County with his all-action contribution to the two senior triumphs of 1991 and '94. He was manager as they reached the 2010 final too.

They weren't able to compete with us, however.

We led by five points at the interval, Down only getting off the mark just before the short whistle. Having laid the foundation, we cranked through the gears to prevail by 3-10 to 0-6. Peter moved out around the half-forward line, leaving space inside in which Tommy and Tomás in particular thrived. Tomás grabbed a brace of goals in a very different role to the one he would have when we made the senior breakthrough 12 years later, while Tommy, who was always dangerous, slotted the other.

I was subdued but I remember so much about that day.

I had an old bag that I'd used for years. It had a few holes and 'Dublin' written on it, believe it or not. We were bought new bags for the semi-final and told we had to use them. Not that most people would have had any objection. The boys started slagging me in the dressing-room when I opened my new bag and took out my old, tattered one. The bus driver knocked great craic out of it.

I had a few *piseogs* like that and there was no way I was going into the cauldron without my bag.

It didn't bring everyone luck though. Bosco had to go off injured after just five minutes. Ger came on and did well. The defence had excelled throughout the campaign and they quelled Down easily. When the team was named, A.N. Other manned left corner-back. With Bosco having missed a bit of training due to the injury, Ger got the nod.

That semi-final experience was the making of me. I couldn't believe I was going to be playing in an All-Ireland for Galway but the fear had gone. The Croke Park factor had been neutralised as a negative force and I suffered none of the nerves that bedevilled me the previous month.

I was asked afterwards whether it was daunting for one so young to be performing on such a stage, in front of such crowds, but my reply was that it was like playing on a pitch with four televisions, one on each side. There were crowds, but they weren't a threat.

It was like they were on a screen, not there with me. It's a cliché now but for me, there was grass and a ball, white lines and two goals, just like Maloney Park.

That mindset and the comfort it brings doesn't always mean you play well but I did that day against a Cork team that had beaten Kerry and Dublin and were the favourites. They had the likes of Stephen O'Brien and Mark O'Connor and it was no surprise that the game ebbed and flowed.

After the calamity of the Connacht final start, we were determined to be at concert pitch from the throw-in and led by five points before the Rebels knew what hit them. They showed their mettle to wipe that out, as they did in the second-half when we opened a similar gap, but doing so spends a lot of physical and mental energy. We never panicked, even as we fell two points down after that initial good start or when we only had a point in hand with eight minutes remaining.

Things were clicking for me.

I caught some good ball and was involved in the play from the start. And it was a dream start, as Tommy Finnerty dusted himself down after being fouled by O'Connor to plant a penalty after only six minutes. Future dual star Mickey Mullins got a goal back for Cork and Adrian Brennan was forced into a great save from Dave Larkin. He was to better that with a stupendous stop from the same player after the resumption, and another when one-on-one with Noel Twomey. These were key interventions in a game that made a pendulum appear one-sided.

So too was Tomás' rasping goal that helped us go in two points ahead at the break and settled us down after a shaky period.

I was moved to centre-forward for the second-half and promptly landed two points in the first five minutes after the restart and though I missed a goal chance, it didn't have a negative impact on me. We stretched five ahead once more but a bad goal after a mix-up in defence placed the verdict in doubt again.

It is Peter who will be remembered for delivering the final, definitive thrust into Cork's heart, rattling the net two minutes from time from the rebound after Tommy hit the post from another penalty, this one awarded for a foul on Tomás. Galway's record of never losing a minor final was maintained.

We were champions on a 3-8 to 2-7 scoreline and for good measure, I was named Man of the Match.

When Carthage Buckley called a halt to proceedings, I felt euphoric. It was the greatest joy I had ever felt and I'm not sure it was replicated after any subsequent game as a player. Not even when we bridged the 32-year gap at senior level in 1998. This was more visceral, rawer. As I got older, the losses exercised me more than winning but that was not the case on September 21, 1986.

That it was something for Galway people to celebrate for the first time at All-Ireland level since the minor triumph a decade previously accentuated the glow.

We were treated to a civic reception in Eyre Square on our homecoming on the Monday night, which was memorable as Alan's father John was the mayor.

CLOSER TO HOME, it was as if we were carrying the community banner into battle.

The number of 'Good Luck' cards and letters that arrived addressed to Bosco and Kevin Walsh before the final, and 'Congratulations' ones afterwards, literally brought it home.

We knew what it meant but we were intent only on creating our own history. Sharing it with people I had a close bond with was special.

But sharing it with Bosco, on the field beside me, and having my parents there to bear witness, was the best of all.

CHAPTER 5

THEY THINK IT'S ALL OVER

Some beautiful paths can't be discovered without getting lost.
– Erol Ozan

THERE HAD BEEN a few basketball scholarships offered by American universities, but I paid them no heed. I couldn't even tell you now where they were from. It wasn't something I thought about pursuing even for a millisecond.

I wasn't keen on leaving Doon for any longer than I would have to, not to mind Ireland. Anyway, it was football I wanted to play. After the minors, all I could see in my future was playing for Galway… as a senior footballer.

I had to start earning a crust though so my work on the farm ended once I completed the Leaving. I worked in a local factory, ECL in Oughterard, just after my Leaving for 12 months, but then I headed for the building sites, mainly plastering for about two years.

My life in the Garda Síochána began in April 1991, when I walked into the Training College in Templemore for the first time. It was never a vocation. My parents wanted me to do it. I suppose my father had the two brothers in it. Maybe he didn't want to see me slogging along all my life.

It was a pensionable job, so I went along with the suggestion.

The best part of being in the service was meeting Mary when I was posted to Mill Street in Galway city in February 1993. She had the same values as me, having enjoyed a similar upbringing, and we hit it off, getting married three years later at St Brendan's Church in Mullagh on April 27.

I WAS IN Dublin during my training but my first official posting was to Blacklion in June 1992. It wasn't my first experience of Northern Ireland.

When I was 13, I travelled to Belfast for a national basketball camp. The train from Dublin was stopped and members of the British Army boarded with their guns, opened our bags and turned them upside down. It was a considerable eye-opener.

The Good Friday Agreement was still seven years away when I arrived on the Cavan side of the border, just across the river from Belcoo in Fermanagh. It was obviously a hot zone and a real element of tension and danger hung in the air. I was lucky to escape without getting involved in anything violent, though you never knew what awaited you as you stopped the next car at a checkpoint.

There was one very stark reminder of this threat on the morning of Sunday, November 15. I had been rostered to be on duty from the previous night but swapped with someone else. The garda station wasn't caught up in anything but it came as a shock to learn that an RUC policeman had been shot by an IRA sniper firing from the Irish side of the border.

Like me, Alan Corbett was pretty much a rookie, a couple of years older at 25.

There were plenty of good memories from my 15 years in the guards, the last 12 of which were in Salthill, and I worked with the best of people – many of my best friends are still guards, as is Mary. But it was never a job that stirred the passion.

As well as that, having both parents as guards with five young children in the house wasn't ideal. More and more, it dawned on me that I did need a greater sense of purpose in my professional life. I didn't just want to be hanging in there for the pension. So I left in 2006 and not for one day have I missed it.

There has been a lot of negative publicity towards the force in recent years and that's a pity. It stemmed from Garda leadership not knowing how to get the best out of people. They were very distant from the rank and file. That sense of 'us and them' is unhealthy and creates an atmosphere of unhappiness.

For any team to succeed there needs to be unity of vision, purpose and action. That didn't exist, the communication lines weren't open and it led to heavy disillusionment.

I had begun building houses as a sideline and decided to dedicate a little more time to construction. I really enjoyed that line of work. There was a process to it that I got a buzz from. There was a variety too. There was so much more to it than bricks and mortar, though I loved getting my hands dirty again.

During my stint with Sligo, I was approached by CMCC Financial Solutions to open an office in Moycullen. The prospect of selling policies hadn't ever exactly entered my head but once I sat down to talk, the idea grew on me. I set up the office in 2014 and I got my QFA (Qualified Financial Advisor) diploma in January 2017.

The job appeals to the caring side of my nature. I want to give people the policy that is best suited to them, not just make a sale to make my numbers look good. People's needs are different and getting to know clients while delving through all the information and finding out what is most appropriate for them is highly satisfying.

♦ ♦ ♦ ♦ ♦

I WAS STILL a minor in 1987, as were the likes of Tomás Mannion, Brian Silke, Peter Maher and Adrian Brennan. In all, 10 of the panel were underage again, so hopes were high of us doing something Galway had never managed before – winning back-to-back All-Ireland titles at the under-18 grade.

We repeated our Connacht success but didn't perform at all in a drab All-Ireland semi-final as Cork got some measure of revenge for the previous September. Galway have only managed one All-Ireland minor title since. We were operating in rarefied air.

The call-up to senior was immediate as Billy Joyce named a 33-man panel for the 1987-88 National League. I had been invited the previous year but felt it would be better to focus on the minors. The folly of commencing the competition in November was evident as just 300 people turned up in Pearse Stadium to bear witness to my debut, as we scraped over Clare in the opening tie of the Division 2 campaign.

I lined out at midfield alongside Hugh Bleahen and scored a point in a 1-8 to 0-9 victory.

The picture of that day remains vivid in my mind, as were my nerves walking into the old dressing-room. If I was shy about joining the minor squad the year before, I was even more in awe of being a senior. Noel Roche was in direct opposition that day and he had been playing for Ireland against Australia in the deciding test of the Compromise Rules series just seven days earlier, won by the Aussies.

Gay McManus was a legend of Galway football and he went out of his way to make me feel welcome. I appreciated that and kept it in mind when it was my turn. Gay cared about the people he shared the dressing-room with, and the future of Galway football, even if he wasn't going to be around to benefit.

I made my championship debut in Ruislip against London in 1989. I was sited at full-forward and did well but we couldn't really have an idea where we were. Unfortunately, Mayo let us know in no uncertain terms at MacHale Park. We just weren't very good.

In the February before my maiden championship, we drew with Kildare in the League, 0-8 to 1-5. It was an anodyne affair and both counties would be relegated to the third tier – a long way from crossing swords in an All-Ireland final, as transpired in 1998.

The *Tuam Herald* had a headline above an article about the selection of a team for the following week's visit to Páirc Uí Chaoimh that read… *In Dire Straits as Cork hold out Division 3 ticket*. It was next to a photo of Jimmy O'Dea and me during the half-time kickaround.

Jimmy was wearing a pair of headphones, listening to music on his Walkman. The article suggested that no blame could be attached to Jimmy for tuning out, given the paucity of the fare on the pitch, and that Dire Straits would be the only appropriate band to listen to in the circumstances.

Sitting next to Jimmy in the dugout that day was the first time I had ever seen a Walkman.

As dreadful as the situation was with the seniors, that particular season had been all about the under-21s, with the '86 minors coming of age. We gave it a good rattle under the management of John Joe Holleran but came a cropper at the last hurdle.

As I had become accustomed to, I was joined by Bosco, who had been named Galway Under-21 Footballer of the Year in 1988. Again, I spent most of the time at full-forward.

We needed a late goal to be sure of escaping from Carrick-on-Shannon with the verdict over Leitrim in the Connacht semi-final and beat Roscommon for the third consecutive season in the provincial decider. Alan Mulholland, who like a lot of us was an established senior by now and would be my predecessor as Galway manager, had the honour of collecting the silverware as captain. It was my second Connacht under-21 medal. I would bag a third the following year.

A pair of goals in the opening two minutes from Tommy Finnerty got us through against Meath in Portlaoise. It was an extraordinary start by Tommy and he was only denied a three-minute hat-trick when his thunderbolt was ruled out by referee Ray Maloney, who adjudged the pass by Tomás Kilcommins to be illegal.

The All-Ireland final took place at the Gaelic Grounds in Limerick and was a repeat of the minor decider three years earlier. This time, it was Cork who came out on top. It was a gut-wrenching defeat, as we rallied against the odds in the second-half but fell a point short, 2-8 to 1-10.

We had a very strong wind in the opening period but failed to capitalise, recording only three points and going in five in arrears after the concession of two goals. That prompted the introduction of John Joyce to midfield, where I joined him, and between us we helped turn the tide, imposing our physicality and athleticism on the Denis Fitzgerald-Liam Honohan pairing.

Like me, John's knee problems were already blighting him. A cartilage operation had caused him to miss the entire campaign until then. He was nowhere near fit and it was a measure of his class that he would influence proceedings so much. It isn't a stretch to suggest that had we the fortune of an injury-free John Joyce at midfield, the result might have been different.

He caught some serious ball after his introduction. Playing into the wind, we had to hold onto possession more and I carried a lot through the centre of the Cork defence, set up a few points and notched up one.

Brian Silke was brought in also and he put the shackles on Noel Twomey, who had been causing havoc. Alan O'Connor had swapped with me and pounced for a goal in injury time to reduce the deficit to the minimum but time ran out.

◆ ◆ ◆ ◆ ◆

THESE WERE DESPERATE times for Galway football and the optimism generated by underage success quickly evaporated. We were at the wrong end of some heavy beatings by Mayo and Roscommon, while falling to Leitrim was considered a disaster in 1993.

Young players need time but before I knew it, I had a decade done and very little to show for it. We endured relegation to Division 3 on a number of occasions and getting well beaten was not unusual.

John Tobin became manager after Billy for 1990. It was a wise appointment, given his influence as boss of the All-Ireland-winning minors. He would surely be the ideal individual to oversee the promotion of so many of that squad to senior level.

Unfortunately, it didn't unfold as any of us desired.

The minors did not progress. We drifted from one season to the next. You're beaten, it's over... you come back and another year slips by. Adrian Brennan, Ger Farrell, Francis McQualter, Tomás Kilcommins and Bosco came and went. Tomás Mannion and Fergal O'Neill were more regular.

I was in and out through injury and getting stick because of it. I often said I wished I had a cast as the absence of any visible signs of a physical problem suggested something less than an iron will. If only people knew what I went through to get on the pitch, what I went through while on it, and what I went through to come back from the latest setback.

My Galway career was drifting away, nothing like I had envisioned it would be. There is no doubt that my passion for Killannin was all that was keeping me in football at this time.

My motivation wasn't helped by being accused after a game by John of drinking that week. It wasn't true, wherever he got his information from. I was stubborn but young and not anxious for direct conflict so rather than say anything, I just picked up my gear bag after the game, walked out and didn't go back.

They sent people to the house.

'Will ya come in?

'Go on, come in!'

No chance. John had crossed a line as far as I was concerned. I get on fine with him now and we have never discussed it since. I'm not even sure he knows why I didn't go back, but I wasn't going explaining.

I always told players I wouldn't be looking in the windows of pubs to see if they were drinking. What would stop them doing it in their sitting rooms? If you didn't prepare properly, it showed between the white lines. If the group decided that there would be no drink for a period before a game, then that had to be adhered to, but I never walked in and imposed a ban.

Even if I had video evidence, I would never accuse a player of cheating in that fashion. To do so in front of the group is really backing a fella up against a wall but I would avoid it even privately, if I could. There are serious issues there for the culture of the squad. Trust is monumental.

If I knew someone had done something, I would try to get them to admit it. There is honesty in that, which might even strengthen the group. Own up, take your medicine and drive on. Throwing allegations and blame around can cause schisms that have an apocalyptic effect on a squad, no matter how well founded they are.

◆ ◆ ◆ ◆ ◆

THE ONE BEACON in this period was winning the Connacht Championship under Bosco McDermott in 1995, bridging an eight-year gap. It is worth noting that after defeating Sligo in the first round, we only got over Leitrim by a point in the semi-final, having lost by that margin in the two previous campaigns, and after a replay in 1994.

The Galway cognoscenti were disgusted when we were taken down by the traditional minnows but I always talk about taking trends from blocks of time and it is clear now that the relative no-shows against Mayo and Roscommon in previous seasons were far worse performances than anything we put up against Leitrim in this time.

Managed by a young, enthusiastic manager named John O'Mahony, Leitrim went on to garner a first Connacht title in 67 years by claiming Mayo's scalp in 1994. They were ultra-consistent around that time and it was a good effort to get over the line against them.

It suggested something different and that was Bosco's impact from his appointment at the end of 1993. Three points down against the champions, who had some sort of Indian sign over us, we somehow pulled it out of the fire to snatch it by one, 0-12 to 0-11.

Our captain, Ja Fallon led from the front with a point two minutes from time and Seán Óg de Paor levelled 60 seconds later. Not for the last time, Niall Finnegan was ice cool in converting the match-winning free – his seventh point of the day. With that, Galway were in a Connacht final for the first time in five years.

I HAD MISSED the two-point defeat to Roscommon in 1990 after leaving the panel temporarily, and there were some nervy moments in the build-up five years later. The first round win over Sligo was the first game I played since the defeat to Leitrim 12 months earlier, when I had damaged my groin badly. It went once more against the same opposition in 1995 but I got patched up and lined out at centre-forward against Mayo.

We needed a strong start and got it, leading by six points after 20 minutes and when Mayo threatened briefly in the second-half, we responded again. I managed to get on the scoresheet but Val Daly was on fire, with four points from play. Tommy Wilson kicked two incredible points, while Niall excelled from placed balls.

Ja also produced a real skipper's performance and when you include me, Niall, Gary Fahey, Ray Silke, Seán Óg de Paor and Tomás Mannion, it is clear that good groundwork was being done for what would follow three years later. It is interesting that Tomás, Fergal O'Neill and I were the only graduates from the 1986 minor team, however.

They are a good team, an excellent team, and they are young enough to have many better days ahead of them. But they must want these better days – want them badly – if they are to succeed, is how Bosco was quoted in *The Connacht Tribune* after the subsequent All-Ireland semi-final loss to Tyrone.

Bosco brought real pride back into wearing the jersey.

That was his priority from the moment he took the job. A hero of the three in-a-row crew, he was an outstanding motivator, which is why I brought him in on a number of occasions during my own management. His assessment was to prove spot on.

We had approached the semi-final with optimism. In the pre-backdoor epoch, you were one of only four still standing once you achieved provincial primacy. Add to that the fact there was no dominant force in that era. The football championship was wide open.

That said, according to the oddsmakers and pundits, we were massive underdogs. We surprised everyone outside the camp with our first-half dominance – as evidenced by the paltry Galway support – but kicked a lot of wides, missed three gilt-edged goal chances and then a typical piece of opportunism from Peter Canavan ensured that the Red Hands were only two points behind. His goal was supplemented by seven points by the conclusion, and they advanced by 1-13 to 0-13.

The narrative afterwards was that we had exceeded expectations. That wasn't how I saw it, and I was bitterly disappointed. It still irks me because it had taken so long to put ourselves in this position and I was a bit of a passenger in the second-half, although I did okay in the first when the team as a whole excelled.

While a mixture of biomechanics, overloading, misuse by various managers and coaches and bad luck played roles in my horrific injury profile, there were a few times I didn't help myself. This was one such occasion, which is why it stings so much.

The groin wasn't right after the Connacht final but in a move that won't be found in any manual of wisdom, I took an injection to play in an A versus B match the Sunday before the Tyrone game and did a lot of damage.

I was desperate to make it back to Croke Park for the first time since 1986 and feared being left out if unable to prove my fitness. That was something I couldn't bear to consider, when I thought we had such a chance of bridging the gap to when Bosco himself was getting his hands on the Sam Maguire.

Tyrone were subsequently beaten in the final in controversial circumstances, with Charlie Redmond staying on the pitch for a few minutes after being sent off and then Sean McLaughlin having a late equaliser disallowed when Canavan, who scored 11 points in the game and wound up being named Footballer of the Year, was deemed to have fouled the ball on the ground by referee Paddy Russell.

So it was a good opportunity spurned and I played my part in that. Nowadays, the medical team would make the call and I wouldn't have played. I wouldn't have been given the injection either. In hindsight, Bosco shouldn't have put me out on the pitch against Tyrone once all those things happened.

He felt I was too important to leave out but I couldn't reward his backing.

AS A MANAGER, you would always go with the medical advice but there was one time, in my first season with Sligo, when I made a massive call against that counsel. Charlie Harrison broke his collarbone in our 2009 Connacht

Championship semi-final against Galway. That is normally an eight-week absence and he missed our qualifier victory over Tipperary.

Next up were Kerry, just 20 days after the injury.

Charlie was in my ear to play. He was a real leader, but my initial response was that there was no chance. My own experience with persistent injury influenced my approach in this department. I would put the player before the team. In truth, doing so served the team best as well. If anyone understood the perils of playing injured, it was me.

As far as I was concerned, Charlie was out.

But as was his wont on the field, Charlie did not relent easily. He would go through a wall for the team and he kept at me, so on the Sunday morning after the Tipp game, I told him that if he were to have any chance, he would have to play a full part in training in the week ahead.

This, remember, is just two weeks after breaking his collarbone. It shouldn't have been possible and not being able to do it during the week would provide Charlie himself with incontrovertible proof that he could not do himself or Sligo justice lining out against Colm Cooper et al.

What unfolded, however, was Charlie flying on Tuesday and Thursday, thundering into the rigours of full physical contact. Now, I had no choice.

The doctor and physio might have said there was no way he could be right but I had seen that he was. And while the championship cauldron is a different devil altogether, Charlie's importance as a leader in the trenches, as well as his ability as a player, allied with what he had illustrated midweek, convinced me to give him his head.

He would go on to play a stormer as we almost derailed Kerry, losing by a point in Tralee to the team that would be crowned champions of Ireland two months later.

◆ ◆ ◆ ◆ ◆

BY 1997, THE battle with injury had begun to wear thin.

I had come on as a sub for the last 20 minutes of the previous year's Connacht final and scored a point from a free but was only on one leg. It was tough to watch Liam McHale have the run of Castlebar, knowing that if my body had co-operated, I would have done something about that.

Bosco stepped down after blooding some future Galway legends and making us competitive again. Val Daly was named player-manager. We had shared a dressing-room for almost a decade but that clearly counted for little, as I was not involved that season.

I did train with the squad before Christmas, but had a knee operation in January and nobody checked in at any stage to see how my rehab was progressing; whether I might be interested in coming back, not even just to see how I was.

My services were not required but it was the lack of care or interest about my welfare that stung most.

After a decade, I was resigned to being finished as a Galway footballer.

Exactly 20 years later, I would give Val's son, Michael his debut for Galway and in 2019, provide another, John with his first outing. Funny how things work out sometimes.

The year away, however, turned out to be a blessing, physically and mentally. When those injuries keep coming, it is difficult to pick yourself back up off the floor, go through the anguish and torment of getting yourself fit and then hit rock bottom again.

In nine years, I had only been able to show glimpses of what I was capable of, while taking blow after blow to the psyche.

The pressure was off now.

I no longer had to deal with the knowledge that people doubted me and my desire to play, or feel like I was letting anyone down.

My inactivity enabled me to accept the invitation to manage Killannin. I was only 26, so it was a tremendous honour and a major responsibility. I relished it and we flourished.

It was May before I kicked a ball and I went on to play some of my best football in years with Killannin.

We reached the county semi-final and totally outplayed Corofin. We should have taken them out but conceded two late goals when leading by four points. They went on to win the All-Ireland. It remains my greatest regret, even though I produced one of my best performances in the blue and white.

In the meantime, John O'Mahony became Galway manager. It was a move that surprised many and angered plenty who felt a county with such a rich tradition should not be going to an outside man to steer the ship, and definitely not one from Mayo.

It was a point of view that would change quickly.

CHAPTER 6

THE '98 RISING

Nuckser Buckley across the field. Martin Lynch will race across. Will he get to the ball
ahead of the defender? A BRILLIANT catch again by Tomás Mannion, the farmer...
for Galway. To Michael Donnellan, the son of a former minister. He gets the ball.
He's made a lot of ground but he's still back in defence... and he gets the ball to Kevin
Walsh. Big Kevin comes past midfield. Puts a Kildare man down on the ground. Back
to Michael Donnellan. He's made a great run... he's 30 yards out. Gets the ball now to
Derek Savage. Savage moves into the centre... hasn't time to kick with the left. Out it
comes to the left half-back and Seán Óg de Paor lobs it... and it's over the bar by Seán
Óg de Paor!
    – Micheál Ó Muircheartaigh, RTÉ Radio 1, September 27, 1998

THE BEST DREAMS are rarely realistic, but even playing for Galway wasn't
a plausible ambition as a child growing up in Killannin. To even get to wear the
maroon jersey at senior level was for heroes and legends.

    Ambitions evolve and the All-Ireland minor triumph of 1986 lit a flame
under the desire to achieve senior success. The 16 year-old optimism had taken a
battering over the course of the years however, and I was ready to draw the curtain
down on what had been a largely underwhelming and unrewarding decade at the
highest level.

My over-acquaintance with the surgeon's knife and the physio's table had brought contemplation of retirement for a few years but when Val Daly deemed me surplus to requirements, that was the decision made for me as far as I could ascertain.

Yet when John Bannon called a halt to the All-Ireland final of 1998, I was not in the Croke Park stands but on the pitch.

Literally stretched out on the turf.

THERE WERE A few reasons for that.

The first was that I was exhausted.

Secondly, I had gotten a right drive in the calf with about 10 minutes remaining, the same calf I tore in the replayed Connacht final.

That meant managing my movements, but this was my game now anyway. It was more cerebral than athletic, though the way some TV pundits went on, you'd be forgiven for thinking that people using Zimmer frames had more mobility.

With my calf hobbling me, I consigned myself to the space just in front of the full-back line, picking up positions to take the ball and give it off. There was one in our right corner-back position that ended with a vital point off his left by Niall Finnegan as Kildare came at us with everything they had.

It meant I had to pull out of the International Rules panel, which was a disappointment. Representing Ireland would have been a wonderful honour, but I was hardly in a position to complain.

The prevailing emotion as I lay there and looked around was more relief than exhilaration. I just could not countenance walking into the losers' dressing-room, the regrets that would haunt you forever already taking hold. I know all about those *what ifs?* so the relief of not having to ask those questions anymore trumped elation.

But that was just me. All around me, the joy was visible on the faces of my teammates and the long-suffering supporters flooding onto the sacred turf in waves.

Nobody would have been predicting my role in this history 12 months before.

♦ ♦ ♦ ♦ ♦

I AM GUESSING that Pete Warren and Stephen Joyce played a major part in breathing life into my Galway career and giving me an Indian summer that would yield another seven years, two All-Irelands, four additional Connachts and three All Stars.

They were John O'Mahony's selectors and as immersed as they were in Galway football, would have been aware of my form with Killannin. Johno saw plenty of me over the years himself but perhaps Pete and Stephen told him I still had something to offer, despite not having been involved in 1997. I had made my peace with closing that chapter but when Johno called, I didn't need my arm twisted too hard.

I knew Galway were close. We were provincial champions in '95 and in the next two seasons lost to a Mayo team that reached the All-Ireland final. They were within seconds and a flukey Colm Coyle equaliser of winning in '96 before falling short by a point to Meath in the replay. The following term, a Maurice Fitzgerald-inspired Kerry defeated them by three.

Meanwhile, we had some young bucks from the 1993-95 Connacht three in-a-row minors and the under-21 unit that claimed provincial honours in '96 to provide depth, competition, energy and a bit of swagger.

At the core of my *Why?* however, was that I loved football, and I could not escape the conviction that I was capable of making more of a contribution, with just a bit of good fortune and some better care. Watching the midfield struggle against Mayo while I was in my civvies in 1997 confirmed that for me.

To be perfectly honest, I look back on that now and think that Galway could have won an All-Ireland that year with a little more organisation, and me helping out. That said, I can't have too many regrets about that season with Killannin. It was good for me.

It was this tantalising prospect of having more in the tank that Johno zoned in on. I told him I was just sick of the injuries, of being shoved in at full-forward on one leg, of being doubted. I was sick of the absolute hardship for a man of my size to build the fitness back up from the latest period of inactivity, to be in sufficient condition to play at midfield against the cream of the crop.

Added to that, Mary was expecting our first child – Caoimhe was born in January – and I had no idea how a baby would affect the sleep patterns. Throw all that in with the shift work and it was hard to see how such a massive commitment could be justified.

I will never forget the words that followed from the other side of the line. It was masterful in terms of man-management and motivation. In a flash, I was all-in.

'We won't be flogging you in the winter, Kevin. We'll get you a full physical assessment and we'll manage that side of it. I want to EXPLODE you in the summer!'

It was like the movie *Jerry Maguire*.

You had me at hello.

I KNEW I wouldn't be wasting my time.

He was saying I would be looked after and playing to my ego, that I would be an essential component of what he planned. What was obvious was that he planned on winning an All-Ireland.

He had come to Galway to do just that, having gone so close with Mayo in 1989. Johno was very professional, detailed and ran a good training session. There was no messing either. His sessions were very organised and enjoyable.

I was very impressed when he set up the biomechanics assessment with Aofáine Walshe. While it has become something of an urban myth that I had an injury-free run from this point on – nothing could be further from the truth – there was a real will to look after me, to get me the proper treatment and work on various physical issues that might be causing some of my groin and knee difficulties. I was being cared for.

By unearthing a lot of core issues, Aofáine was able to address them and there was an immediate improvement just by getting orthotic insoles for my footwear. I owed a lot to Aofáine, as well as Mick Byrne, the Republic of Ireland soccer team physio under Jack Charlton. While there were a number of other injuries, there would be no more groin issues, having had three of them up to that point.

With a decent bank of fitness from the club season, I was able to join up with the panel in September and put in all the winter training for the first time in six years, without having some injury knock me off course.

I had a tailored programme and Johno got Eddie O'Sullivan, the future Ireland rugby head coach, to work with me on short, sharp, high-intensity sessions, with more recovery time. It was a testament to his attention to detail.

As a result, I lined out in a number of league games and caught the eye of the Connacht selectors, at a time when the Railway Cup was still something you liked being involved in. But Johno was onto me quickly.

'Kevin, do you mind if you step back from that? I know you're playing well but do you mind just stepping back from that and we'll *explode* you in Castlebar in May.' He was at it again.

Massaging the ego while stopping me doing something I sort of wanted to do. What he was doing was managing me though, and that was what I needed. When it came to injury prevention, I did not need to add Railway Cup mileage.

We played Kilkenny in Freshford in March, which was a fairly unusual occurrence brought about by a new structure. The reason it sticks out in my mind was that I had to rush back home straight after because we had organised a surprise party for my father's 70th birthday.

I was just building up minutes, confidence and fitness.

Getting ready to detonate.

♦ ♦ ♦ ♦ ♦

THERE WAS ONE other important element to my form that season.

It started with an article I read about the great Spanish golfer José Maria Olazábal, who had endured years of agony with pain in his foot, that was ultimately traced back to a biomechanical defect in his back. Olazábal had tried everything and as someone who had been to the local Holy Well, I knew that head space well.

Prior to this, I had given Japanese bioenergy a twirl, at a practice on Merchant's Road in Galway. It is based on the Japanese belief that there is an aura around the body and that pain can be caused by a blockage to your energy channels.

I found bio-energy treatment very helpful and went back regularly as I got some relief with my groins and an old neck injury from an under-21 club game. That was healed without ever being touched and has been 100 percent since.

So when I read Olazábal had gone on the Nutron diet, I felt it might be the kind of radically different approach I needed. I began in March, when I was blood tested for 200 different allergies. Anything you had an intolerance to was removed from your menu.

That was dairy, gluten, any frozen food… anything in a package, wheat, flour and yeast. It was brutal. After the first week, I got a lot of headaches and back aches, but that was just the body looking for what it had been accustomed to.

After six weeks, I was meant to start re-introducing one or two foods at a time so I could nail down what might be having a detrimental effect on me. If there was none, you kept it in the diet and moved to the next.

I went an extreme route that the nutritionists wouldn't approve of. I kept going as I was right through to October. Seeing pictures now, I was like death warmed up. You could see the sinews in my legs.

My face was gone to nothing. I played the All-Ireland final at 15st 2lbs. I'd be fit at 16st 4lbs. I lost some power but was still strong. The real benefit was that I had massive relief on my knees, hips and groins.

I could jump more often. I FELT GOOD!

Obviously, it would have been unhealthy to continue such a regime and I gradually returned to normal but the positive impact remains to this day. My weight used to balloon when I was out of action but since then, I can eat like a horse. I still weigh in at 16st 7lbs, albeit with a lot less muscle.

Nowadays, if you were missing out on protein, like I was, the nutritionists might meet you halfway and recommend some supplements. When I went to Sligo, I put Alan Costello on the Nutron. I had a target for him to lose more than 2lbs per week.

I would pull the weighing scales out of the boot and get him to stand on it, surreptitiously. We wouldn't do it in front of the lads. Weight is a very sensitive issue and I was working with Alan. He didn't need slagging, he needed encouragement.

I knew from my own experience what the benefits could be for him and he turned out to be a superb player for me. His native Mayo never got the best from him, never helped him reach his potential, but he was outstanding for Sligo.

♦ ♦ ♦ ♦ ♦

COROFIN WON THE All-Ireland club final on St Patrick's Day, comfortably accounting for Erin's Isle by five points. It was a painful reminder of when Killannin had them on the rack and I couldn't help thinking what it would have been like for our little parish to be known for having the best club side in the land.

Ray Silke was presented with the Andy Merrigan Cup and we all hoped it was a portent of things to come.

Back on the county scene, we lost to Offaly in the league quarter-final at Dr

Hyde Park. It was a decent effort in that we created more than enough chances to win the game. Personally, I was feeling fit. Offaly were the reigning Leinster champions and they progressed to claim what remains the Faithful's only Division 1 title, overcoming Derry by two points in the decider.

If I was reasonably pleased with the performance, Johno maintained we were missing a fundamental ingredient. He reached out to Ja Fallon, who hadn't lined out for Galway since the 1996 Connacht final when he led from the front despite injuring a knee that eventually forced his departure in the second-half.

After that, he went playing rugby with Galwegians and his form in the AIL around a time when the oval ball code was transitioning to professionalism, brought him to the attention of Connacht director of rugby, Warren Gatland. There was talk of a contract offer.

One of Ireland's greatest rugby players, Ronan O'Gara wrote in his *Irish Examiner* column in 2015… *When you walk down a mean street with someone, you know exactly what he is made of.* We had a real breath of fresh air in the likes of Pádraic Joyce, Michael Donnellan and Derek Savage, to join men of the calibre of Seán Óg de Paor and Gary Fahey who were now bedded into the team.

But I had been down some real dark alleys with the likes of Ja and Tomás Mannion. I knew they could be relied upon. It was a fantastic boost to see Ja ambling into training that first night. Others got more plaudits but Ja was our best forward in my opinion. He was capable of the stupendous but had consistency, could win his own ball and was an outstanding link man as well as a score-getter.

Johno had sprinkled his magic dust once more and another piece of the puzzle was in place.

♦ ♦ ♦ ♦ ♦

WE HAD A lot of attack-oriented players, so for me, the game plan was very simple. I would win it, give it and mind the house most of the time.

Seán Ó Domhnaill was my midfield partner. A lovely fella, 'Fada' was a mountain of a man, two inches taller than me at 6'6". And his hands were so big! We used to say he was so tall he could tie his shoelaces without bending his back. He was a free spirit who enjoyed the craic, could talk for Ireland and liked to do his own thing on the pitch.

Seán has said often that his best days in the maroon were alongside me and I do think it was because I was the one person he would listen to. The only time his sunny disposition became cloudy was when he was told what to do but whatever language I used, or however I delivered instructions, he seemed to go along with them and I could cajole him around the park. When you had him on side, he would do anything for you and he had a huge campaign.

The players called me the daddy of the team, though I was still only 28, but I was happy to take on that role. It was in my nature to be pointing and issuing instructions. I directed traffic and rarely stopped talking; coaching even before I considered it something I might be good at. That was definitely Mary Nihill's influence, having placed such a high emphasis on on-court communication.

The entire focus was on the first round of the Connacht Championship and another clash with Mayo, arguably the best team in the country. That their victory the season before was their first in Tuam in 46 years was a nice little additional piece of motivation as we headed up to Castlebar on May 24.

All the planning and preparation on a personal level got off to a disappointing start when I got a dead leg in the first aerial challenge after 90 seconds. As I was in agony, I thought to myself that if this were more of the same, the boots were going over the fence.

I shook it off though and went on to have a very productive day.

Ciarán McDonald kicked two first-half goals either side of a peach of a lob by Derek Savage but we found another level in the second-half. We still needed a bit of luck when McDonald struck the underside of the crossbar with us leading by three points. We won a free from the clearance and Niall Finnegan slotted for his fifth point to seal the triumph.

These are the fine margins that determine people's judgements of players, managers and teams. Had McDonald's shot been an inch lower, we could have been out.

Pádraic, Derek, Gary Fahey and Ja all had big games, and Martin McNamara made a couple of big saves. I was named Man of the Match. People might not believe me but the feeling after that victory was the sweetest of the entire season. I remember it more fondly than the All-Ireland final itself.

This felt like the justification for everything and you don't replicate that a second time. To put in the work I did, with tremendous support from a lot of people, and get the actual rewards for it was incredible. There wasn't a medal on offer.

There wasn't even a place in the Connacht final.

The reward was me at my best and only a year after I had been discarded. It was Galway beating Mayo, as good a team as there was in Ireland, when it was do or die. It was just glorious.

What's more, we did it in front of a sea of maroon. I had never seen such support. It was the first time we had ever been held up in traffic at Claremorris. The outpouring of emotion from the stands matched what I felt at the final whistle.

It was the greatest buzz of all.

♦ ♦ ♦ ♦ ♦

DESPITE STARTING SLOWLY, we blew Leitrim away by 14 points in the semi-final, displaying a really good attitude. Niall, Pádraic and Derek were responsible for 1-12 of our 1-16, while Seán and I dominated the middle. The one negative, and it was a considerable one, was the fractured fibula suffered by Paul Clancy.

Roscommon lay in wait in the Connacht final on July 19. The acrimonious Munster hurling final replay in which Clare trounced Waterford the same day dominated the headlines. That suited us because the post-mortem wouldn't have been pretty from our perspective. Once again, we rode our luck and it looked like curtains when Eddie Lohan pointed a free in front of the posts with three minutes remaining.

Martin, who made two splendid first-half saves from Lorcan Dowd and Tommy Grehan, responded sharply by taking a short kickout to Gary. He launched it long, a free was awarded and Niall was the personification of composure once more to rescue us.

Roscommon played the guts of 20 minutes at a numerical disadvantage after the dismissal of substitute Jason Neary. While wastefulness had almost cost us dearly, our attitude had been poor. It was evident that some players took Roscommon for granted, which history has shown us is a perilous and foolish policy any time.

It was a nice lesson to learn, without paying the ultimate price.

Johno made a big point on the culture of the team too when taking Fada to task for his head-shaking reaction to being substituted. No-one is happy about being hauled ashore but the manager persistently emphasised the importance of the team over the individual. Seán took the message on board and responded very positively.

In the dressing-room before the replay, which was back in the Hyde again, Johno produced a newspaper article with the headline… *Galway Fancy Dans get the simple things wrong.* In it we were labelled a nice team and it wasn't a compliment. The article also said that Galway… *don't have a midfield pairing capable of winning a majority of team possession.*

I always used any sense of injustice or unfair commentary, or even the perception of it, to try to find that extra bit as a player – and did the same as a manager – even in the era of high-performance preparation. There is nothing like feeling slighted to get a little bit more and with two evenly matched sides, you are always chasing the one-percenters.

None of which is to say it was any easier second time around.

We played better but Roscommon had good players and possessed a ferocious workrate. The game went to extra-time after finishing 0-13 apiece when we came from two points down in the last 10 minutes to hit the front, but Eddie Lohan levelled from a 35-metre free.

The defining score was an opportunist goal by Michael Donnellan at the start of extra-time's second-half. There was nothing fancy about it, being rooted in the industry by Shay Walsh, who had come off the bench. He closed down Roscommon goalie Derek Thompson and forced an error. Michael pounced on the spilled ball and drove it to the unprotected net with glee. That was the margin of victory at the end.

In the process, Johno was winning a Connacht Championship with a third county. It is an amazing achievement.

◆ ◆ ◆ ◆ ◆

I HAD COME off six minutes from the end after tearing my calf. Rather than hit celebratory mode, my thoughts turned to the All-Ireland semi-final.

After the disaster against Tyrone three years earlier, I was going to do everything to be in mint condition back at HQ.

The lads hit the town but I went straight home to begin my recovery.

From there it was an intensive programme of physio and ice. I did not return to work until the following Saturday and though I didn't train much, apart from a bit of jogging, I knew the week before that I would be good to go.

I would need to be. Derry had a much-touted midfield pairing of Anthony Tohill and Enda Muldoon. Tohill earned most of the plaudits and was a fine player but it was notable for me that his form had waned for a few years after Brian McGilligan's retirement. To me, McGilligan gave Tohill the freedom to focus on being an attacking force. He was the one doing the donkey work.

Because of our struggles against underrated Roscommon, Derry were heavily tipped to have our measure. The lowered expectations definitely helped us.

The optimism generated by the Mayo win had dissipated among the Galway support too and they did not travel in force to Croke Park.

Seán and I silenced the pre-match doubters once more by getting the upper hand around the centre, and Fada kicked what was becoming a trademark bomb from the right wing to signal our growing confidence.

We were well on top, even before Kieran McKeever's second-half sending off. Their goal came from a 68th minute penalty by Gary Coleman but Ja rounded the day off with an exhibition score using the outside of his left boot from the right flank well inside the 14-yard line. There was no angle at all for a *ciotóg* but he made it look easy.

It was a fitting exclamation mark on a fantastic performance that yielded a five-point victory and a coveted All-Ireland final berth.

◆ ◆ ◆ ◆ ◆

CONTEMPORARY FOOTBALLERS WON'T believe it but we had club championship the following week. Fortunately, everyone came through unscathed. It was nice, too, to see Paul back in the ranks after breaking his leg earlier in the campaign.

I enjoyed the build-up. I was generally a relaxed type anyway. I would be at the back of the bus going to games, playing cards, trying to take a few quid off some of the lads if I could. I loved the over and back of a bit of slagging.

One thing I got a great kick out of was answering the questions for the pen pics. When it came to my favourite footballer, I can imagine a lot of people scratching their heads wondering who John McEvilly was?

That was pure divilment.

John is a seriously good character from Killannin who went to America in the mid-80s. He continued to be a massive Galway supporter who was savage craic. But he couldn't kick snow off a rope. That's the type of messer I was. I wanted to give a really good supporter a mention, while knocking a slag out of it too.

John is still in America and he's bragging about his big mention to this day.

It is important to keep things light, particularly when the season is reaching boiling point. There is a time and a place for everything and a few characters add to a group's morale. With the minors and under-21s, Tommy Finnerty was the messer. Some of the winter training nights, Tommy might go to training early, park the car behind the bushes in Claregalway and whistle at the lads running around that corner. I was with Tommy one or two nights aswell.

Fada was a full-time messer but there was never an ounce of malice in his jokes and pranks. His only goal was to have a laugh and elicit one from everyone else.

On one team holiday, he pulled down the togs of a county board official in public. Intent on revenge, our county board man snatched Seán's wallet while the big man was catching rays on the beach. I'm not sure what his plan was from there but Fada jumped up and chased after him.

Before he could be caught, didn't your man throw the wallet into the ocean.

Rather than erupt in anger, Fada burst out laughing, which he could afford to do since the wallet didn't belong to him. He had actually been minding it for someone who had gone swimming.

Seán and I roomed together on overnight stays or team holidays. One year, after a few pints in New York, a few of us decided that an accumulation of smaller tricks demanded one decent one. It was time for him to taste some of his own medicine.

Nicely lubricated, we went up to the room and took the bed, chair and table out of it. We had to take the legs off the bed to get it out. The whole lot went into the lift and was sent to the bottom floor.

Payback.

◆ ◆ ◆ ◆ ◆

I WAS SURPRISED we were such massive underdogs, even if Kildare had accounted for the previous three All-Ireland champions. As they would know well in the Thoroughbred County, 2/1 in a two-horse race is insulting.

Locally, Fada and I had been dubbed the Titanic Twins but nationally we were portrayed as mummies such was our apparent immobility. We had considerable respect for Willie McCreery, Niall Buckley and Dermot Earley as ball winners and runners though, so Martin and I devised a plan, using our reputation to our benefit.

Kildare expected the kickouts to be bombed down the middle, because the perception was that this was the only way we could win primary possession. They would have backed themselves to pick off a few of them.

We decided to hit the flanks – Martin hit the spot and I had to be there. Fada would pretend to move one way and then go another. I would do likewise but was heading for the flank Seán Óg was vacating.

You look awfully foolish when you make the run and the ball goes directly to your man but Martin was dialled in, so I just had to be sure with my handling.

I was delighted it worked out so well for him. He had borne the brunt of some supporters' criticism for his kickouts in the previous year's loss to Mayo and it stung him. It was brave to commit to a plan that would require pinpoint accuracy off the deck given that galling experience but he wasn't lacking courage.

And his execution stood up.

We got so much ball as a result, while also dragging McCreery, Buckley and Earley around the field, and it was a key element of the 1-14 to 1-10 triumph.

◆ ◆ ◆ ◆ ◆

WE BEGAN QUICKLY, totting up three rapid points.

Michael was enjoying himself, his pace and energy flourishing in Croke Park's wide expanses. He slotted the third of those opening scores after soloing clear, having run most of the length of the field just before to help set up the second, by Seán Óg.

That run was actually voted top GAA moment by RTÉ viewers in 2005. It was a magnificent team score, rooted in the stout defensive play by Tomás, who beat Martin Lynch in a battle for possession before laying off to Michael inside the '21'.

No-one seems to remember that, or the fact that Michael didn't actually go through the entire Kildare cover himself!

His speed was electrifying though and using him from deep positions made him a serious threat. He spent a lot of time in our half of the field. It's funny that such tactics cause such wailing now, yet there it was, reaping significant rewards more than 20 years ago in what was considered an attacking unit.

You would see it to very good effect again for Declan Meehan's goal two years later – possibly the greatest ever scored in an All-Ireland final – when Pádraic was on the ball on our own 14-yard line in the build-up.

We were flying but at the end of the opening quarter, Earley palmed a pass from McCreery to the net and Kildare pushed into a four-point lead. We needed Pádraic's pointed free just before the break to steady the ship.

I don't remember much at all about what was said at half-time. Johno focussed on a few of our abiding principles, such as creating more space and delivering the ball more quickly into the full-forward line. Afterwards, Niall joked that we took our Viagra.

Really, we just needed some time to reset, remove the junk flurrying around the mind. There was no panic, just an understanding that we had much more to give.

The other 15 members of the panel lined the tunnel as we emerged to resume hostilities. This was the absolute epitome of what Johno had worked so hard to build. The collective being more important than the individual, and being stronger for its unity. There could not be a bigger boost resuming battle.

As John Divilly said in *A Year 'Til Sunday*, after that injection of adrenaline, 'We ran out, ball thrown in. *Sin é*.'

Michael and Ja moved a little deeper to make some room for the lads inside but it had the added impact of Ja finding a bit more freedom. He piled all the years of hurt into a third quarter of rare quality. His leadership and genius propelled us back into the game, starting the fightback with a sensational point from the left wing.

Then came Pádraic's goal, just four minutes into the second-half that rocked Kildare back on their heels. It was a composed finish after being put through by Michael, who had gathered a long kick from John Divilly. Pádraic sidestepped Christy Byrne with ease and shook the net.

Interestingly enough, Pádraic and Michael had been watching *Match Of The Day* in their room in The Berkeley Court Hotel the night before when the

Newcastle-Nottingham Forest highlights came on. Alan Shearer had a shot saved by Dave Beasant when one-on-one and the boys agreed that if presented with a similar situation the following day, they would round the 'keeper. So Pádraic knew exactly what to do.

It was a form of visualisation, which was an innovation Johno had introduced. He had brought in a Scottish fella who worked in human resources in the city, Bill Cogan, to work on the mental side of things. I wasn't open to it at the time, though I would learn to place a lot of value in sports psychology as I become more informed later on.

Bill liked to use visualisation as a tool and some of the lads benefitted from talking to him. It showed again how revolutionary the manager was in so many ways in terms of preparation.

Ja bettered his previous score with an absolutely absurd effort from a sideline kick on the right. We were absolutely humming. Tomás, Gary and Seán Óg were leading a stern defensive resistance.

No-one was talking about the madness of having Tomás in the corner now, although by his own admission, he didn't like the role himself. A scoring forward when we enjoyed minor success 12 years previously, he had developed into a top rank half-back. But John foresaw a man-marking role.

The young lads were enjoying themselves up front, inspired by Ja, while Fada and I had established midfield dominance. I fed Fada for another point from a different post code. He raised his fists in delight and defiance.

There would be no hard luck story today.

Kildare fought as you would expect of an excellent side. Gary deflected an Earley piledriver that was heading for the top corner over the bar. That made it a three-point game but Seán Óg popped up at the end of another lovely move, in which Paul was involved after coming on, and we were home.

♦ ♦ ♦ ♦ ♦

I AM GENUINE in saying that I felt more jubilant after beating Mayo.

Even the Connacht final provided more of a buzz. It probably doesn't make sense to people, after 11 years, for winning an All-Ireland not to have elicited the greatest emotion.

I just think it would have been hard to better what coursed through me after Castlebar. That set of circumstances could not be replicated.

Don't misunderstand. There was a deep-seated sense of satisfaction. We had scaled the mountain top and I had done my part. To have my parents there was fantastic, as were Mary and an eight-month-old Caoimhe.

For the second time in six months, Ray climbed the Hogan Stand steps to be presented with an All-Ireland trophy – another All-Ireland-winning Galwegian, the late Joe McDonagh doing the honours as GAA president. Like Joe, Ray is a fine orator and got plenty of opportunity to display his skills that year. This speech was classy, particularly Ray's remembrance of Shane McGettigan. Shane offered stern resistance on his championship debut at centre-back for Leitrim against us in May but was killed tragically two months later in an accident on a building site in America. He was just 21.

The homecoming was a marathon. It was crazy with some amazing scenes crossing the Shannon, through Caltra and Ballinasloe. Tuam was just incredible.

I am not great in tight spaces and found the bus massively claustrophobic. It was wedged, with every kind of a divil on it. I couldn't wait to get off.

We sat down for our meal in the Sacre Coeur at 3.30am. Mad stuff.

The year would end with an All Star, and another, less well-known award that came from Mick Byrne. He really was a larger-than-life character, a tremendously positive presence in the dressing-room. We had great fun.

Mick was a keen golfer and though I wasn't into it that much, he told me at the start of the year he would give me a driver he had in his bag worth £500 if we won the All-Ireland. Though I couldn't say it was one of the more impactful motivational tools I used, Mick arrived at a subsequent function and presented me with this driver in front of the lads.

In later years, I gave him a few jerseys and he sent a few my way. Damien Duff's jersey against Germany was being worn by the lads for years after. John O'Shea's togs too.

1998… it just kept giving.

CHAPTER 7

FALLS TO CLIMB

There comes a point of time where it's just you in front of the mirror.
And that mirror gonna tell all.
– Dwayne Wade, D. Wade: Life Unexpected (2020)

In some ways he was like Muhammad Ali in his pomp. When he was on the Galway
team, you just felt way more confident.
– Seán Óg de Paor, Thank GAA It's Friday, July 29, 2016

YOU NEVER REALLY know about someone's mettle until they are forced to deal with setbacks and the same applies to the collective of a team.

Some come back, others don't.

On a personal level, I was almost as acquainted with getting back on the horse as a jump jockey, but the end of 1998 was probably the only time in my last eight or nine years with Galway that I didn't consider calling it a day. I felt good and wanted to help establish this Galway team as a great one.

We were the most consistent side in the country between 1998 and 2003 and a second All-Ireland was imperative in ensuring a certain standing, but we should have won at least one other and probably two. That we didn't still galls me and it has been interesting during this process that I remember much more about the games we lost around this time than either of the All-Ireland successes.

We lost grip of both the Nestor and Sam Maguire Cups with an unsatisfactory whimper, after the conclusion of the 32-year quest to attain ultimate glory.

I was hugely motivated to add to the kitty but noticed some danger signs in the form of a hint of over-confidence among the younger lads. Having gone so well in their first season, they began to stray from the team ethic and play with a degree of individuality. As the saying goes… 'Slow success builds character. Fast success builds ego'.

I was at one end of the scale, aware of how hard it was to reach the peak and desperate to squeeze as much as I could out of what was left in my career. They thought they had all the time in the world and that the continuation of the good times was inevitable. It was just another lesson to be learned.

Injury remained a constant companion. In 1999, my knee gave me a lot of trouble. I had another operation in February and only got a couple of run-outs in the league. A thumb injury against Donegal stunted my progress further and I would have to put in a lot of lonely hours to try to get to the required level of fitness.

I played no part in a workmanlike defeat of London in Ruislip; Pádraic helping himself to 1-5 in a 10-point win. Tomás and Michael were unavailable too so it wasn't the worst effort in a potentially tricky environment.

The only takeaway from the drawn semi-final with Sligo in Markievicz Park, however, was that we survived. I was back though far from fully fit. Tomás and Michael had returned too, but the new absences of Ja and Niall were keenly felt in an attack that failed to hit its stride apart from Paul, who contributed three points.

With the help of a Derek goal, we moved seven points clear early in the second-half but then proceeded to self-combust, conceding three goals. Brian Walsh and Paul Durcan grabbed the first two and when Walsh nailed his second, we were trailing with time almost up.

While all about them were losing their heads, Martin reprised the clear-headedness that had followed Eddie Lohan's late lead point for Roscommon the previous year with another quick and accurate kickout. It ended with a foul on Paul and Pádraic saved our bacon.

The attitude was much better for the replay at the Stadium and Mickey Moran's charges were unable to lay a glove on us in the second-half. John Donnellan justified his selection with seven points, six from play and many of those out of the top drawer, as we pulled away for a 13-point win.

It proved a false dawn however, and our campaign perished in Tuam a fortnight later at the hands of Mayo. There could be absolutely no argument about the four-point verdict, as we were unable to trouble the scoreboard operators from the first minute of the second-half, when John Donnellan put us 1-10 to 1-6 ahead.

There was a lot of chatter afterwards. The most common trope was that we had partied too hard. I can knock that on the head. We had a lot of work done. There was no-one who took their eye off the ball in that regard.

That's not to say the focus didn't waver.

Too many of our forwards were flat against Mayo and I think that was mental, in terms of not being attuned for the reasons already mentioned. Some of them thought it would just happen again and that their previous form gave them a licence to try do it all on their own.

Getting the star treatment can turn a young man's head and it definitely impacted on a few of the lads looking to exhibit their party tricks. That's part of growing up as a person as well as a footballer but some of them should have been taken off against Mayo, because they were making no contribution at all.

On the day, it might have given us a chance to pull it out of the fire, and longer term, it would have delivered the message loud and clear that nobody was bigger than the team.

◆ ◆ ◆ ◆ ◆

I HAD BOTH my knees scoped in September 1999 while having a meniscus tear addressed. They scraped away the debris that had accumulated behind the knee-caps. The plan was for it to be the last knee operation. Yeah, right.

I returned for 15 minutes against Cork in the league in February but felt a little strain in the groin once more in a challenge against Derry the following week, so sat out the next month. Then I aggravated it again in my first game back against Tyrone.

Killannin had championship in April, prompting me to take a chance and tog out a week or two earlier than advised. Given what had been occurring, I should have been going a week or two the other way but the draw of the club was always too powerful for me to resist.

Bad idea.

I paid the price and I made absolute shit of it. Five minutes in, I felt something like a bomb going off. Some of the lads on the line thought I'd been hit off the ball. The pain was so bad, Mary drove me directly to Aofáine's house for treatment.

The right groin was completely ruptured. The ligament had come clean off the pelvic bone and away from my stomach. I felt it might be the end of my football days at that point.

I had physio with Aofáine twice a day, five or six times a week for six weeks. There was hydrotherapy three or four times a week with Emily O'Rourke at the Corrib Great Southern Hotel. It was an arduous regime even before the process of getting myself in physical condition to line out.

The test was mental as much as anything because I didn't know if I would return to fitness and even if I did, there were no guarantees Galway would still be in contention by the time I was moving well again.

But I had to try. I did a lot of cycling, gradually got myself right and made it back for the last few minutes of the Connacht final against Leitrim, which we won by eight points in Dr Hyde Park.

We had beaten New York by 10 points in Tuam, when Richie Fahey and Joe Bergin made their championship debuts. Michael was on the bench, having only returned to training about a month before after a stint playing soccer with Galway United.

Sligo were next up, after they had scuppered Mayo's hopes and we strolled to an 18-point success and though Leitrim were resolute, we picked up Galway's 40th Connacht title with ease, despite totting up 11 wides.

The game was over when I came on but it was nice to hear the ovation as I jogged out towards my position. I wanted to see where I was so when the first ball came on top of me, I thought, *To hell with it*, jumped and the groin held, though I misjudged the ball by a mile.

That was some relief.

A week later I lasted the hour for the club against Barna, with Mayo midfielder Pat Fallon in direct opposition. I played very well and that was another injection of confidence.

NEXT UP WAS a box office All-Ireland final reunion with Kildare.

Tickets were at a premium because the Hogan Stand was being rebuilt but Mary was there with Caoimhe (2½), Orlaith (1½) and Cathal (five weeks), who must have been the youngest in attendance.

That is Mary for you. She wasn't missing the games even if it meant hauling three children under the age of three with her. In the week before the Kildare game, I had to go into the station at Salthill for the start of my 10pm shift directly from training. As a guard married to a guard who was a county footballer, it wasn't easy but Mary did it all without any fuss.

Many pundits thought Kildare would have the greater motivation, but we had no shortage of it, having made a mess of 1999. We were anxious to prove that '98 was not a one-off, attributable to Kildare being affected by the hype or injuries. Most of all, we wanted to establish our squad as one of the best of its generation.

The big difficulty were the injuries, which would become more significant as the obstacles became more difficult. Things had gone well for me since the Connacht final and I would be capable of more if required this time around. Ja and Tomás would play no part however, the former after tearing his cruciate in the club championship in June, the latter due to a crippling back injury.

Apart from the quality that duo brought, their unavailability left a chasm of leadership that manifests itself in tight corners. We were far from perfect, failing to add to four sharp points notched up in the opening seven minutes for the rest of the half, leaving Kildare leading by one at the interval thanks to Tadhg Fennin's goal.

Ja would not be one of those people who is in your face all the time, talking for the sake of it, so when he spoke during the break and you heard the hurt and desire in his words, you steeled yourself. We had to do better.

Paul, Pádraic and Michael kicked three points but Karl O'Dwyer replied with a treble of his own and when Brian Murphy goaled, we were three behind. I managed to get on some possession when making my entrance six minutes into the second-half but of more significance was the solid screen that blocked Kildare's ability to break forward. Willie McCreery, in particular, had been rampaging through the middle but I blocked that route to goal.

Gradually we assumed control, with Pádraic and Michael excelling. That said, we were still a point in arrears with five minutes remaining, though Kildare were down to 14 following the sending off of John Finn 10 minutes earlier.

The key to the strong finish was our experience of this sort of situation, rather than the numerical advantage. Rather than waiting for things to happen or being afraid of making a mistake, we went for the jugular.

Pádraic kicked a pair of lovely points before Michael lofted over a free from nearly 55 metres. Niall won a free and converted it himself and we were back in another final, thanks to a 0-15 to 2-6 scoreline.

♦ ♦ ♦ ♦ ♦

IT CAME AS a shock that I wouldn't start the All-Ireland.

Before the semi-final, when he was mulling over the idea of picking me, I had told Johno that neither Fada nor Joe deserved to lose their places after three good wins. We were going well, so why change?

That didn't apply now. I had to come in just after half-time because we were in big trouble. Something had shown itself not to be right and I had been called upon to turn it around. So I was annoyed.

I felt it was a necessity, for the betterment of the team that I start.

At the time, Maurice Fitzgerald was seen as an impact player for Kerry. Maybe that's what Johno had in mind but it was something I never believed in. I knew at the time that Maurice probably wasn't good enough to get his place. Of course you can have an impact when you're as talented as he was but I don't see it as a defined role like that. I think if you're good enough, you start.

I couldn't let the disappointment show. I just had to be ready when I got the nod but I think to this day it was a costly decision.

As it transpired, the nod came far earlier than anyone would have wished for, 18 minutes in. The puncture that could have been mended from the start had to be fixed now but we had a lot of ground to make up.

'Warm up', is all Johno said to me. I didn't have to be asked twice although there was a part of me wondering if I was being thrown to the lions.

IT WAS ABOUT making a difference and I was intent on imposing myself on Donal Daly, who was fetching kickouts at his ease, while Darragh Ó Sé had been enjoying himself too.

I caught the first ball that came into our alley. Kerry actually went a further three points ahead but the flow of the play had started to change. There was a battle now. I needed to make that statement.

You're dealing with me now boyeens!

Relocating Pádraic to centre-forward was a good decision as he began influencing matters more too. He occupied a couple of Kerry defenders and we began to get a toehold in the game.

Slowly but surely, we inched our way back. People liked to talk about our array of glitzy skills but this was a performance of grit and determination. To be within three points at the change of ends said a lot for the progress we had made in this regard, particularly without Ja and Tomás.

That said, when Kerry extended their advantage to five, it was worrying because we had far less time to reel in the deficit now. I had to banish a feeling of disillusionment that had attempted to creep in. It was time to dig deep into the reservoirs of fortitude and that was demonstrated by the entire team.

We never led and Pádraic only made it 0-14 each with four minutes remaining, but we were making all the running in the final quarter and should have won it in the end. We dropped three shots short into Kerry goalie, Declan O'Keeffe's arms, including one by Derek off his weaker right boot, when he had Pádraic in position for a simple score.

Of course we might have lost it too. I was the nearest to Denis O'Dwyer when he had his shot from 35 metres.

Near but not near enough to get a block in or put pressure on.

I felt physically sick as he drew his boot back and can tell you now, a silent prayer was muttered as he did so. I thought we were gone and it was some relief that his shot tailed to the left.

Journalist Kieran Shannon put some stats together after the drawn game. Before I came on, Kerry had won nine out of 10 kickouts, with Daly catching three clean. Ó Sé had been in possession 11 times.

When I threw myself in amongst them, we claimed nine of the next 13 kickouts; Daly managed only one more clean catch in the remaining 51 minutes and Ó Sé would touch the ball on just eight more occasions.

Meanwhile, I caught three kickouts, broke two to teammates, scored a point, gave the last pass for a point and played a part in another. I also found a teammate with 11 of 13 passes.

Another journalist, Alan Milton – now the GAA's head of communications – calculated that only Michael, with 18 touches, and Pádraic, with 16, had more on-ball impact than I, with 15. What is notable, for those that don't buy my *79:1 ratio*, is that Michael was on the ball for 62 seconds and Pádraic 45. I had it 40 seconds.

That leaves a long time without the ball.

THAT'S WHERE THE invisible game comes in.

Shackling the Kerry boys wasn't just about physical pressure. It was what you did away from the contest, the invisible stuff.

Taking their space, under the ball of course, but also denying room for a run, clogging up the passing lanes. Our full-back line had been under too much pressure. I took it upon myself to provide a shield. I always took it upon myself to provide that shield.

That type of analysis wasn't done too often in that era. It isn't done too often now, so it was a credit to Kieran and Alan. It showed quite clearly the madness of not coaching players for all that time when they did not have the ball.

Mary's sister, Triona got married the Friday afterwards. It was strange, being congratulated for playing well but feeling disappointed. And of course, there was another All-Ireland to go in eight days, so I couldn't celebrate in the way I might have liked to.

All along, I had thought the season would be over.

The possibility of a draw never enters anyone's mind.

◆ ◆ ◆ ◆ ◆

THERE CAN'T HAVE been much discussion about whether I would start the replay. Richie would also start, in place of Ray, who had a tough time against Mike Frank Russell. This meant three Killannin men would march behind the Artane Boys Band – a momentous achievement for such a small outfit.

We resumed battle with Kerry on October 7 – a Saturday – with the International Rules test being given the Sunday slot. They were good value for the 0-17 to 1-10 margin, and that was despite us getting off to a flier with Declan Meehan's seventh-minute goal.

I don't think there have been many better goals in an All-Ireland final, in terms of total football, team play, movement, accuracy and as convincing a finish as you could ask for.

It started as I managed to prevent Dara Ó Cinnéide's '45' going over the bar even as the Kerry supporters were celebrating a point. The ball made its way out to none other than Pádraic, who was standing on the 14, exhibiting the benefit of a forward coming deep to make an impact once more, as Michael had done so often.

And to think many consider this an evil, modern Ulster-generated evolution, and that I introduced this black plague on Galway.

Pádraic, John Divilly and Tomás Meehan escaped a tight spot cleverly to send Seán Óg scampering down the left.

I had begun to move my way forward and even as Seán Óg cut in and passed to me, I could see Pádraic sprinting past him tight to the sideline. So I quickly gave him a fisted pass off my left. Fada pulled a man out of the middle, giving Pádraic the gap to drill a lovely low, diagonal kick pass into Paul.

Paul's peripheral vision was in top working order and not alone did he spot Declan scorching through on his left as he gathered under pressure, but he was also aware that the space he had vacated was now uninhabited. He just had to get his kick pass right.

Without looking, working on feel and a subconscious calculation of where his lightning quick teammate might have progressed to by now, he pinged it. Declan never had to break stride to collect it and unleashed a scorcher into the far corner of the net.

I don't think you can beat that for quality. Ever.

Soon after, I got the ball to Derek and he transferred to Niall, who pointed the free awarded after he was fouled.

I HAD DONE some damage though.

My knee was really sore. I tried to run it off but had to come off in the 17th minute. It was devastating but I still hadn't given up hope of bringing something to the party. I was in and out to the dressing-room, getting an injection and some treatment. Kerry dragged us out to the wings and profited from the space through the centre. What bit of the game I did see, was hard to watch.

So when Johno asked if I was willing to go back on for the last 20 minutes, there wasn't a prayer of me turning him down.

WE HAD GOTTEN level but Kerry had too much firepower. Johnny Crowley, Liam Hassett and Aodán Mac Gearailt kicked three points each from play. Michael was our only multiple scorer from play with two points.

I managed a point myself after returning to the action but x-rays afterwards revealed that a chunk of my kneecap had broken away. Coming back on was crazy and assuredly made matters worse but you do what you can and I actually did well following my reintroduction. All you are thinking about is winning an All-Ireland.

The failure to bag this one represents the greatest disappointment of my senior county career. To have taken Kerry down in a final would have been perfect, given their status in the game, and it was my only chance of doing so.

Not having Tomás and Ja was distinctly damaging to our chances but after what I had done in the drawn game, and how I'd begun the replay, there's no-one who will ever convince me we wouldn't have won if I had started the first day.

I don't know why Johno was so cautious, given he had planned on starting me in the semi-final. I had been free of injury and training since before the Connacht final and unlike that game, we needed to make changes early against Kildare. What's more, I had an influence. You would not have had to be justifying the decision to anyone.

Saying that makes me sound cocky and I hate to come across that way but it is my fervent belief. The defeat was avoidable. That's what hurts.

I should have started, Ray shouldn't have been left so long on Russell. He shouldn't have even started on him given he'd openly admit he's not a corner-back and you had Richie sitting next to me on the bench.

And we should have finished those chances in the closing 10 minutes that would have seen us home comfortably.

I don't spend every day thinking about it. But I won't ever forget it.

♦ ♦ ♦ ♦ ♦

ONCE AGAIN, THE pull of Killannin proved irresistible and with us qualifying for the final of the senior championship for the first time in our history, I wasn't going to sit in the dugout. I strapped up as best I could and lined out at full-forward against Corofin, hoping I might win a few frees or something.

It was the end of the year and the Stadium was like a bog. I was in agony and finally conceded defeat with 10 minutes to go. We fell short by a goal. More heartbreak.

I was getting older. Mary and I were very kindly invited to Renvyle's GAA dinner dance at the end of the year and they produced a lovely booklet, that included a piece on me. A typo had me being a member of Galway's All-Ireland-winning mob of 1886. There was great craic about that as we wondered were people trying to tell me something.

Despite the knee hurting as I walked up the stairs at home, sat in the car or played with the kids, I was intent on avoiding another operation. I rolled the dice and let it fall where it may.

When I couldn't even play a game of table tennis on the team holiday in Cape Town the following January though, I had to concede defeat on that score. So, in February, I went under the knife once more.

The urgency was due to the delivery of the message that my services were still required and given how I had performed in two All-Ireland finals, I had no doubt in my mind that I still had enough in the locker to offer the cause.

I was ready to go again once fitness was restored.

Good idea.

CHAPTER 8

RESURRECTION MAN

Pádraic Joyce and Michael Donnellan rightly get a lot of credit for their roles in our success. Yet the man that orchestrated the whole show for us was Kevin Walsh. He was the guy who could see the moves and pulled the strings and won the ball for the forwards.

Anyone who doubts his importance to the team need just look back to see the differences between our performances when he was missing, like the defeat to Roscommon in 2001, and the way we played when he was there.

– John O'Mahony, The Best Of The West (2008)

I WAS SEETHING.

The mood wasn't great anyway, after a back spasm consigned me to a non-playing role and there was nothing I could do about Seamie O'Neill being given the freedom of Tuam. Watching us being figured out so easily, doing the same things we had always done and having no answers for Roscommon almost drove me over the edge.

How long do we want to live off '98? That was three years ago.

We were poor in 1999 and then blew a glorious opportunity in 2000.

Yet still we went with 'same old, same old'… the Rossies said, 'Thank you very much', and consigned us to the very first qualifier series in GAA history.

At least we had that.

I CAN SMILE about the qualifiers now, all these years later. I wasn't a supporter of the concept. Galway had actually voted against their introduction.

What a delicious irony.

From where I was sitting in Tuam, a second chance didn't seem to be much good if we continued with our jaded approach. September seemed a long way in the distance and time was running out for me.

I couldn't afford to think of next year. There was only now. Keeping my thoughts to myself was not an option.

I shared them in a frank exchange of views. Johno seemed unmoved so I delivered the ultimatum. Unless something changed… 'I'm out'.

Consistent with how he had responded to similar situations since riding into town, he stuck to his guns. So that was it.

It was June 2001 and I was finished.

◆ ◆ ◆ ◆ ◆

THIS WASN'T THE first bump in the road.

Because of the elongated nature of the previous season, we didn't train at all before Christmas as a group. The break was needed and we had a great holiday in Cape Town in January. In February, Ireland was ground to a halt by the first outbreak of Foot and Mouth disease in 60 years.

Martin and Niall retired, and in the meantime, the injury count soared. The upside of that was the introduction of some fresh blood during the league, a lot of them under-21s. Kieran Fitzgerald and Matthew Clancy would have big roles later in the year, while the return of Ja and Tomás was a priceless boost.

Somehow, we reached the Division 1 league final but despite leading by three points on three occasions, we lost to Mayo by the minimum.

The management introduced county hurler, and now international humanitarian, Alan Kerins to the panel the following week and when he was selected for the championship opener against Leitrim just a fortnight later, it caused ructions.

John Donnellan was the one to lose his place and he left the panel. Michael, being his brother, departed in sympathy. It was front-page news locally and neither of the siblings were in Tuam that Sunday as we accounted for Leitrim by 3-24 to 3-5, with Alan one of five championship debutants along with Kieran

Fitzgerald, Pádraic Lally, Lorcan Colleran and new captain, Kieran Comer.

I don't know how discussions unfolded but the two lads were back in training on the Tuesday night, having been gone no more than a week, albeit missing a championship tie. There were no recriminations but Johno stuck to his guns with Alan throughout the campaign.

♦ ♦ ♦ ♦ ♦

IT WAS ABOUT five weeks later when I almost fell out with him.

I only wanted what was best for the team and it was obvious, watching from the line as goals from Frankie Dolan and Nigel Dineen put us to the sword, that we had become stale.

Pádraic kicked six points, four from play, but we could not get the rest of the forwards into the game. Meanwhile, the defence was unbalanced, and our pattern of play had become predictable. I went home that evening thinking that this had been coming.

I would never undermine a manager or question him in front of others, but I never had a problem in putting my view forward privately for consideration.

I mulled it around in my head for a about a week before resolving to call Johno. I drove over the bridge from the station in Salthill, pulled the patrol car up behind a garage on the Headford Road – the old Advance Pitstop – and dialled the number.

An hour later, the conversation finally concluded.

It wasn't a bitching match and there was no bad language, but my offerings weren't well received. I put everything I was thinking out on the table and there was loads coming back.

We needed a Plan B at least for when our go-to methods weren't working. And a Plan C.

I mentioned a roving corner-forward and spoke about tightening up in certain areas. I referred to certain individuals, their roles, their contributions. I just threw out ideas.

I couldn't argue with Johno when he said he was the manager and would make the decisions. What I was hoping was that he would listen to a senior player, someone I hoped he respected, and maybe give a commitment to consider what I was saying, to think outside the box.

It seemed obvious to me that he either placed little value on what I had to say or felt that I was out of order to be offering an opinion on such matters. So out it came.

'You won't see me Tuesday night.'

This was not for show. I was deadly serious. For all the opportunities I had, I only retired once. I would have hated to do so and rock back in a few months later. So, I meant it.

We had Wicklow in Aughrim the following Saturday, a dirty, rotten little challenge when things aren't going well. I stayed at home that Tuesday night, and a couple of county board lads called to the door the next day.

'Will you come back in?'

'I won't… and you'll go back and tell him I won't.'

I didn't go to training on Thursday either. On Friday, the call came and the tone had softened substantially.

'Look… we've been thinking about what you've been saying. All we can say is we'll keep it in mind and we'll look at a few options. But for now, will you just keep the ship afloat?'

That was all I had wanted.

WE WENT DOWN to Aughrim and changes were made.

Tommy Joyce was withdrawn as a rover, to act as a third midfielder and additional defensive screen, leaving more acreage inside to increase our attacking threat. With John Divilly injured, Tomás, who had been put through the ringer by Frankie Dolan, was relocated to centre-back, where he was more comfortable and could exert more influence with his great positioning and reading.

Alan Keane was handed the goalkeeper's jersey, and Gary and Richie resumed their duties in the full-back line.

We emerged unscathed with nine points to spare and the renewal had begun. What's more, the management had shown flexibility, having been jolted into considering other options.

Of this I am 100 percent sure. Galway would not have won the All-Ireland if I didn't dial John O'Mahony's number and had that difficult exchange. The changes were pivotal and turned our year around.

Credit to the management for making them.

WOULD I BE open to that sort of conversation as a manager?

Absolutely.

I placed such emphasis on having open lines of communication with players that I developed a conduit system. It started in Sligo and developed over time, where we created pods of four or five players, with a leader to be their conduit to management. Subsequently again, I appointed a deputy leader, to keep the leader 'honest' and make sure he was doing his job.

I was thinking about the fella that wouldn't have the balls to say something to me. Dialogue with number 40 is as important as with number 1. You want everyone to be happy and comfortable.

Apart from that, everyone has different information. Why should that information be just gathering dust in the recesses of someone's mind? I like to work with a cement mixer of ideas. Throw everything into it.

I learned so much by having these communication lines open. You've got to park your ego and be as open-minded as you can.

Communication is a critical component in the creation of a positive, caring culture.

◆ ◆ ◆ ◆ ◆

OUR ROUND 3 qualifier with Armagh was fixed for Croke Park, which was a tremendous advantage given our experience at that point. Armagh were very strong and would be All-Ireland champions the following season.
We had played them a few weeks previously in a challenge match and they beat us by 16 points – we had a lot of ground to make up.

Kieran, Gary and Tomás were outstanding in defence and Tommy helped keep things tight. We weren't humming up front but Armagh were strong defensively and had a really industrious, no frills midfield.

I made my first appearance of the year in the closing stages in a bid to stem the tide as Armagh established superiority. Paul and Derek announced their returns from injury as subs as well. I won a few throw-ins with Paul McGrane, one deep in our own half with the teams level on 0-12 each.

Michael made the decisive defensive play, blocking Justin McNulty's kick and hitting them on the counter. His kick pass found Paul and he verified his well-being after his broken ankle with his second point... the winner.

We had a fortnight to regenerate for Cork in Round 4, back at GAA HQ. They were a real threat, had been in the All-Ireland two years previously and shown their form by pushing Kerry to three points in the Munster final.

Fada got married the day before.

We all attended, though obviously there was no night made of it. A goal from Seán Óg put us in a strong position the next day and we were six points ahead when Seán came on for me at the end of the third quarter.

Cork gave us a scare as they recorded the next five points but Gary led a stern resistance from the back and the lads showed real steel to wrestle back the initiative. Ja strained his hamstring, which was a worry, but Matty went on and helped himself to two points in an eye-catching cameo. We won by four and had passed another major test.

The first qualifier series had been navigated.

A fabulous innovation.

◆ ◆ ◆ ◆ ◆

WE GOT ROSCOMMON in the All-Ireland quarter-final. It was a dream draw for us, a nightmare for them. We were a completely different outfit from two months before and John Tobin's men would see a completely different picture.

A thirst for revenge provided further fuel.

It was all over by half-time, with the scoreboard reading 0-9 to 0-1. We weren't at the same level in the second-half but never needed to be.

My fitness was improving all the time and I enjoyed myself, even kicking a point but spending a lot of my time blocking the passing lanes into Dineen and Dolan. Pádraic slotted seven frees. Our restructured defence was dominant and unusually for us that year, the game passed without drama.

◆ ◆ ◆ ◆ ◆

DERRY WERE UNBACKABLE favourites to end our rehabilitation process and when a 20-minute famine of scoring on our part found us five points in arrears with time running out, nobody was questioning the layers.

I was enjoying my tussle with Anthony Tohill and the supply to our attack was regular, but Derry were more constructive and economic. Pádraic ended the drought with a couple of pointed frees before Matty justified his introduction once more with a 65th minute goal from a thunderbolt. We were buoyant and prevailed by 1-14 to 1-11.

To come from behind, having won all our games since the Connacht semi-final from the front demonstrated real resolve and spirit. We were in a great spot heading into the marquee day of the GAA season for the third time in four seasons.

◆ ◆ ◆ ◆ ◆

ALL WE COULD hear was… 'Meath this' and… 'Meath that'.

Apparently we had to beat Seán Boylan's charges to win a proper All-Ireland, as if beating Kildare, who had toppled the previous three champions on the way to the final in 1998 counted for nothing.

When did Meath become the barometer for greatness? Remember how lucky they were to beat Mayo in '96? Well 12 of that unit were lining out against us.

Yes, I knew they had obliterated defending champions Kerry by 15 points to get over the penultimate hurdle. That just piled pressure on them. On RTÉ, the way Colm O'Rourke went on, you'd think Meath had 20 All-Irelands won.

Meanwhile, Johno played the poor mouth to perfection.

Then there was the personal criticisms.

One of O'Rourke's I had stored was when he said after the replayed All-Ireland that it was time for Fada and me to stand aside, that we had no more to offer. That was harsh, very unfair, but most of all, ill-informed. I had played very well until the injury.

That was actually a major motivation for coming back in 2001. To finish the year with a second All-Ireland medal and another All Star was exquisite.

THE MEDIA WERE playing up talk of a double, with the hurlers also in the final. It never really permeated the dressing-room, though it was obviously very real for Alan.

That all ended once the hurlers were beaten by Tipp by three points.

Again, that must have been difficult for Alan, because there is a grieving process after losing an All-Ireland. But then maybe the involvement with the footballers was a Godsend in those circumstances. Certainly, he wasn't moping around the place in training.

We were secure through the entire duration of the game. Some maintain that it might have been different had Trevor Giles goaled from his penalty to cut the deficit to four points with 12 minutes remaining, or had Nigel Nestor not been sent off a little earlier. You never know the ripple effect of one event but whereas I would point to a number of days in the course of our campaign in 1998 when fortune was our friend, we were completely dominant in this game.

But listen, it was no penalty, whatever Michael Collins was thinking. I was near John McDermott and he threw himself to the ground, in my opinion. All he was missing was the Triple Salchow.

What kept Meath in touch for as long as they were was our recklessness in front of posts, with Pádraic the chief culprit. He kicked three wides he would normally convert with his eyes closed in the first-half but still had some part in all of our six points.

It was criminal that we were level at half-time.

I wasn't much of a talker in the dressing-room normally but on this occasion I told the forwards if they had gotten as much ball in training, they would have dusted our backs. It was time to buck up.

Pádraic held his hand up and promised he would produce if we kept feeding him. He finished with 10 points, half of them from play. Talk about keeping your word.

Declan covered every blade of grass and Michael, Joe, Tommy and I helped establish the whip hand around the middle. Michael and Joe were more attack-minded, while Tommy and I focused on clogging up the middle and cutting out the supply to Ollie Murphy. And with Pádraic and Derek in plenty of space inside, we could find them with ease.

Most satisfying was that our workrate was far superior than Meath's. They were renowned for their industry, their physicality, their hardness. They wore teams down. They broke them down.

Every team has physical players. We outworked them and we outplayed them. It was full throttle all the way to the line and it was authoritative at the conclusion, 0-17 to 0-8.

TO HAVE THREE Killannin boys on the team that gave Galway its ninth All-Ireland was incredible. For Gary to be the first man from the west of the county to collect the Sam Maguire Cup was plucked from the realms of fantasy. What a great little club.

Needless to say, I didn't emerge completely unscathed. There was one incident where McDermott and I were going for a ball and his head slammed up into my lower jaw, snapping my mouth shut. That led to two upper molars being shattered and a few more fillings loosened.

It was sore but you don't even want to think what might have happened if my tongue had been sticking out.

The one disappointment about the entire day was that Mary and the kids couldn't get out onto the pitch. I would have loved that because I wouldn't be out there if Mary didn't facilitate it.

She contented herself with taking photos of the presentation and the players celebrating but clearly Orlaith didn't want to look back on the day her old man won his second All-Ireland, even though as a two-year-old, she wasn't going to remember.

When Mary was distracted, most likely with Caoimhe or Cathal, she opened the camera and pulled out the film. We still give her stick over it.

They say you never forget your first time but the joy from the second lasted a bit longer. Proving critics wrong is the sweetest supplement.

CHAPTER 9

OUR LEADER

In this era, Kevin stands out as the big man. He was at midfield, catching the ball with one hand when the referee threw it up, and laying it off. He's an inspirational man. For fellas of my vintage, he would certainly be one of the greats of Galway football, certainly in the top half-dozen.

               – **Bosco McDermott,** *The Sunday Times,* **May 19, 2002**

It was a second-half full of passion and effort but with Kevin Walsh an Atlas like figure in the middle of the field with the Galway football world on his shoulders, a victory was secured from the very clutches of defeat.

               – **Francis Farragher,** *The Connacht Tribune,* **June 7, 2002**

KERRY BEAT US well in 2002, after we had annexed the Connacht title, but the failure to go back-to-back in the All-Ireland championship was the least of my worries.

My father was ill with cancer.

He had been diagnosed at the end of 2000 but started getting quite weak during the summer, when he was moved to a hospice.

I would call in after my shift at the station, whether that was in the morning or later at night. We staggered our visits so that he had someone with him as often as possible. It was tough, going in maybe at 10.30pm and coming home at 5am but for the man who had worked himself to the bone to help provide for us, shaped our principles and given us such a *grá* for sport, there was nothing we wouldn't have done.

With Galway, there were some good days but others when nothing happened. At the time, I did not consider what was happening with my father to have any impact but it must have. Even in terms of just being physically tired and lacking focus.

He died in September, a month after the Kerry game.

I hope I made him proud. You never knew because he didn't share his feelings too much but I think I did.

I was proud of him and it meant so much that he was in Croke Park in 1986, '98 and '01 along with my mother, as they had been at all the games and athletic meets when we were children. They set us on the path. They wanted us to have something else other than life's grind. I hope those days were some form of payback.

My father was a quiet man.

He was a great man.

He was our leader.

♦ ♦ ♦ ♦ ♦

THE LADS USED to joke that I would be wheeled out by the time the Silver Jubilee of 1998 was celebrated. I'm looking good to make it out under my own steam but even as my chronic injuries were being managed well, there always seemed to be something.

We dispatched Roscommon ruthlessly in the opening round of the championship but I began to feel some discomfort in my thigh in the immediate aftermath. I sat out training but the pain worsened.

I was brought into hospital on the Wednesday night before the semi-final against Mayo and it was discovered there was a cyst growing into the bone on the inside of my thigh.

They put me on an intravenous drip and scheduled the operation for Monday under general anaesthetic, but by Friday, I couldn't take the pain anymore. I pleaded with them to consider some other alternative to a procedure that required general anaesthetic.

Well, they could root it out under local anaesthetic?

Grim. Grisly.

Luckily, I had no idea how grim and grisly and I told them to bang away.

It was excruciating, the worst pain I have ever felt. More than once I wondered if local anaesthetic was any anaesthetic at all.

They let me out on Saturday, wrapping me up with reams of padding, and a pair of fishnet tights to hold it all in place. And that's what I wore under my shorts as I strode out of the MacHale Park dressing-room the following day.

WHAT I MANAGED over the next 70 minutes and change was astounding really. I hadn't just not trained for a few weeks, I had been in hospital for four days, had my inner thigh drilled into and was sore as a boil.

But something clicked.

Whatever position I took up, the ball seemed to arrive there. When I jumped, it stuck in the paws. When I gave a pass, it hit the mark. Just behind me, on a day for the old stagers, Tomás was excelling.

Yet we trailed throughout, Michael Moyles goaling with a mere 15 seconds gone. It wasn't always easy for the forwards but Pádraic and Paul came up with some huge scores.

I could feel the petrol gauge beginning to empty early in the second-half. It was the 43rd minute when I saw David Brady getting ready to come on for David Heaney.

Now I used to enjoy playing against Brady and would always be confident of handling him. He normally started around that time but I would always tell him he would be heading back to the bull pen shortly enough. He was very emotional so I would try to press a few buttons to get him wound up.

He was honest as a footballer, gave his all and was physical. He wasn't the biggest but you knew there was going to be a lot of niggly rooting and pulling and dragging. The physical aspect of midfield play never held any fears for me for obvious reasons but I hadn't the gas left for it.

My far-from-ideal build-up had caught up with me. I was wrecked.

Being Brady, his first move was to drive an elbow into my side.

Normal behaviour.

I knew I wouldn't be able for 25 more minutes of this.

It's either you or me here buddy, I said to myself, just before Mayo goalie, Peter Burke launched his kickout.

Brady fielded it, fell and when he got up I drove my right fist into the left side of his chest and shoulder. He went down like a sack of spuds with his arms outstretched like he was on the cross but to give him great credit, that was probably just an instinctive reaction, because he bounced back up immediately.

In doing so, he may well have saved me.

I had never really thought about where the referee Niall Barrett was, which was an indication of how frazzled I was mentally. He couldn't have missed the incident.

It might have looked from the stands that I struck Brady in the jaw. I had always been conscious of not hitting anybody above the shoulder. It just wasn't in my nature. I had never been a fighter. I knew it looked bad though and I couldn't be sure I hadn't gotten it a little wrong.

I was convinced I was gone. It was some relief when the yellow came out.

Thereafter, Brady kept his distance and I was able to play within myself again without too much stress, just coaxing people away from our central channels.

Had I been dismissed it would have been disastrous and there was no doubt that I was lucky to stay on the field. The fortune extended to after the game because while Pat Spillane was screaming from the pulpit that I should be getting a three-month ban, the fact that the foul had been dealt with on the pitch meant it could not be revisited subsequently.

So while it wasn't a move I pulled out often, I didn't regret it for a second. It was what the circumstances demanded, with my energy levels on the floor.

I had one option, I took it and it paid off.

The conclusion of the game was highly dramatic. After Paul had brought us level, Conor Mortimer had a chance to put Mayo back in front from a relatively straightforward free and missed. From that wide, Alan Keane hit me a quick kickout; I transferred the ball inside to Richie and he launched it long to Pádraic, who gave us the lead for the first time, in the 71st minute.

Tommy added another almost immediately after and the great escape was complete.

It was one of my best performances for Galway. It was very satisfying on a personal level to be still doing it at 32, after the week I'd had and my father so poorly.

◆ ◆ ◆ ◆ ◆

THE CONNACHT FINAL against Sligo was a dogfight and Derek converted a penalty just before the interval that proved the difference between the sides.

That set up an All-Ireland quarter-final against Kerry. Between us, we had won four of the previous five All-Irelands and it looked like the expected humdinger was on track when Michael scored a sensational sixth minute goal.

On an individual perspective, this was far more impressive than his run in the 1998 All-Ireland final, for which he seems to be best known. Richie started it all with a brilliant fetch and supplied Michael inside our own half.

Michael then played a 25-metre kick pass to Pádraic and was close enough to take the pop pass back. Then, unlike in 1998, he had to evade defenders, the first two as he burst beyond the '45', the other pair around the '20', wrong-footing them with a neat side-step. To finish then, with a low left foot shot off the inside of the post was prodigious.

It was a false dawn however, for us and the game.

The 2-17 to 1-12 scoreline brooks little argument. We missed some really good goal chances but in truth, the five-week break left us a little off the pace coming up against a crew as good as Kerry, who were razor sharp having come through the back door.

A month later and my father was dead.

◆ ◆ ◆ ◆ ◆

I DIDN'T HAVE much enthusiasm for football when the season concluded and even told Johno I thought the time had come to hang up the boots.

We went on an All Star tour to San Diego and I spent most of the trip avoiding him.

There was a priest out there who invited the Galway crew to a dinner in his house. All I was thinking was that Johno would be on the same table as me and

I would have no way of avoiding him. It nearly took the good out of the week trying to steer clear of him. He got to me in the end. And once Johno began talking, his magic took hold again.

There was a piece of me, deep in my sub-conscious, that wasn't ready to sign off, not that I was aware of it in that moment. He might have sensed it. Performing so poorly against Kerry was not how I would have liked to ride off into the sunset. Johno might not have been pushing an open door but it was slightly ajar.

Then he mentioned the captaincy. That was an undoubted honour for me, my family and my club at that stage of my career, not that I would be changing anything. Plenty of on-field directions, no loud fight-on-the-beaches orations.

It showed that there was no residue of ill feeling from our brief stand-off in 2001. Johno understood it had never been about personalities but wanting what was best for the team.

I combined being Galway skipper with the role of Killannin manager, so it was a hectic year. A fifth Connacht medal arrived as a result of seeing off Roscommon, Leitrim and Mayo and I was thinking of my father when handed the Nestor Cup.

It remains the last time Galway would go back-to-back in the province. I wouldn't have believed then we would only lift two more provincial titles before I was appointed manager and helped double that return.

Sadly, we fell at the next hurdle once more but unlike 2002, the defeat to Donegal can be found filed in the folder marked… Ones that got away.

Earning a third All Star at the end of the season was justification for continuing. While I would have swapped it for another All-Ireland, it was recognition that I valued. That it took so long for Galway to receive another one was sad and I was delighted that that particular drought ended under my own watch, when Ian Burke was honoured in 2018. I would be confident that there will never be a father of four winning an All Star again though!

The irony, given that I derived such enjoyment from neutralising opposition midfielders and inside forwards with my movement, strength and ability to win primary possession, was that it was the more visible act of my last-ditch equaliser from outside the '45' that had people talking.

That is natural of course. People enjoy great scores and I am no different to anyone else in that regard. It's just that I appreciate, value and recognise the invisible game as much, knowing it has more of an influence on the overall proceedings.

Brendan Devenney was inspired in the replay and though we exhibited a lot of spirit to reduce a seven-point margin to three at the final whistle, we had given ourselves too much to do by missing some great goal opportunities.

Donegal went on to play the champions Armagh and were leading by four points when their full-back Raymond Sweeney was sent off early in the second-half. And though they lost by four, Armagh only confirmed their progress when Oisín McConville found the net from a 75th minute penalty.

I think Donegal would have won the All-Ireland if Sweeney hadn't been lined. So seeing as we threw it away against them, I will believe until my dying day that we should have won it all.

It went back to missed chances, and missed chances cost us in 2000 as well.

It makes me think twice when I read or hear descriptions of the traditional Galway style, with the swashbuckling, free-scoring forwards. But 15 years after losing to Donegal, I stood on the sideline in Croke Park as manager and watched us butcher chance after chance when we had Dublin under pressure. It was like Groundhog Day.

Gutting.

♦ ♦ ♦ ♦ ♦

IN CONTRAST TO 12 months earlier, my form made it very easy for me to come back in 2004 but the year proved to be a wipeout.

Initially, I picked up a knock on my foot that was only diagnosed as a fractured toe after a third x-ray. That wrote off most of the league. We reached the final but lost to Kerry again.

Then, just as I was returning and feeling good, Joe landed on my foot in training and broke the toe once more. I was only able to come on with 15 minutes left when Mayo overcame us in the Connacht semi-final. I returned for the defeat of Louth in the qualifiers but that would turn out to be my last game for Galway.

A week before our date with Tyrone, I tore my hamstring. I arrived late to training because of work and didn't do a full warm-up so I could take part in the trial match. Stupid.

After hitting the oxygen chamber in the hospital the first night, I had regular oxygen therapy through some contacts Aofáine had at Galway Sub Aqua Club, who helped out a number of Galway footballers over the years. I also flew to Dublin for some laser treatment. We threw the kitchen sink at it but it was all in vain. I failed a fitness test in The Citywest Hotel the night before and had to watch as we bowed out to Mickey Harte's champions.

Two more days and I'd have made it. Might as well have been two years.

◆ ◆ ◆ ◆ ◆

A LITTLE STORY about that hamstring injury that indicates Mary's high degree of saintliness.

I hadn't my mobile with me the Saturday morning I did it, so I had to ring her from a payphone just to let her know I wouldn't be home for a while yet. She started to talk but I cut across her, impatient and urgent.

'Mary, listen… I'm after making a mess of my hamstring.

'I have to play against Tyrone. I have to push this as far as I can so I'm heading straight into the oxygen chamber at the hospital now.

'I'll talk to you later.'

With that I hung up, went into the oxygen chamber and came home. But nobody was there. I rang Mary's mobile and after a few rings… she answered.

'Where are ya?'

'You wouldn't let me tell ya.'

'Where are ya?'

'I'm in labour.'

'Where?'

'In the hospital.'

'Jesus I'm only just after leaving it. Why didn't you tell me?'

'You didn't let me.'

The patience of Job.

Luckily for me, Dara wasn't in a huge hurry to join this world and waited for me to be present for the occasion of his birth.

IT WAS MARCH 2005 when I called Peter Ford to tell him I wouldn't be coming back in. I could have gone on but the possibility of breaking down again was always there. I had played in the All Star game in Hong Kong and survived, but hadn't exactly over-exerted myself.

The group of youngsters that had come in in 1998 were now around the age I was then. That left a real strong core that could combine with the next generation to bring further success.

Meanwhile, the family had expanded from one to five fairly quickly, Dara having been born safe and sound despite me not letting his mother tell me she was in labour. I was back working nights and now 35 years-old.

I might just have been doing Peter a favour too, though he did try to persuade me to stay on. He had succeeded his fellow Mayoman, having done a good job with Sligo. With Johno departing, and all of my generation retired too, it just felt like the right time.

I will forever be thankful to Johno. I am certain that we would never have won an All-Ireland without him,.

His arrival was like a *Sliding Doors* moment in my career because I was on the scrapheap when he rejuvenated and regenerated me with his vocal massage.

Oh the times we had.

CHAPTER 10

THE BATTLEGROUND

In 1998 and 2001, he was untouchable. People couldn't compete with him. Between
1998 and 2003, Kevin was one of the best midfielders in Ireland.
— Ray Silke, *Irish Independent,* July 30, 2015

ANY GROUP OF people will have a portion of warrior and wavers. If the ratio is tilted towards the wavers, as in those that tend to falter when forced out of their comfort zones, the prosperity of that group is threatened.

I played with and against members of both categories but have tremendous respect for most midfielders I tussled with. We were all trying to do the same thing in an era when it was *mano-a-mano* far more than is the case nowadays. We just had different ways of going about it.

Midfield was the engine room then, the battleground where kickouts landed, long and straight. Win the ball. Or lose it.

When I was starting off in the late-80s, my primary opponents were Roscommon duo John Newton and Seamus Killoran, TJ Kilgallon, Willie Joe Padden and Liam McHale of Mayo, Sligo's Paul Durcan, Dublin pair Paul Bealin and Jack Sheedy, Anthony Molloy and Brian Murray from Donegal, Derry's Brian McGilligan and Cork's Teddy McCarthy and Shea Fahy.

Later you had John McDermott (Meath), Rory O'Connell (Westmeath),

Eamonn O'Hara (Sligo), Willie McCreery, Dermot Earley (both Kildare), Seamie O'Neill, Fergal O'Donnell (both Roscommon), Anthony Tohill, Enda Muldoon (Derry), David Brady, Colm McManamon (both Mayo) and Paul McGrane (Armagh). I didn't mark Kildare's 'Nuckser' Buckley in the 1998 final and he gave it up soon after.

A younger crew I didn't play against very much included Darragh Ó Sé (Kerry), Pádraig Clancy (Laois), Nicholas Murphy (Cork) and Seán Cavanagh (Tyrone).

If an opponent's strength was athleticism, you'd coax him down the wide channels. Someone like Earley or O'Hara might do you for pace, so you were careful to avoid getting too tight to them. It was all about shepherding them down blind alleys.

McCreery wouldn't kill you for speed but he'd stay going all day, up and down the field. He had some engine and was a real workhorse. You had to know where he was and be prepared to run with him. Beforehand, you knew a day at the office was not going to be fun when Willie was your direct opponent.

You'd cover ground. He was also up for a bit of horsing too around the aerial contest, appropriately enough for a man who even then was immersed in racing and is now a very successful trainer on the Curragh.

What I tried to do to Willie when he had the ball was to exert some standing pressure. His skills weren't as strong as his running ability so I tried to force an error by making sure I was just close enough to ensure he hadn't an easy outlet and might have to solo. If I got too close, he had the strength to relish that and win a free.

Too far away and he could get a kick off, so I had to get that gap right.

Those that weren't going to do me for speed, I would look at imposing physical pressure off the ball. That's not boxing or wrestling. That's jostling, using the hips and shoulders to claim my ground, particularly just before the ball arrives.

With the likes of O'Neill, Brady and O'Hara, the physical pressure worked for going after them a little bit emotionally too. If there was a propensity for losing focus, I might contribute to the acceleration of that process.

O'Neill loved the big fetch so I could really get into his head if I timed my step across him as he made his run. Do that a few times, deny him the oxygen of the soaring leap and the roar from the stands, and the frustration would take hold very quickly. The next step then was to smile at him, and the head would go completely.

That was the bit of emotional pressure, just as when I'd tell Brady he would be back in the bull pen soon. That would have no impact on some fellas but it would get to others.

Without a Plan B, and another method of winning the ball, players like O'Neill tended to fade out of the game once I stopped them going for the 'Hollywood' catch every time. It just got to them.

For our own kickouts, where I couldn't even afford my opponent to fist the ball back towards our own defence, I would pick out maybe a square metre of ground where my feet were going to be when the ball landed. I had to claim my ground against the likes of a McCreery, McGilligan or McGrane, men who were willing to compete with me for the standing jump. I had to box them out, get my arse into them and reverse them out of that area.

If my rival was an O'Neill or McDermott and wanted the big running skywards spring, I wouldn't leave *terra firma* at all. My sole intent was to mess up their run. If I timed my step across their intended line properly, they would bang into a static object, either conceding a free or, if I was sufficiently anchored, be forced to watch helplessly as the ball floated into my arms or hit the ground in front of me allowing me to gather it from the bounce.

I don't think too many of my contemporaries were at that kind of thing. McGilligan might have been alright. Ó Sé was young and we rarely crossed swords, but he was already doing a bit of it.

IT DOESN'T MATTER how you win the ball.

While it's lovely for the crowd and the cameras to see the high fetch, if you miss five out of seven, is it effective? And if I cause you to miss five out of seven due to good body position and footwork, who's doing the better job?

I liked going airborne as much as the next man and there are plenty of samples of my work in that area. The knee and groin issues forced me to choose my moments in that regard however from the mid-90s. I needed to think about how I would compete a little more and became a far better player for that.

Teddy McCarthy was an outlier in that he wasn't tall but possessed an incredible spring. He loved what the AFL commentators call a 'speccy' – a spectacular catch.

I didn't get to play a lot against him, but I would take the same approach to him as I would to O'Neill and Willie Joe Padden – they all lived for the 'Wow' factor.

O'Neill had a huge game in 2001, the day I missed out with my back spasm. He didn't have too many games like that when I was alongside him and it wasn't because I was out-fielding him. I just didn't let him do what he wanted and worked the body a lot.

That would be a common theme through my last eight years, I felt. Opposing midfielders were often criticised for playing poorly against Galway, and it might be opined that I had done so too. But I knew that making an invisible impact just by taking up a particular position had the same value as a visible one.

Cumulatively, invisible impacts counted for more given the 79 minutes you weren't in possession of the ball in a county game.

So, there was a lot going on in my head depending on who was in the opposite corner, even though I wasn't breaking it down in terms of pressures at that time. The strategies existed – I only began to give them categories later as I studied coaching in a far deeper way.

While the game has changed irrevocably, I am sure that the best of my era would still flourish today because being a top midfielder was about brains, movement, awareness and understanding.

McGilligan, McGrane and McCreery were among those I admired the most, and McGilligan was the best in my opinion. He had excellent footwork and was such a physical specimen. He churned it out consistently, doing the simple things right. He was courageous and consistent but most of all he was caring.

He brought it every day so that his teammates could get the limelight.

Once Derry won, he didn't care who was getting the love from the terraces or the media, but he was the heartbeat of that team.

CHAPTER 11

WHERE THE HEART IS

Guess who has come down to the sideline, taken off a black cap and is about to come into the county final? You won't believe this... the Galway football manager is in the game!
– Ollie Turner, Galway Bay FM, October 5, 2014

I will do my best, for the credit of the little village.
– Mat 'The Thresher' Donovan, Knocknagow, 1879

'OH SHIT.'

Eamon McDonagh was injured and getting treatment. I was in the stand, like a Western spy in Cold War Russia, in deep disguise, with a cap pulled down over my eyes, attempting to look as inconspicuous as possible

'Get up Eamon.'

Eamon wasn't getting up. I was asked to get stripped.

A lot of things were going through my mind but I could not shake a feeling of trepidation. I had played in countless big games over the years... All-Ireland finals, Connacht finals, the big local derbies. I had worn the t-shirt out in the wash and rarely felt nervous, but I was suddenly feeling very uneasy.

Well, I was almost 45 and hadn't played a game in five years. Even 20 years earlier, my body was rebelling.

In the same week that I had been named Galway manager, I was standing in the middle of the field about to face a kickout. Paul Clancy was on one side of me, Gareth Bradshaw on the other, and Cathal Sweeney watching on.

I decided I'd have to go for it.

Kevin... make or break.

♦ ♦ ♦ ♦ ♦

NOT WINNING A senior championship with Killannin is my greatest disappointment in football. It would have been an extraordinary feat for a club as diminutive as ours to get over the line. We were so close a few times and should have registered one title at least, even with the might of Corofin knocking around.

Killannin is a townland in the parish of Rosscahill that gave its name to the GAA club. Prior to its establishment in 1958, people from the area like my Uncle Michael played with Moycullen and Oughterard predominantly.

It was Pullagh man, Pack Walsh, Ted O'Connor from Rosscahill West and Tommy Kinneavy of Rosscahill East who came together to found Killannin GAA. Training took place in Rosscahill East and in Tullykyne for more than a decade before John Maloney donated around 12 acres near the church in the 1970s after he moved to America with his family.

The grounds we use now are known as Maloney Park in his honour, and some of our benefactor's family flew over to attend the official opening on October 14, 1990. It is not a GAA facility exclusively, however.

It is a community one and that distinction is very clear.

I PLAYED THAT day, for Killannin against Oughterard.

It was the so-called curtain-raiser to a clash between Galway and Kerry but was the priority for everyone in the locality.

Although a small club, we won a couple of county junior titles in 1967 and '72 and three other Western titles around that era. We are such a proactive outfit driven by a municipal spirit and like all good teams, unity has made us far stronger than the bare sum of our parts.

We had a bit of inter-county representation here and there, and Tom

O'Connor, Patsy Kinneavy, Bosco and I brought Celtic Crosses home with us.

Killannin had made it to senior but struggled and were relegated in 1990. It was a temporary reduction in standing however, and we made our return in a blaze of glory, securing a league and intermediate championship double the following season.

I was named Man of the Match in both finals, but couldn't have given a damn about that. Being established as a leader, with eight years behind me already despite not yet being 22, I was only doing what was expected and needed of me. It was all about getting back to senior. Getting there, having won a county final made the relegation worthwhile.

Our tiny society deserved to be king of the hill. Or the mountain.

We were a physically imposing side, especially down the spine, with Bosco at centre-back to mop up anything that got past Finbarr Thomas and me. We eased past Glenamaddy in the semi-final and made sure of the final in the first-half against St Brendan's of Ballygar.

It never stopped raining in Corofin but that didn't bother us. We were outdoor folk. We were five points ahead at the change of ends after Johnny Kelly touched my kick from a sideline free to the net.

Brendan's had been relegated with us 12 months previously and their hunger undoubtedly matched ours. They just couldn't get the upper hand on us around the field and though they reduced the margin by two points, they were never really a scoring threat.

In this period, there is no doubt about it, that playing for Killannin far outweighed playing for Galway in terms of my priorities. We had a good party that night.

◆◆◆◆◆

WHEN I DIDN'T get the county call in 1997, I was asked to manage the club. With some more free time on my hands than I was accustomed to, I accepted what was a considerable honour but also one to be treated with utmost gravity. By then, I was probably beginning to think about the game a bit more, though football was nowhere near the evolved sport it is now.

As I've explained already, I had a great championship in playing terms and it got me back in with Galway when John O'Mahony took over as boss with Pete Warren and Stephen Joyce for 1998. We failed in our overall target of winning the championship however, although we gave it an almighty rattle.

Corofin were our semi-final opposition. They were super powers and could draw from a far vaster population, but we revelled in boxing above our weight and had taken their scalp two years previously. There was confidence we could repeat the dose.

We set up perfectly and the various roles were carried out to a tee. Most of the individual battles went our way. Gary and Richie were part of a strong defensive unit. We had a few others like Finbarr, Mickey Walsh, Enda Fahey and Ray Gibbons who played National League for Galway.

It all translated to a four-point lead with 10 minutes to go. It was as well as we ever played. And it wasn't good enough.

Corofin sucker-punched us with two goals. We didn't react well to the first, a bit of panic set in, and number two stole a famous victory from us. It is the most painful defeat of my career. That Corofin went on to win the All-Ireland club final at Croke Park the following March, captained by Ray Silke, did not serve as any balm whatsoever. It only accentuated the what-might-have-beens. *If we could win one county senior title.*

Losing the final in 2000 hurt, too. This was after Galway had lost to Kerry in the All-Ireland replay. I had taken an injection and come back on after breaking my kneecap, causing significantly more collateral damage.

I played no part in the semi-final defeat of Dunmore McHales, who were without the also injured Michael Donnellan.

The final took place on my birthday, November 5 and I don't recall my 31st with any great rapture.

Again, it was Corofin in opposition and this time they had three points to spare. They were captained by future coaching *compadre* and former minor, under-21 and senior teammate, Brian Silke on this occasion, and had his brother Ray, Martin Mac, Kieran Fitzgerald and Jason Killeen in their ranks.

The game should never have gone ahead. It was held in a monsoon, so bad that the parade was dispensed with. The biting cold and rain made it nigh on impossible to execute the simplest skill. That it concluded 1-3 to 0-3 provides more details than any words can do.

I was held together with glue and duct tape. I stood on the square and couldn't move, but just hoped I might catch a few balls, entice a foul or two. It wouldn't have needed much more. It was useless though. I finally departed with around 10 minutes to go.

Talk about ones you regret. It raises the hackles again. If we won the All-Ireland the first day like we should have, I wouldn't have even been out on the pitch to wreck my knee a few weeks later. Taking an injection and going back out probably prevented me even being slightly more mobile in the county final but you don't think of tomorrow when all of life hinges on today.

Still, an All-Ireland blown and a chance of at least a county title with the club. It would have meant so much to our manager Peter Lee, to our selectors Breda Molloy, Mattie Maloney, Tony Osborne and Pat Ryan.

Breda is my sister, married to Packy Molloy, proof positive that the love of the GAA was not gender-biased in our house, but with my mother as interested as anyone, the girls had a great role model.

Pat must have been involved in every team down at the pitch over the years from underage up. He was my under-14 manager when we won the County B final against Glenamaddy. Pat was also a great supporter of mine and would travel the country to watch me play for Galway and then the same when I was a manager. He is the epitome of what is good about Killannin.

I was desperate to give Pat and all our community an unprecedented glow, to pay them back for helping to make me.

It wasn't to be.

♦ ♦ ♦ ♦ ♦

I WAS MANAGER again in 2003, while also captain of Galway. We had four young children at home, too, at the time. It's just as well I never had much interest in television.

They were on to me again once I called time on my management stint with Galway at the end of 2019 but I want to step back from that scene a bit, for now, though I will be there in the background to help out if needed. I also want to help put a real structure to the underage, which combined with the incredible passion and selflessness of the people around can produce an ever better yield from our resources.

I love the idea of going back to my roots.

People talk about that glibly at times, without thinking about it. The roots that ground you to a place, from whence you grew.

I never took that for granted.

It is why I'm still here and why I will always be here. The opportunity to put professional processes in place and marry them with the enthusiasm of the volunteers is one I am so glad to be able to avail of.

My lads have gone through the club like I did and there will be a new crop starting next year and the year after. It is the same with the basketball club. They provide the same service so I am intent in giving them as much support as I can too. I have really enjoyed my involvement.

There is great beauty in the wheel turning, generation after generation.

Family has always been the most important thing in my life. Killannin, and Corrib, are families also, playing anchoring roles in the region. They will be there long after me but there will be a little bit of me in them forever.

◆ ◆ ◆ ◆ ◆

THERE WAS A great kick for me, lining out for our second team to win the county junior B title in 2008. I was feeling good at that level, keeping it between the two '45s' and using the grey matter, what bit of it there was buried beneath the greying noggin.

That really should have been it but six years later I played a small role as Killannin garnered another intermediate championship, just a month short of my 45th birthday.

And just days after being appointed Galway manager.

I had finished up with Sligo and Michael Breahtnachs the year before and again, with a bit more time on my hands, I decided to just go down to the field to do a bit of training and maybe lose a few pounds that had built up with five seasons of little exercise.

We were going well and coming up to the final against our neighbours Moycullen, I was asked to tog out. I thought it was absurd. I had six weeks of kicking a ball done and thoroughly enjoyed it, but I was an old man in football terms, with nothing done in years.

I fobbed them off but they kept coming back. The panel was small, and they felt I could do a job if required. Then it was that the players wanted me there and that certainly removed the fear of upsetting the apple cart in that regard.

I relented.

I was on edge all day, worried that they might bring me on. I couldn't figure out why I felt like that, given that I never feared a big game.

It was only the following year when I had Bosco McDermott talking to our group that the question was answered for me. He was saying to them that you play the game because you love it, but then added the kicker.

'Never forget, every time you put on a jersey… you're taking a risk.'

The light bulb finally went off in my head. It was obvious really.

I hadn't played for a number of years. I was going out into an environment that I couldn't feel as confident in as I used to because of that, and if I was to make the mistake that caused us to lose the match, I would carry the regret of doing that to my club forever.

In addition, because of my profile, the reaction would have been very predictable. The egotist trying to be a hero, chasing another medal, sticking his nose in as if they couldn't do it without him.

We had been winning throughout with Patrick Sweeney putting on an exhibition but Moycullen were throwing everything at us in the closing quarter of an hour and were on our tails when Eamon got injured.

I had been trying to keep a low profile. When the subs warmed up, I went behind the high wall in Tuam and did a few groin stretches, so I wouldn't be seen. But I couldn't avoid it anymore. On I was going, the sense of apprehension multiplying.

The memory is as vivid as any from my playing career. The first ball was kicked right on top of my head. It seemed to be in the air for ages.

Kevin… make or break.

I ELEVATED, PRAYING that the groins would manage the take-off, and the knees would hold in the landing.

I remember coming down with the ball in my hands wondering… *How the hell did that stick?*

I could have jumped and missed it by yards because my timing would have been so off. But I jumped with Gareth and Paul, and came down with it.

I couldn't believe it.

I will never forget the massive roar from the Shedeen in Tuam, and the banging of the sheet iron when a free was awarded. It was an unbelievable moment, me going back to the roots, the club that I loved so much.

People say that catch turned things around as Moycullen had closed the gap to three. It certainly seemed to have a galvanising effect on our wonderful supporters and the lads responded to the ear-splitting noise from the stands. From there we finished with a couple of points to win by three.

I work in Moycullen and we still have the slagging about it.

To be out there with these young lads, 31 years after I first walked out on a Killannin adult team, 29 years after playing a West final and 23 years after we had last won the intermediate championship was a gift I absolutely did not take for granted.

The people of Killannin GAA absolutely deserved that day.

I pulled my hamstring when coming on as a sub again in the Connacht championship. Now, I could call it quits for good.

It wasn't a bad run.

PART THREE

Managing the Game

CHAPTER 12

THE BOSS

Basketball really helped him in Gaelic football. Kevin was really aware of space on the field and was light on his feet for a big man. He'd always tell us to remember the basics. Mind the ball and keep the game simple... Kevin always had the capacity to be a manager as he was a born leader.
— Pádraic Joyce, Irish Daily Star, July 15, 2010

The cerebral part of the game intrigued Walsh. He admits that he got to the stage where not only would he demand of himself total concentration for the 70 minutes but that he could detect when his marker let up for a second in those 70 minutes; a shake of the head, a glance down to the ground was interpreted by Walsh as a sign of weakness, as a chance to make a telling run. It might explain why the idea of managing the county a few years' down the line appeals to him... he likes the idea of advising players one-to-one, of giving them the odd subtle hint here and there that could make the difference between winning and losing. Just like he so often was in his playing days.
— Kieran Shannon, The Sunday Tribune, March 20, 2005

CREDIT TO DUBLIN, Mayo and Kerry, they have been among the most reliable teams in the country in recent years but it can be a bit tiresome to be treated as if they have reinvented the wheel, just because they have more resources than anyone else.

It is natural that media professionals will attempt to lift the lid on these counties to examine what gets them to the pinnacle, or as I always targeted, consistently being in the position to win.

But if you are doing a deep dive in that sense, aren't you investigating what they have that is different? Where they are innovating?

What resources they might have…financially and otherwise? Rather than making them out to be pioneers in an area where they are not.

We have had quite a few giggles in my house when various reporters have treated the use of basketball coaches and strategies as some sort of left-field innovation.

I STARTED TAKING the Sligo players to indoor halls and walking them through moves in 2009. But before I would ever get them on screens, V-Cuts and leveraging players to make space – or using a variety of pressures, blocking off or angle defending to take it away – I had to show them proper footwork, something that is incredibly poorly coached in Gaelic games compared to basketball.

First good movement, then the use of the stutter step… the drop step… the slide step.

You would think Jim Gavin had solved the secret of Fatima and the question of whether there was life on Mars in one fell swoop, just because he brought Mark Ingle in. Kerry followed up with James Weldon and then Mayo, with Deora Marsh and Terry Kennedy. It is fantastic that GAA coaches are looking outside of the narrow confines of convention to embrace other sports.

Though Sligo's improvements were acknowledged, considerable as they were, they were in a different grade and nobody had any interest as to what tools they were kitted with to fashion that progress.

It was the same when Galway made equally significant gains.

Because there is this notion that Galway should be winning Connacht titles every second year at worst and the odd All-Ireland with that – even though a cursory glance at recent history will expose the nonsense of that expectation – credit didn't even come the players' way for the strides they had made.

Had we gotten over the line in 2018, and we really could have with a few more things going our way, the way we did it would be the only show in town.

Five years earlier, Jimmy McGuinness won an All-Ireland final with Donegal and everyone wanted to ape his methods. James Horan got Mayo to the brink and was pilloried. There is no basis in reality between those polar treatments, for what in truth, is a tiny margin.

But that's the gig of a county manager.

◆◆◆◆◆

THERE WAS SOME surprise expressed when I pitched up in Sligo.

Externally it seems, I wasn't viewed as management material and I hadn't done a big senior club job. Apparently, that's a necessity to be a top coach.

There wouldn't have been many of my former Galway teammates shocked. They knew how much I thought about the game and I had been coaching all my life. Just because it wasn't on Broadway didn't devalue it.

Killannin, Corrib, Aran Islands… Galway ladies football.

All levels, all age groups, different codes, both genders. I had a holistic experience, fine-tuning my methods.

I had an ambition to manage at county level but there were stories going around that I was peeved at being rejected for the Galway minor job, which was why I went off to Sligo.

In a huff, don't ya know.

Bullshit.

I never applied for it and never heard about it. I learned afterwards when coming across the story that someone nominated me. Nowadays, a nominee must confirm his willingness to let his name go ahead.

The only person to contact me was Dessie Sloyan, who I had played against many times when he was a top forward for Sligo. I was playing golf in Portugal with the Lake Society from Oughterard when he called. It was the only golf trip I ever went on and it wasn't really about the golf as much as a break.

Dessie was on the committee set up to fill the vacancy left by Tommy Jordan's resignation and for some reason, my name popped into his head.

I didn't fancy the commute and tried to put him off a few times. We met in Claremorris and I laid out my principles, but I wasn't going all out to sell myself because I didn't really think I was a good fit, given the geographical hurdle.

Gradually, I was sold on the potential and convinced myself I couldn't wait for the perfect job. This was a good chance to put my ideas to the test at a higher level.

I needed three passionate Sligomen with a good pedigree and knowledge of the domestic game, so I went for three lads that I knew were made of the right stuff. I had huge respect for Dessie, so after drawing me in, he could hardly decline. It was great to get Paul Durcan and Paul Taylor involved as well, another pair who had worn the jersey with distinction over the years.

♦ ♦ ♦ ♦ ♦

NO MATTER WHAT ideas you might have about coaching, you would be a fool not to have your eyes and ears open when exposed to different methods, characteristics and principles. Nobody knows it all and a nugget might come from anywhere.

You need to park the ego to be open to learning.

I have already explained the massive influence Mary Nihill was on me in terms of creating a good culture, discipline, communication, teaching the skills of footwork, and maintaining the courage of your convictions in the face of resistance.

My exposure to John Tobin's training when I went into the Galway minors was a real eye-opener and very good for me. It was at a level of endeavour and intensity I hadn't experienced before and was central to my development. I was prepared for the senior set-up once I had two years of that.

Billy Joyce was my first senior manager and I will always be thankful that he had the faith in me to call me up quickly. Blooding new players, increasing the depth of the squads was an early aim of mine with both Sligo and Galway.

That was why I took over the juniors at Sligo and winning the All-Ireland in 2010 was a tremendous achievement that nobody should ever downgrade as being 'only the junior'. The group was treated to a huge reception in the town. It was only the county's second ever All-Ireland – the first, also a junior, coming in 1935.

Crucially for the development of the seniors, we got the likes of Shane McManus, Eugene Mullen, David Rooney and Colm Magee from that source.

I did the same at Galway for a few years and brought Johnny Heaney, Declan Kyne and Bernie Power through. Bernie was Corofin's third 'keeper when I introduced him to the squad but progressed to be No 1 in their three in-a-row All-Ireland winning side, and a county regular.

The junior grade is great for picking up a handful of lads that have slipped through the net. There is a tendency to ignore players that didn't light it up at underage, due to life circumstances or just being late developers. If they have great attitudes, they can flourish with good coaching.

In Galway, we had a couple of under-21 All-Ireland winning squads but they don't just translate into seniors automatically. Like racehorses, some were more precocious than others. In the longer term, the slow developers might often prove to be more reliable as shooting stars fizzle out.

But we went outside the box to have a look at players too. In all, we invited 144 players from 38 clubs. Not everyone took us up on the offer, especially in the first year or two, but the trawl was extensive and as Pádraic Joyce acknowledged after succeeding me, he was taking on a far healthier squad than the one I inherited.

In other words, I did my job.

JOHN CONTINUED BILLY'S transitional process when he came in. Of course, he knew all the minors but for some reason, very few kicked on.

Again, the training was fantastic but the incident where he accused me of drinking before a game informed my thinking on dealing with players. It is detrimental to the good feeling in a group to do that. You need a guy to come clean if he has done something.

The big issue in my case is that wherever John got his information from, it was duff and ended with me walking away until the following season.

I rated Bosco McDermott so highly as a motivator, I brought him in to talk to the players a number of times when I became manager. His passion is contagious and that's the type of contagion you want in a group. He got us believing that Galway were capable of more, while at the same time giving some future heroes their first taste of top-flight competition. Bosco did very important work that John O'Mahony built on.

Johno was outstanding in terms of organisational skills and preparation. Training was very good too and he introduced weights to our programme. The culture of the group was important, emphasising the team over the individual and remaining consistent on it, which is the critical component.

He was all about details and our preparation was meticulous as a result. He was the first manager to bring us in to look at some video. It was basic compared to the Hudl app we have now, where players can look at clips and visualise anything they want.

It was something we had never done before and Johno was all over it.

He would make plans for months down the line.

He knew where he was heading.

One-on-one, Johno was terrific. I thought Galway were finished with me and was feeling a bit sore and disillusioned about it all but in one conversation, my mood elevated completely. He made me feel valued

As a manager myself, I would always want players to feel looked after, would work on building relationships from the very start of our time together and maintain a line of communication for as long as we were working towards the same goal.

Coaching and tactics would not have been a great strength of any of the aforementioned, apart from Mary Nihill, but then it wasn't a big part of football at that time, so you couldn't consider it a criticism. It was a different era.

You got players really fit and strong, you made sure they were treated well, and you sent them out on the field ready for battle.

There were exceptions. Any of the lads who had been in St Jarlath's would have been accustomed to a level of coaching not too many others in Galway got. Down's All-Ireland-winning teams in the early 90s under Pete McGrath looked very well coached to me. They had a definitive style. But most teams played conventionally.

That was one thing I was going to do differently once I was back on the county beat.

I had a clear view of how players could be improved by taking up clever positions around the field to vastly increase their chances of carving out scoring opportunities, as well as cutting down on coughing them up at the other end.

Time to bring it to a bigger stage.

CHAPTER 13

KINGDOM COME

Things had slipped but Kevin was a huge appointment for us. He was a huge presence. He's a big, strong man anyway but his achievements added to that reputation. He was a great character. He had a nice way about him. He was very modest. He never talked about what he had won, even though we often wanted him to.

There are only a handful of guys out there who have the X-factor as a manager and Kevin definitely had it. In 2009-10, he really had us playing as a unit. He had this ability to make players want to play for him. Under him, you felt you could do anything.
– Philip Greene, Irish Independent, July 30, 2015

THE FIRST COURSE of action at both Sligo and Galway was the same.

Morale was low in Sligo after a torrid season just past. Whereas Galway were riddled by doubt after gradual decline, with a massive turnover in managers and only two Connacht titles since my own retirement, the most recent of them in 2008.

You couldn't be under any illusions about the extent of either task, so I had to inspire and motivate, while always keeping an eye out for the inhibitors and energy sappers… be they players, county board officers or anyone else.

This is an ongoing process – building blocks upon blocks gradually.

At Sligo, I reminded the players that I hadn't won a whole lot for most of my career. I had one Connacht medal, just as they had. I was very fortunate that success came in the last few years, but it came because I had kept at it.

There was supreme talent in Sligo, but you end up where you are for a reason and winning the Connacht title in 2007 counted for nothing the following term. Relegation to Division 4 was disastrous.

Mayo sealed Sligo's fate with 13 points to spare and a lot of the players made themselves unavailable for the Tommy Murphy Cup. They bowed out to London, having beaten them by 16 points when they got their Connacht championship defence under way two months earlier.

I challenged the lads to prove they shouldn't be in Division 4. If they were too good for it, they would earn promotion.

◆ ◆ ◆ ◆ ◆

THE DIFFICULTY AFTER working for a sustained period on basketball courts and in indoor halls is to translate it to the larger surface of a GAA pitch, with a lot more moving parts in terms of 15-a-side as opposed to five-a-side in basketball.

It took me a long time to learn how to do that and like all coaching processes, it is an ongoing evolution. The tight space is ideal however for showing a plan and working on the nuts and bolts of it. I built an outdoor basketball court at the back of my own house because the kids were playing with Corrib and we could practice out there.

I began to use it to stress test ideas and drills, using my own kids as guinea pigs.

Basketball had a big influence on my playing and coaching but a good coach should be looking at a host of sports. The various pressures used in rugby and hockey are also useful, but the one common denominator with them all is good footwork, the desire to create space in an attacking environment, and make it disappear in a defensive setting.

Footwork is overlooked in a lot of sports.

Jacob Stockdale is a try-scoring machine in rugby but his footwork was absolutely atrocious in the concession of two tries by Ulster against Toulouse in the Champions Cup quarter-final in September 2020. He didn't know how to keep a high shoulder and coax the Toulouse players wide. His angle and balance were all wrong and they did him back on the inside.

I start doing footwork drills with the under-8s at Corrib Basketball Club. You can't do much without good movement.

This isn't intense, spirit-raising training, where you go at it like the clappers and collapse on the ground exhausted when it's done. This is skills coaching, a different beast. You must make sure the players understand that it is going to be slow and they will have to concentrate for long spells.

It's more difficult at county level because you are doing some basic stuff at the start and it must feel like doing multiplication tables for your Leaving Cert. But you don't build a house on poor foundations. You must get those basics right and if you must walk an adult through a child's drill to do so, that's what you do.

As we worked on improving the skills, we also built them up in their minds. I talked a lot about value, attitude and belief.

VALUE IS ABOUT why you are contributing so much time to this.

Why are you giving up on holidays, not going to family weddings, giving up on nice food and all the other things your peers are immersing themselves in?

How big is your *Why?* If it isn't big enough, if you are only in there because you were asked and it's what is expected of you, there will come a point in time where you will be found wanting.

You are the person who looks out the window before going training, sees it's pissing rain and thinks... *I'll wait another 10 minutes.* Now you'll still go, but if you had a high value on it, the first you'd have known about the rain was as you bounced out the door to get into the car.

If your value is good, your attitude will follow, doing whatever it takes to get better. Value and attitude equals belief.

That doesn't mean you'll win, because Babs Keating was right, a donkey will not win a Derby. But it gets you operating at close to your optimum level consistently. Then you're in with a chance of winning more games than you lose.

◆ ◆ ◆ ◆ ◆

THE SLIGO PLAYERS rose to the challenge of extricating themselves from Division 4 and showed me a lot in the process. We finished level on points with

Antrim at the top of the table, achieving the primary target of promotion.

The final took place in Pearse Park and there was plenty to like about the team's attitude and mental strength as they carved out a 1-12 to 1-10 triumph. Stephen Coen scored an opportunist goal and Adrian Marren continued a high-scoring spring by recording six points, including five from play.

Antrim were always on our coat-tails however and when Seán Davey got the line with 10 minutes left, I was getting the chance to see how much progress had been made between the ears.

Thankfully, the players redoubled their efforts and finished strongly, with points from Gary Gaughan and Adrian to secure treasured silverware.

IN THE CHAMPIONSHIP, we gave debuts to Neil Ewing, Eugene Mullen and Alan Costello. We fell short by four points to Galway but it was obvious that significant strides had been made. Seán Armstrong hit us for 1-3 from play but in subsequent years I would have our defence set up to send him down the sewer channels as I called them, away from the danger zone of the central channels and into the shit.

Seán would not trouble us to that extent again and when I enticed him back into the Galway panel a few years later, we worked together to counteract that and make sure he was always operating in the scoring zone.

The game plan had been applied brilliantly and Eamonn O'Hara was an effective shield and ball winner when dropping into a deeper role. We were level entering injury time when a ball broke in midfield. Galway just latched onto it and Joe Bergin launched a point from distance. Seán got his goal then to finish it.

We ground out a result against Tipperary in Semple Stadium and drawing Kerry provided training with a further impetus, even though the game was in Tralee. Now we would be able to get a more accurate measurement of our progress.

We also sniffed an opportunity.

Kerry were not motoring well and having lost to Cork for the second year in-a-row in Munster, they staggered over the line against Longford, only scoring two second-half points.

When I spoke to the lads on the Thursday night, I told them that with 10 minutes to go, they would either be leading, or just trailing by a point. The game would be there to be won.

'Whatever happens… don't stop', I emphasised.

'Don't think, "Hell, this is Kerry… we're not good enough to win this." Because you are good enough!'

I had to force them to visualise being in that position so that when it happened, it wouldn't come as a shock. When it happened, they would remember my words, the belief I had in them and realise that the belief was justified.

This was where I expected them to be. I needed them to expect it too so that they would not retreat in fear of the situation but embrace it.

It was a proud day, if also an absolute stomacher.

The players were magnificent. We marshalled Tommy Walsh and Colm Cooper well, keeping them scoreless in the first-half. Charlie Harrison was like a man possessed, 20 days after breaking his collarbone. Ross Donovan wasn't far behind.

David Kelly ran Marc Ó Sé ragged and the former Footballer of the Year was withdrawn at the interval. David's goal just before the change of ends gave us a two-point lead, though Kerry had a very strong wind in the second-half.

But the players exhibited their understanding of all we had done through the winter in the halls, and we suffocated Walsh and Cooper. Declan O'Sullivan and Paul Galvin were Kerry's most influential operators and they moved ahead but we wouldn't go away.

Syl Doyle had no option but to award a penalty three minutes from time, when Johnny Davey's powerful run was crudely brought to a halt. But it was heartache for David, as his shot was well saved by Diarmuid Murphy.

Even after that, there was no sense of feeling sorry for ourselves, or satisfaction that we had put it up to football royalty. Ken Sweeney was back in a flash to kick a point and leave just one between us. It told you everything that Kerry had 13 players inside their own '45'.

Charlie almost got a kick away, but Mike McCarthy got a great block in. We just couldn't source the leveller and it finished 0-14 to 1-10.

When the final whistle went, we all felt sick but there was one man who felt sicker than anyone else. My first thought was to go to David. The photographers caught up with us, which I wish they hadn't, but I just wanted him to know that getting a penalty is not the same as scoring a goal.

There is a chance it will be missed or saved, in a pressure situation.

I put my hand under his chin and told him to hold his head high. He had torn

Kerry apart and put us in the position where we had a chance of winning.

A defeat is never on one individual, anymore than a victory is. He needed to be reminded of that at a low time. He is a smart young fella.

He didn't let it affect him in the long term.

Management is not about kicking buckets around the place for five minutes and apologising afterwards. You have to control your emotions.

You are all in it together.

The loss hurt but success is about improvement and it was evident that my methods and principles were applicable and effective at this level, and that the players had bought into it. That first year would boost their confidence in themselves and in the management group, even more so when Kerry advanced to win the All-Ireland.

There was a lot to look forward to.

CHAPTER 14

HISTORY

There's a way about Kevin. No matter what he does, he's excellent at it.
– Gary Fahey, Thank GAA It's Friday, July 29, 2016

THERE WAS REAL enthusiasm for the following campaign, with a strong sense of purpose; a confidence that we were capable, not just of rattling cages, but claiming some scalps of note.

Again, the league was important in terms of keeping the momentum going. Ironically, it was a repeat of the previous year's campaign in that we finished level on points with Antrim at the top of the table.

The only difference was that Wexford were also on 10 points and so the placings were decided by scoring difference.

Antrim were well clear on +24 and we finished with five points in hand on Wexford, on +14, to cement Division 2 status for the following season and a coveted final at Croke Park. What was really satisfying about that was delivering in the last round, when we went into it deadlocked on score difference with the Model County. Wexford had an Antrim side already assured of promotion, and duly defeated them by two points.

We were playing host to provincial rivals Roscommon and totted up 20 points in accounting for them by seven. Impressively, only four of that tally came from frees. Mark Breheny, David and Alan were flying.

Antrim had beaten us in the first round by a point but when the silverware was on offer, we had too much firepower, shooting 19 points this time around to win by five. We had four players scoring three points or more.

We were moving well, creating so many opportunities and had tightened up a lot defensively overall, despite the concession of a goal 10 minutes from time. We were never threatened and a second league title in 12 months was secured.

◆ ◆ ◆ ◆ ◆

POSITIVE RESULTS ADD to the bank of belief, but it was the manner of some of the wins before we started to click offensively that were as significant as anything. Chiselling out dogged affairs such as the 12-11 win over Offaly in Markievicz Park, a week after we had failed to turn up when beaten by seven points at Wexford Park, was critical. We eked out a one goal win over Cavan the week after.

Emerging from the trenches covered from head to toe in blood and muck but with the type of warm glow that is unique to the hard-earned success, infused confidence and was the catalyst for the freedom of subsequent performances.

That type of experience stands to you when you concede a goal to a penalty early on, as we did against Connacht champions Mayo in the championship in June and still strode away to win by four, 0-15 to 1-8. That was even more convincing than the margin indicates and sparked delirious celebrations.

It stands to you when you go behind with the seconds ticking away in the semi-final against Galway, because you have been here before; you trust the process, you trust each other and you dig it out.

It was strange seeing Johno in the opposite corner now that he had returned to his native county to take over the reins. You don't want to inflict pain on someone who has given so much to you, knowing that afterwards, the knives would be out for him regardless of his stunning record – a manager who finished with eight Connacht championships for three different counties.

It was the same with Galway and any of the lads I had played with.

I had thought about the prospect of facing Galway when offered the job initially. Any club job I took, it was never in Killannin's grade. I could never plan against my club.

I REASONED THAT we would not meet in the league and might not meet in the championship, and if we did beat them – as we did two out of the three seasons we faced off – we would not be knocking them out of the All-Ireland championship.

But I was Sligo manager now, with a job and a responsibility to the players, the board that appointed me and the GAA family of a proud county. That took precedence over friendships and previous loyalties.

We were in our second year together now and had developed a system whereby Charlie and Ross could have a major impact running from deep. It worked so well that we would later try Charlie at wing-back. He had nothing like the same effect. It was just easier to lose a corner-forward than a wing-forward.

And Charlie could run all day, so he did not mind totting up the mileage.

He wasn't like the contemporary soccer full-back, who is brilliant going forward but cannot defend. He was a watertight marker and was getting better as he took our coaching on board. For him to be rewarded with an All Star at the end of the season was well deserved and a pat on the back for everyone.

It was very gratifying that Mark, a stalwart of a decade's service in the black jersey, was willing to take my messaging on board. It said a lot for him, who had been a central plank of everything the team had done for a long time, that he wasn't afraid to change and develop his game.

Mark added more industry and hard tackling, moved deeper to pick up ball, finding a little more space and helping create some more for the inside men like David. And he was still a scoring threat. So, it was *79:1...* contributing without the ball when we had possession and when the opposition had it.

Our work on the basketball courts was really paying off.

At half-time against Mayo, the line was quite simple. We had no more interest in moral victories. That was fine in our first year, to compete against Galway and even Kerry. Now, when we knew we had Mayo on the rack, we had to bury them. It was very pleasing that they could finish the job.

We needed two bites of the cherry against Galway, having let a six-point lead slip in the drawn encounter, with an extra man for much of the second-half. There was a lot of criticism after but the path to progress is never smooth. There are always trials and it was a good reminder about sticking to the process.

David was now one of the most talked about forwards in the country, showing he had grown from the disappointment of Tralee. That was a measure of his mental strength. His talent was unquestionable, but we did a lot of work with him to make sure he was winning the ball in danger areas rather than running away from goal.

He got his V-Cuts down and was reaping the rewards, thanks to the supply and workrate of the lads outside. He scored 1-3 of our 1-10 in the drawn game and the goal was a glorious finish.

It was interesting to see the Galway fans celebrating at the final whistle. That was great for our dressing-room. It was telling us where we stood now, that Galway were relieved to get out of jail. As management, it was our job to reinforce that because the white noise spoke of underdogs never winning replays and the chance being lost.

We were the dominant outfit on the first day.

So, we could be the dominant outfit the second day.

We didn't dominate. At times, we had to be dogged. But the belief never wavered, and another famous triumph was registered, 1-14 to 0-16. It was Galway's first loss in Markiewicz Park since 1975 and Sligo's first replay victory since overcoming Mayo at the second attempt in the Connacht final that same year.

It was also Sligo's first replay win over Galway and a first ever replay defeat for their manager, Joe Kernan.

These were all the kind of landmarks I liked to set as a player, and I carried that into management. It was personal motivation, but you fed the nuggets to the players. Success cannot be all about the cup or the medal.

One team wins a competition.

So that can never be the only, absolute measure of success.

Those landmarks captured the magnitude of this win. They did not come often in these kinds of circumstances for Sligo. There was no residue from spurning such an advantageous position at Pearse Stadium and when the game was in the melting pot, it was Sligo who found the definitive strike. Colm McGee got the headlines coming off the bench to kick the winner and it was a glorious finish.

That showed the strength in depth we had built up.

Colm had scored five points in the league final but responded brilliantly to losing his starting berth. Another sub, Ken Sweeney kicked a point to bring us back to within one of Galway and Mark brought us level. David had kept us in touch earlier with another goal and Adrian's radar was on. Overall, we played much better than in the drawn game.

Galway did too but it was our day.

There were no mixed emotions.

I was with this group of players 18 months. The bonds were tight; I knew what they had given me and given to the cause. I was overjoyed for them.

♦ ♦ ♦ ♦ ♦

THE JOB WAS different now and I was aware of that as soon as the final whistle sounded. Having been constantly attempting to build the players up, I now had to get them recalibrated. In my post-match interviews, I played it low key.

Nothing done.

Nothing major achieved.

Nothing won yet. We are only into a Connacht final.

Inside, I was jubilant, but mass celebrations can be draining. And if you have achieved something massive, it can lessen hunger. So, I reminded everyone, publicly and privately, that no medals had been handed out. I had to.

The hype was all around us.

Sligo were in a Connacht final and because we had taken out Mayo and Galway – it was the first time in 63 years one of them was not in the decider – we were favourites. It was not a position the players were accustomed to.

The supporters revelled in it, but it was a mental challenge inside the dressing-room. We had to stay in the present.

Losing that game to Roscommon in MacHale Park is one of the gut-wrenching disappointments of my managerial career. One damn point, 0-14 to 0-13.

And we never really turned up.

IT IS IMPOSSIBLE to shield the players from all the hype because they are in their communities. They are working and meeting people, constantly lauding them for their two huge wins and talking about what it would mean to them to be Connacht champions.

The Rossies would be tough but they weren't as good as Mayo or Galway.

Ergo.

Having seen this play itself out as a player in the Galway team, especially prior to playing Mayo in 1999, I had the rest of the backroom team primed to do all we could to ward off any sense of complacency. We described it as a heavy mist that kept coming at us.

Could we tie up our anorak as tight as possible to let none of it seep in? I think some of it did get through.

Fear can be mistaken for complacency too because they produce similar results. I do think there may have been a bit of both in some of the players. The fear can relate to worrying about not performing on the big day, of failing to live up to expectations that hadn't existed before, of the crushing disappointment that would come with defeat after taking care of business against Mayo and Galway.

Identifying this fear isn't easy because players are adept at putting on false fronts. It is a very male trait anyway, and a dressing-room only heightens that disinclination to show any hint of weakness or uncertainty.

Another factor was how much the emotions of the three previous games left the players a little flat. They had to contend with three big pitch invasions, tumultuous events that occur only on huge occasions.

And it sapped some of the energy out of them.

In the dressing-room before the game, I overheard one player wondering which shirt he was going to wear after the game. You need confidence but not over-confidence. I was slightly worried by that.

We never had the same 'cut' that had characterised our performances through the latter half of the league and the championship. In addition, Roscommon were desperate to honour the legendary Dermot Earley Snr, who had died tragically after a brave battle with illness.

I was proud of how the lads gritted their teeth after a disappointing opening, knowing it wasn't happening for them. Alan was like a man possessed, kicking five points.

The key moment was an exceptional save by Geoffrey Claffey from David at a time when we were clawing ourselves back into the game, having been six points down at half-time. We did get level but could not get our noses in front, having worked so hard to claw ourselves back into it, and Donie Shine kicked the winner from a free.

The loss and the circumstances of it made recovery on a six-day turnaround impossible. The physical exertions were one thing – it would have been all about recovery. But that was not enough time for the mind to recover.

The hurt was going to linger a lot longer than six days.

So, we went to Breffni Park to play Down and it was one-way traffic... 3-20 to 0-10. We never stood a chance.

I would not let that detract from the obvious improvements made. But we all knew a tremendous chance to do something special, to win a Connacht title by beating the big three, had passed us by.

We were all deflated.

CHAPTER 15

IN OR OUT

The first thing he brought was his man-management skills and he was never going chasing after fellas... Kevin's attitude was that you came on board straight away because he wasn't coming looking for you at a later stage.

– Eamonn O'Hara, *Irish Independent*, August 9, 2010

It's crazy but if you mentioned Cristiano Ronaldo to a 12-year-old, they would immediately say, 'Yeah, he was a brilliant player for Manchester United'. But if you said, 'Ji-sung Park', they may not know who he was. Yet all of us who played with Park know he was almost as important to our success. That's because of what Park gave to the collective and I want to talk about teams. They – not stars – are the most important thing in sport.

– Wayne Rooney, *The Sunday Times*, May 17, 2020

THE HANGOVER CLEARLY followed over into 2011, when we lost to Leitrim in Connacht and Wicklow in the first round of the qualifiers, making it a very short campaign.

That gave us time to take stock after three years.

At the end of each season, speculation hovered around me taking charge of Galway. I felt tremendous loyalty to the players though and that's a two-way street. They were giving me everything. I couldn't walk away on that note.

There was more to do.

The consistency returned in 2012 and we made another Connacht final, getting the better of Galway once more in the semi-final having enjoyed a fruitful trip to New York prior to that. The 2-14 to 0-15 scoreline reflects the merit in the victory but once again, we fell agonisingly short in the decider, losing 0-12 to 0-10 to a Mayo team that got to the All-Ireland final.

There was no consolation in these types of effort by now, as we were trying to shake off the notion of a moral victory, but Sligo were operating at an exalted level around this period. Think of Kerry winning the All-Ireland in 2009, Mayo getting to the final in 2012... and Sligo beating Galway and Mayo in 2010.

Silverware was the next step and that it didn't arrive is an undeniable regret because it was a reward that group of players deserved.

A FACTOR IN that was the change in county executive after three years.

In the final two seasons, it went from being pro-active to reactive, and sometimes inactive. You need that support in many ways, without having to be haggling and fighting. It is more invisible stuff that makes a massive difference.

Adrian illustrated the type of confidence in the camp when blitzing Galway for 2-6 in Pearse Stadium, a first ever championship win away to the Tribesmen. But the highlight for me was the composure of the players when trailing by four points at half-time; the trust they had in each other and the system of play.

I put up a few slides of some of the things we had done together in a variety of team-building events, trying to inspire them. Helping each other climb a mountain. That sort of thing. Just little triggers.

They had each other's backs. There was a bond.

Then it was just a reminder of our basics once more, and that if they replicated the teamwork they had shown before, they would win the game.

The individual inspiration came from Adrian. Some of his point-taking was from another dimension and Galway just could not handle him.

I liked the calmness too once we were making the running. There was no hint of fear or sitting back after hitting the front. It didn't come as a surprise. It was what they expected.

My teammate with the All-Ireland-winning minors, Alan Mulholland threw on Pádraic Joyce – still putting his shoulder to the wheel 14 years after we won the first of our two senior All-Irelands together – and Michael Meehan.

But nothing was going to take this away from Sligo. We were the better team; we knew it and played like it.

◆ ◆ ◆ ◆ ◆

SOMETHING THAT HAPPENED in the build-up to that game reflected the growth of the team and the evolution of a player-driven culture, which had been my goal from the outset. It also showed the maturity of players, the willingness of an individual to accept his fate for the greater good of the collective.

Johno had pushed this all along at Galway and it was a key element of our success. It would have always been what I espoused, how I had played anyway. My ideal is for it to come from players though – it has a higher value, rather than something being imposed.

Prior to the Galway game, the leadership group approached me, telling me that Stephen Coen had contravened their culture by doing something that was against the agreed values of the Sligo panel and they wanted it dealt with.

Stephen was flying at the time, one our best forwards. But he was part of the group that had set the agreed behaviours and now that the leadership had come to me, I had to respond to maintain the standards.

If they agreed, after every game, we'll have three pints together, then that's what we'd do. If they said, we're off it for three weeks, that's what we do. And if someone goes his own way on that, there has to be consequences.

So I decided Stephen would be dropped entirely from the panel for the game. It was a massive call before such a big game, but long term it would have been worse to play him.

We went back to the group leadership and told them our decision. They were a little taken aback when I said that he wasn't togging at all and asked me to reconsider. I pointed it out to them that they had brought the situation to my attention.

They said, 'We feel we need him'.

'I do, too', I said. 'But I need a team more.

'I need a team believing in each other going out that door. I don't need anything inside the set-up that's going to upset the apple cart.

'You know what', I continued. 'You lads go have a meeting and come back and convince me. I'd love if you could tell me Thursday night why he should play.'

When they came back, they accepted it was the right call.

We didn't hang Stephen out to dry. We put it out that he had a hamstring injury. We also agreed that if he knuckled down for three weeks and didn't say a word, we would protect him. And that's what we did.

It said a lot about Stephen and his commitment to the team that he still wanted to serve the team on the day. He knew it was about something bigger than him and he ended up doing stats. There was no strop, no self-indulgence. He hurt like hell but recognised the fault was his own and did not resort to lashing out.

It made us stronger.

It illustrated that we weren't in a dictatorship, that our leadership system was working and that we teased things out. And to come through that was another evolution.

No doubt the fact that we won in those circumstances was huge for the group. And the fact Stephen was there with us added to that.

But if the result went the other way, I would be very clear that everything was done right. The standards had been set by the player leadership, who were also starting to drive other individuals who may have been sitting in the comfort zone due to their talent. This was real leadership.

We had a lot of them now... Charlie, David Kelly, Philip Greene, Ross Donovan, Mark, Alan.

Caring, consistent and courageous.

THE CONNACHT FINAL was a tighter affair, with huge, physical contests. In contrast to two years previously against Roscommon, we began well, leading by three points after 15 minutes and Mayo were frazzled.

We had some chances to extend our advantage but spurned them, keeping our opposition involved in the game.

Mayo had a strong wind in the second-half and though we threw everything at it, we struggled for attacking fluency. Another opportunity slipped by.

Just as in 2010, there was a no-show in the qualifiers against a Kildare unit building up a head of steam. They were on a roll of winning games; we were coming off a two-point loss in a final.

And though we had 13 days to try build the players back up this time, it proved an impossible task. They carried the devastation into the game at a windy Hyde Park and only scored four points. We were unrecognisable from the Sligo we had become.

The psychological buffeting had left its mark.

◆ ◆ ◆ ◆ ◆

I THOUGHT LONG and hard about whether to stay on for a fifth season into 2013. Very few managers do that at county level or are given the opportunity. The driving was a real chore. I had to really have a value on the involvement to keep doing that.

We met with the group in October and had an open discussion. If they felt it was time to freshen things up, we would move on. If they wanted us to stay, we would really have to push the boat out in a bid to find the extra little bit that might – *might* – get us over the line in Connacht.

It was their call.

At the meeting it was agreed by players and management that players who could not commit to the team values at that point – i.e. train together and prepare together – that they would not be allowed to rejoin the panel later. Every player was asked that question.

In or Out?

If there were not enough 'in' then we said we would move on as a management team, but that if there were enough committed players we would be staying with them. Of course, if there was an emerging young talent who wasn't part of the existing panel and wasn't given the opportunity at the beginning of the season, then he could be added later.

But there was no pressure on any one player. Everyone was given a few days to think hard about the 'In or Out' question before getting back to management with their answer.

The overwhelming contention was that we would all give it one more year, come in and work really hard in every sector to try make small gains that would have a cumulatively positive impact. That was what the players wanted so we agreed and committed to that.

Eamonn O'Hara decided it wasn't for him and left the panel, ending a long career of tremendous service. You had to respect that decision. He had earned the right to do whatever was right for him.

I can have no complaints with the commitment of the players to the programme we put in place. But we suffered a shock one-point defeat to London in Ruislip.

This was the other end of the confidence graph.

We had succeeded in building belief, but the positive results over the years had brought that element of expectation that is not easy to contend with when you are not used to it. Along with that might come the danger of believing you will always beat the so-called weaker teams, that you have hauled yourself out of that group by virtue of stacking up those sorts of wins.

We were targeting a provincial crown now, not just winning a game.

You cannot take your eye off the immediate challenges though.

Ever. To relax is to die and the Sligo players learned that to their cost.

This ranks alongside the Connacht final loss to Roscommon as the lowest point of my Sligo tenure. I do not want to discredit London's feat, even though complacency was a factor. You must be good enough to capitalise. Remember, Mayo had been brought to extra-time in Ruislip two years before, having trailed by two points with time almost up in James Horan's first championship outing as boss.

London were a good team in that period.

We did not perform at our optimum level though. And we didn't get the rub of the green either. Pat Hughes hit the post twice. It was the type of game that if you would have scraped through, you could have built on it because of the reality check it provided.

If.

You feel really isolated after a game like that. It is all on you, the brickbats are coming from every angle and it is hard to cocoon yourself from it. You would wonder why you bothered leaving your youngest son's Communion celebrations early, to have to put up with that stuff.

Players are a group and if they are criticised, it is as a collective. There is a management group too, but it is only the manager who gets nailed and that is wrong; as it is that they receive all the praise.

Ex-Clare and Dublin hurling manager, Anthony Daly wrote about dealing with the devastation of defeat in the *Irish Examiner*. He had his own way of processing it and defeat hit him hard.

He captured the sense of isolation very well.

The 'we' of players doesn't exist, is how he wrote it. And that's it in a nutshell.

When you lose a game like that as manager, you are on your own in a sporting sense. I could not wait to get home.

◆ ◆ ◆ ◆ ◆

EAMONN O'HARA WAS now a pundit on *The Sunday Game*.

His desire to make an impact, it seemed to me, coupled with a bruised ego perhaps, wiped the memory of how highly he rated me and my man-management skills from his hard drive evidently.

He was given a forum to launch a volley of baseless bullshit surrounding our preparation and tactics and he grabbed it with both hands.

It was staggering to be honest, from someone who hadn't been in the camp all year, but then that was clearly the problem. It was poor journalism by the show's producers not to ask him for a bit more detail on that, to back up what he was saying and at least acknowledge the possibility that he might not be coming at it from a balanced perspective.

For the sake of good television, he was let loose.

There's no point saying it's not hurtful and having had to miss my son's Communion, and then suffer that sort of a defeat, before putting up with that unchallenged stuff was hard to take.

Most of all though, I felt he was casting aspersions on his former teammates.

By this stage, the narrative surrounding his departure had changed. I was being told that I had refused to give him an easier pre-season, in deference to him being 37 and the mileage he had on the clock. So, I was informed, I had cut him from the panel.

That was not the case. Of all people in the world, I would have understood the failure of a one-size-fits-all approach.

We had empowered the players to drive the culture and standards at this stage and they wanted exceedingly high values. That meant everyone rowing in together. Nobody would be feeling they were doing more than anyone else, or worth more than anyone else.

Did that mean everybody having the same workload?

Absolutely not. Eamonn said he felt he needed a break and that coming in on January 1 would give him that. I explained that it was just about maintaining the culture, showing his commitment. He would not have to do the heavy conditioning until the new year. It was in nobody's interests to put his body through that before then.

Different individuals would be given different programmes depending on age, physique, fitness levels; everybody would be working together. If that meant sitting on a bike or being in the pool while others were doing harder yards, so be it. Eamonn needed to show his commitment because he had missed a lot of sessions previously due to work and other issues. It would be a strong, positive message.

It was a chance to be a leader.

Apart from that, we would be doing coaching work at this time on skills and set-ups. So being in attendance was vital but would again, not involve any significant physical exertion.

Primarily this was about showing his teammates he was all-in, and allowing someone waltz in two months after all of them could not be countenanced.

We had no pedestals for anyone.

THAT WAS THE last conversation I had with Eamonn.

I never heard from him again. So, he was never cut from the panel. He just opted not to come in. He had a column in the *Sligo Champion*, and began throwing in little lines here and there suggesting he was still available if required.

But the ball had been in his court and he chose not to buy in to what his peers placed most value on. He wasn't available when his colleagues wanted him to be available.

Something else he said on *The Sunday Game* made me laugh out loud. He said the cracks had been showing for two years and that the tactics and training hadn't been up to scratch for some time. That would include the year we beat Galway on Galway soil for the first time ever and lost by two points in a Connacht final to subsequent All-Ireland finalists.

I think it probably says a lot that there was absolutely no kickback within the squad, no negative reaction at all. He even had clubmates in the panel and there was not a murmur. They had set the bar.

He wasn't willing to meet it. It was as simple as that.

IT WAS EVIDENT that the psyche was battered after London.

Derry inflicted a seven-point defeat in the qualifiers, and we played like a team that had the stuffing knocked out. I had known this was going to be my last year and it was time to say goodbye to a great bunch.

We had some fantastic days and I made some great friends.

Sligo improved so much from where they were as players and a team. We had those league successes and those big championship wins over Galway twice and Mayo. Setting all those new landmarks with the replay win over Galway in 2010 and the junior All-Ireland success was significant.

The one negative was not winning a Connacht title. That was a goal that we got agonisingly close to achieving, especially in 2010.

You just hate the ones that slip away

CHAPTER 16

CULTURE CLUB

Soldiers have to eat soup together for a long time before they are ready to fight.
— Napoleon Bonaparte

Men do not engage in combat for motherhood, the flag, or apple pie. They do not fight
for patriotism. They may have volunteered for these reasons, but when their lives
are at risk, and the incredible stress of close personal violence is immediately
at hand, the key truth emerges. Men fight for their friends.
— Major Brendan McBreen, Improving Unit Cohesion: The First Step in
Improving Marine Corps Infantry Battalion Capabilities, 2002

'THAT'S NOT FOOTBALL.

'That's a horrible… filthy style.'

I smile inwardly as a Mayo supporter unloads, despite his team recording a championship victory.

My mood is not as dark as one might expect for being on the receiving end of such delightful discourse after losing. In fact, the ranting and raving from someone who should be joyous is grist to the mill.

We have narrowed the gap considerably in a short period. Mayo have been rattled and we have gotten under their skin. They had not expected a Galway team of steel and resistance, one that would not allow itself to be steamrollered.

We are not strong enough to win a game of this magnitude against one of the best teams in the country, but four points flatters them a little and a freak own goal, coming after Mánus Breathnach booted the ball into Finian Hanley just after half-time, rocked us back on our heels after Gary Sice's brilliant goal just before the interval.

Aidan O'Shea seemed to get a free every time he and Finian Hanley contested possession. Finian did have his hands on him a few times, but two or three of the calls were unbelievable.

We hadn't done a whole lot in terms of physical development, focusing on individual qualities and culture. I liked what I had seen in that regard, for the most part. We fought all the way.

Responsibility, accountability, commitment.

They were there in abundance.

The gentleman from Mayo was not such a fan though. He would prefer Galway to lay down and be rolled over.

Those days were gone.

OVER THE NEXT three years, we deployed a strategy for Mayo that reaped the richest dividends – three championship victories in-a-row.

We had their number. It was some turnaround from being laughed at in Salthill two years earlier.

I looked on the opprobrium as a compliment to what we had done in under a year. Mayo struggled and we hit them hard and heavy. This was something I could take into the rest of the year and the following season.

It was a vastly different Galway, no longer a pushover.

And they knew it.

♦ ♦ ♦ ♦ ♦

AFTER A YEAR to re-energise, the opportunity came to take the Galway job when Alan Mulholland resigned. The timing was right, and at some point, you want to take the reins in your own county. When the offer came, I did not have to think twice.

I took in Brian Silke and Seán Conlon as selectors. I would have been in touch with Brian quite a bit from the minor days. He was on the 1998 panel and had been a fine footballer. When I was in Sligo, I brought the juniors to play challenge matches with Corofin, who Brian was over.

Seán was in the senior panel with us around 1994 and '95. He was also a Galway minor and under-21. He was a very good player with Barna. He had done a lot of club coaching with Leitir Mor and Barna, and both teams improved markedly when he was coaching them. He didn't get much credit for it, but I saw it.

I wasn't looking for big names. I wanted people I felt would be good workers and without an ego, but that obviously could coach.

I had been lucky in Sligo with the backroom team I had there and it was the same in Galway, albeit that I identified the kind of people I wanted. I did a bit of background work, looking for people with high personal qualities who were open-minded and willing to learn, while bringing their own ideas and developing on what I brought to the table. They had to be heavily committed once they were involved and they agreed to that.

I need to give credit to Alan Mulholland for his help and sharing of information and knowledge with me when I took over after him. I also need to credit him with beginning the process of improving the team. He got a hard time from loud, so-called supporters which was unjustified. Alan and myself met a few times to ensure a smooth handover for which I am very grateful.

There are many different aspects to a rebuild but you must consider it a long-term project. I am not naïve, I know there are no guarantees in that regard, but my aim was to do it properly and that meant planning three and four years down the line. The pillars of my first two years were personal qualities and coaching. Greg Muller played a major role in terms of breaking the personal qualities down and categorising them into the four Ps.

Personal.

Psychological.

Physical.

And performance!

PERSONAL QUALITIES REFER to character, conduct, how individuals are in the community, how they hold themselves, what sort of standards they look for.

Psychological pertains to an ability to deal with setbacks, not getting things all their own way. Can they reset or do they sulk?

Physical qualities apply to a work ethic, strength, powers of recovery.

Performance is about technical and tactical abilities, a game sense, tackling, scoring and many things.

EACH PLAYER WAS categorised A, B or C based on a scale of 1-10.

High performance/trainable (8-10).

High potential/tolerate (4-7).

At risk/terminate (1-3).

You will never get an A in all 4 categories but every individual is trying to improve in each area.

We assessed each player continuously and got them to provide their own feedback on their performances, what they needed to improve on and how we might help them achieve their goals.

The communication was constant. Players were provided with KPIs (key performance indicators) every six weeks or so, and we went through them together.

If you don't work on KPIs in a county set-up, you have a problem. We met as management weekly to discuss these, as well as before and after every match.

It was continuous assessment and reassessment.

At club level, you may not have the time to work on three or four areas simultaneously. You might just have to accept that and emphasise the area that needs attention most. In that instance, what is imperative is that everyone is rowing in the one direction.

We wanted to build relationships while finding out about players.

Are they coachable?

Can they accept new ideas?

Can we build some of the necessary qualities in them if they do not possess them?

Are they warriors or wavers?

Weak or winners?

Are they chess players, gunslingers or seagulls?

GUNSLINGERS TEND TO be flashy, outgoing mavericks, good shooters for the posts, but there is a question mark about whether they can be relied upon, in particular, to stick to the process in the last 10 minutes of a tight match. Or do they start trying to win them on their own.

They are drawn to the notion of being heroic… of being *The Man*.

You need to show the gunslingers how to be team players without neutralising their strengths or losing them. If they cannot adapt, they will cost you against teams that are well set up because the frustration will inevitably lead to them trying low percentage shots or kick passes.

With a gunslinger, or any other personality, I would never go after them in front of the group. Sometimes, the idea of teaching individuals a lesson in that manner is alluring but it will invariably backfire.

Confrontation is particularly dangerous with gunslingers because of the ego. They always have the gun out and when under pressure, will pull the trigger. If they back you into a corner, and they have to go, the team doesn't win.

One-on-one is the only way. It's personal. It's honest. It's private. Look each other in the eye and talk it out.

CHESS PLAYERS DO everything right.

They are organised. The boots are clean, the kit is ready the night before. They follow all directions, the process.

They will be assiduous in all ways.

They are always solid and reliable but when pressure comes on in games they can get very cautious – and what was a simple 10-yard pass earlier, can now feel like a 30-yard pass. They can go slightly into their shell and as management, we have to bring them forward and breed more confidence into them.

They might lack self-belief though, which is positive in terms of their hunger to improve but might also prevent them from playing to their optimum. So, you work on them psychologically because they are wonderful characters and examples within a squad.

SEAGULLS WILL PROBABLY let you down as they are there for themselves.

It's about whatever they can get handy – the handy ball, the handy score. It is quite incredible how seagulls can be chirping away negatively in the background.

You must try to nurture each personality but there can come a time when you must cut a recidivist seagull loose. I need my gunslingers and chess players, but I need to shoot the seagull.

When I started with Sligo, I was a bit slow to do that. I saw other attributes in skill, physique or athleticism that clouded the fact that the seagull was killing me because he just took too much time. I was much better at cutting him loose a decade later, but you still had to be wary not to jump to conclusions too quickly and the sports psychologist has an important input there. Gerry Hussey and Mick Toland were brilliant in this department.

What I found, and this was quite unifying for a team and its culture, was that the players would, at some point, root out the seagull for you. They knew he had to be taken down, regardless of how good a player he was, because he was eroding everything that had been built.

PERSONALITY ASSESSMENT IS not new. Most coaches do it without thinking. Even with your under-12s, you are assessing and analysing personality traits.

How do players react to kicking a wide, misplacing a pass... being dispossessed or their direct opponents scoring a goal?

Are they losing concentration while berating themselves?

Good coaches will try to address that in young people by telling them not to worry about the mistakes; try to teach them to psychologically reset, that they are harming their ability to play with their fits of pique.

If you don't address that as a coach when you see it in eight year-olds, you are not helping them, and they are going to have a bigger problem at 14. More importantly, by helping them at this time, you are providing young boys and girls with coping tools for the inevitable setbacks that come with living.

Personality traits that thrive on the football pitch prosper off it.

♦ ♦ ♦ ♦ ♦

I WANTED PROFESSIONAL expertise in terms of nutrition, strength and conditioning, doctors, physios and sports psychology. I was far more open to the latter area than I had been as a player.

You needed to help in every way you could.

Greg Muller was from New Zealand, where he worked with legendary Rugby World Cup-winning coach, Graham Henry at the Auckland Blues when they enjoyed phenomenal success. He came from a military background and was responsible for the physical fitness of the New Zealand Elite Forces before moving to Galway to take up a role with Connacht Rugby.

I met him with a view to bringing him in on strength and conditioning, but as we talked, his skills in leadership and creating an environment conducive to constant self-improvement came to the fore. He stayed for three years and was top class.

You must be honest with yourself as a coach. Sometimes players will not take lessons on board, but you have to consider whether your practices are poor. You must hold a mirror up to your own performance.

I would have felt I was fairly good at that with Sligo, but Greg really drove that message home. He was all about challenging each other as coaches. Self-assessment leads to self-improvement and that is as applicable to coaches as to players.

He always said to me, 'Ego will stop you from learning', and I will talk to anyone in the hope of learning.

Striving for consistently high standards and a culture that demanded the maintenance of those standards was a big driver for him and so he could be extremely critical. It made me and the management structure better. Greg was always talking about being in the forest and needing someone looking into the forest from the outside.

You need someone you can trust to give an honest assessment of what they see, even if you don't like it. Greg had no problems with honesty.

With Galway, the management questioned ourselves all the time. We held ourselves accountable and that environment continued after Greg moved on. We would meet every Tuesday for two hours in a 'Challenge Me' setting.

We would go through each sector... S and C, physio, medical, welfare, training, coaching... and management. Because players weren't involved, we could delve into the minutiae of what we were doing and call each other out on issues if necessary.

I was not immune from that.

Greg lived in Moycullen and called into my office every morning. It was not a shoot-the-breeze type of engagement. It was intense. An hour or more of deep conversation, and I would not be spared.

Nowadays, he does one-on-ones with high-ranking people in a variety of sports that visit him in Moycullen from all over the world. I was incredibly lucky to have access to all that knowledge free of charge.

Greg is the third member of my Holy Trinity of management influences, along with Mary Nihill and John O'Mahony. On culture, putting a good environment about you and questioning yourself, I learned a lot from him.

He was intense and you could not be sensitive but being ultra-honest with yourself isn't always comfortable. It is how you get to the truth though, and you cannot afford to fool yourself if you want to make progress in a high-performance unit.

♦ ♦ ♦ ♦ ♦

THE WORD 'CULTURE' comes from the Latin word *cultis*, which means 'care'. The first thing I did was meet with each member of the panel for one-on-one conversations.

I wanted to get to know them, for them to become more comfortable with me.

Yes, I was trying to determine the type of people they were for the journey we were embarking on, but I was genuinely interested in them as more than footballers. You cannot spend the amount of time we would together without caring. Or I can't anyway. If you've a happier person, you've a better player.

You need to make them feel valued. You want to help them and that might extend to their lives away from the pitch, personally or professionally.

It was nice to read Shane Walsh talk about his good experience with us as he discussed a truly traumatic time in his life in an interview in *The Sunday Times* last October. He was in a car crash in which a man died and must have been going through hell. I kept in touch with him, just to offer any help I could, to offer an ear if he needed it, but most of all just to be sure he was okay. Our team psychologist, Gerry Hussey did as well.

Obviously, there was no pressure on Shane to come back in. That was a decision for him but he knew we were there, supportive, and that he would have a warm welcome should he choose to return.

In the article, he talked about the first evening he called into a session and everyone stopped to applaud him. It showed we cared and it was nice that the message was received. Because that would be very important to me as a manager, that this was the type of environment we cultivated.

In time, another of our sports psychologists, the former Galway hurler Tony Óg Regan steered players towards some of the invaluable services provided by the GPA to aid their personal welfare, whether it is dealing with stress and anxiety about work, study, personal relationships or indeed football, or any other issue. It was fantastic that those services were available and Tony Óg , who did a lot of brilliant one-on-one work with the players, was in a position to recommend them to anyone he felt might benefit.

But before we even got there, in our first year there were 30 conversations that lasted between two and three hours. I gave them each 10 questions on a sheet, which they answered and we both signed. They were for no-one but us. It was time-consuming, in and around 80 hours, but it was a way to illustrate early on the type of manager I would be.

I wasn't going to be a military officer. I was going to be approachable and they could be comfortable with me.

IN TIME, WE developed the Maroon Book.

It took about 18 months. People outside of high-performance environments scoff at such documents but really, it was just a reference point, a refresher on all we had agreed in terms of culture. It was all about high standards in everything we did, with the express goal of being a team that consistently competed to win.

There were a lot of reasons why we got to that point, of consistently competing to win. Changing the culture would be right at the top of the list.

In latter years another sports psychologist, Cathal Sheridan, who has joined the Cork senior hurling set-up for 2021, used to tell us about a sign on a gate when he spent three months with elite forces in America, that quoted three of the Ten Commandments.

You shall not lie.

You shall not cheat.

You shall not steal.

They were the tenets by which that group lived by as a means of engendering trust and team spirit. They were a band of brothers who had each other's backs in times of strife, even if they might never go out for a drink together.

That can apply to any sports team, with clear guidelines for what constitutes lying, cheating, and stealing within the context of their discipline. In a sporting context, and in particular in a team environment, 'lying' is pretending to be doing stuff, but not following through on what you have promised. 'Cheating' is not putting in the same effort as others. 'Stealing' is taking away the potential trophies that are on offer when you truly have not earned them the same as everyone else in the squad.

These are the three worst things you can do but below that is the overriding principle. If you, as part of a group, know that anybody is doing anything like that and allow it to be tolerated, that group is doomed.

IT ALL GOES back to workrate, heart, process and outcome.

If you have the first three, you give yourself a chance but there are no guarantees at the elite level where outside factors – bad luck, poor finishing, refereeing decisions – can have an impact. The first two are non-negotiables.

Workrate and heart will probably take out a team that is not well set up against you. A process without workrate and heart is useless.

That's why we put them in the order we do.

That is why the warrior is your number one. Warriors are in the trenches all the time. Gunslingers get the headlines, the sponsorships, the Man of the Match awards for kicking the winner though they might have had a nightmare. Gunslingers do not tend to get their hands dirty.

That can be a problem within a group that you have to keep your eye on.

Most of the time though, warriors are unbothered because they are not in it for personal glory. They are selfless and care most about the team. They are courageous and go for every ball. And they are consistent in that.

It was probably no coincidence that Galway's wane coincided with the retirement of warrior figures such as Gary Fahey, Ja Fallon, Ray Silke, Tomás Mannion and Seán Óg de Paor. When I was with Sligo, I would have identified the increasing number of wavers in Galway, seen it as an Achilles heel and targeted it.

So, it was no surprise that I would prioritise the return of the Galway warrior when I became manager. Much to my Mayo friend's disgust.

CHAPTER 17

SEWER RATS

Football changed and we probably didn't adapt well at all. We were probably stubborn the way we tried to play football for a long time, going man-on-man at the back, leaving six up front, the traditional way. We had some good results, but we weren't winning and we were conceding a lot of scores.

— Kieran Fitzgerald, The 42, May 10, 2020

(Mayo) did develop a machine over a five-year period, they dominated Connacht completely through organisation, through ruthlessness, through what I could only describe as bully tactics. They really played senior football. The two under-21 teams that came through weren't given the tools to live at senior and Kevin has now given it to them. He's given them a set of tools to play senior, and lo and behold they've turned around and beaten Mayo.

— Gary Sice, December 21, 2016

THERE WERE HUGE deficiencies in areas that should have been addressed through the development squad structure, at minor level and even under-21. We had won two All-Irelands in 2011 and '13 at the latter grade but I was astonished by how ill-equipped some players were in so many facets of the game.

The ball skills were there but game understanding, awareness and footwork were nowhere near what I would have expected. Many of the players had no idea where to be and what to do for the 79 minutes that they did not have the ball in their hands.

We had to put a lot of time into the basics of footwork and progress to the other related skills, just as we had done with Sligo. That was the focus over the opening two years, along with establishing a strong culture and building collective responsibility for attack and defence – a broader comprehension of space, how to create it, how to use it, and how to take it away.

I didn't target winning every game, but we did prioritise the FBD League that first year and it carried on. In five seasons, we won 14 games and lost three.

Obviously, I wanted to see what we had and after conceding four goals to Roscommon in the final, it confirmed the impression that we had defensive issues. You might say it was only the FBD League, but it was how those scores were conceded that was concerning. We were far too open – and it was a trend from previous seasons.

GALWAY HAD NOT won anything in years.

The county had garnered only two Connacht Championships since I had retired. I talked to the players about having an empty medal box and wanting to put something into it. So again, people might not have made much of winning the FBD League in 2016 and following up the next season, but winning is nothing to be scoffed at when it's not something you do a lot.

When you are that long without silverware, to stand up on a podium, with the family there, has meaning. You need it to build confidence.

We had two good championship wins before giving Mayo such a rattle. The first was in New York, just five years after Galway narrowly escaped humiliation at Gaelic Park. Despite conceding an early goal and playing with only 13 men for the last 15 minutes, New York were within a point in the closing minutes, before Galway notched up 1-3 to post a flattering triumph.

So while you wouldn't be jumping up and down to post a 16-point triumph, in that context it was pleasing. It showed a commendable attitude. Complacency is always a danger for Galway football teams because of an innate sense of superiority that has been at the core of many spectacular implosions.

Not here. The lads went out and did the job professionally, following up with a comfortable if slightly workmanlike victory over Leitrim.

We continued to build after the defeat by Mayo with an away win against Armagh, when Damien Comer goaled, and then defeating Derry in Salthill. We only conceded eight points in that outing, having yielded 12 a week earlier. The goals against column was looking considerably healthier, just the one to Mayo conceded in five championship ties.

Donegal showed how far we still had to travel though, raising the green flag three times to beat us by 10 points. That said, we were within three with 10 minutes remaining, but Donegal were a lot further down the road than us at that point, still genuine contenders for All-Ireland honours after going all the way in 2012 and reaching the final in '14.

It was a very pleasing first year.

♦ ♦ ♦ ♦ ♦

THE PLAYERS HAD taken our new methods on board. There were a few sideways glances as we had them go through these basic footwork movements and built them up through slow, painstaking progressions.

They were programmed to value high intensity output, which is important, of course, for fitness but not for learning. Learning takes time.

We had put in the time and would continue to do so, but sufficient advances had been made to use what had been learned and establish some different game plans.

The league served us well in bedding down systems and blooding some new players. Cavan beat us in the final round, when a win would have secured promotion to Division 1 and a place in the Division 2 final at Croke Park, which would have been a worthwhile experience for the squad at that time in their evolution.

I wasn't upset though. Losses have their place if they aren't habitual, and we had begun to win more than we lost. We just were not ready for the step up. The process was still being applied so the consistency wasn't there yet.

It was a continuation of the learning curve.

There are four stages to the habit curve, and we were probably in around the second stage of conscious incompetence. We just had to keep working on it, which we did and by 2018, we had attained unconscious competence. We had the process fine-tuned and it was applied seamlessly.

MAYO WERE SCHEDULED to be our semi-final opponents if they got over London – and I knew of their capabilities better than most – but we focussed on June 18 and MacHale Park from a long way out.

We had a back four of Bernie Power, Eoghan Kerin, Declan Kyne and David Wynne. Three of them were championship debutants and Kyne only had a few minutes in the bank as a late sub against Leitrim the year before. The league had delivered for us.

Francis Farragher wrote the following in *The Connacht Tribune*.

Galway are limited enough on defensive options and they will need to have a strategy in place to cope with the physical power of the Mayo attack. On that sword, the Galway challenge will either prosper or perish!

Well, we did have a strategy that would bring great delight and praise, though by my final year, having a defensive strategy became something abhorrent to many observers.

We designed a plan specifically for Mayo and it would bamboozle them. For three years, they had no answer to it. They finally edged us out in 2019, when we were hobbled by injuries, but not before we caused them all kinds of bother.

Mayo's threats were from off-the-shoulder runners down the centre. Dublin struggled with the tactic. Keith Higgins, Colm Boyle, Lee Keegan, Aidan O'Shea and Paddy Durcan were among those who invariably prospered from it.

We dropped off and let them have their kickouts before sending them down the sewers of lanes one and five – the sideline channels. Using coaxing pressure, a line of three people would shepherd them down each sideline.

They were going where we wanted them to go, not where they wanted.

During the warm-up in Castlebar in 2016, I picked a gate into the stand around the '45' and told the lads not to be afraid to let the Mayo man in possession go that far. We would entice them deep into our half but in an area where they were no threat.

Unbeknownst to them, we would close off the avenue of escape behind them. Then we would attack, forcing countless turnovers and mistakes because there was nowhere to go only trouble.

We were supposed to get hammered – Mayo had taken Dublin to a replay in the All-Ireland semi-final the year before and us getting to within four points of them was not considered relevant. But we squeezed the life out of them, frustrated them, closed the cordon on them. We took away the space.

We got in their faces too. It was wonderful to see Declan grabbing Keith Higgins up by the lapels of his jersey. It was after a nothing foul, but he was marking his territory.

You are mine. We are not going to be walked on.

Plenty will express disdain at such a reaction and my praise for it, but you won't find anyone that operates at this level criticising it. The Fancy Dan crap did Galway no favours and even when we were winning, teams thought we could be got at. It really stood out and attracted such negative commentary because it was Galway.

The same so-called experts would be talking about Meath's need to return to that old traditional, physical style in the next breath.

Tom Flynn came up with the goal 15 minutes from the end that separated the sides, but it was the execution of the game plan when Mayo had possession that was decisive. Needless to say, the analysis afterwards revolved around Mayo playing poorly. As usual, it did not credit the reason Mayo played poorly – Galway didn't let them. To be fair, the analysts probably couldn't see what was going on because they didn't have this experience of coaching.

THIS WAS THE biggest victory in my time as Galway manager, though following up to win the Connacht final when the expectation levels had rocketed runs it close, as does the defeat of Kerry in Croke Park two years later.

This triumph, the minor success of 1986, the defeat of Mayo when I was playing in 1998, and managing the first Sligo team to beat Galway on Tribe soil in the championship are among my most satisfying days in more than 35 years of county involvement.

We had been dismissed and insulted within Galway.

Some of the commentary in the local press on individual players was extremely harsh and close to the bone, I felt. Nobody gave us a chance. But the team put in a huge performance to topple a side chasing a sixth consecutive provincial title.

As is their wont, Roscommon made it difficult in the decider and we needed a replay to end Galway's eight-year wait for the Nestor Cup. We should have taken care of business at the Stadium but were unable put them away until 'Take Two' in Castlebar, which held very recent happy memories for us.

It told me that the players could find another level in the replay, having failed to see the drawn game out with a two-point lead and the wind late on. Mentally, you might feel sore about being caught by an injury-time equaliser, but there wasn't a hint of that, and we blew Roscommon away to win by 3-16 to 0-14.

The first game had been very tactical, but we did a lot of video analysis and were confident we could unpick the lock at the second time of asking. By now, we were getting labelled as a defensive team, but we created some fantastic scores and attacking play was central to my game plan.

As I will say every day of my life until I draw my last breath, taking players deep isn't always about having a defensive mindset. It is a very legitimate offensive tactic in terms of creating space to be more effective in attack.

The front three favoured by Liverpool is considered among the best in the world but its success is dependent on Roberto Firmino dropping deep so that Mo Salah and Sadio Mané can profit from the resultant gaps.

No matter what the sport, space is king.

Roscommon had no answer. Danny Cummins banged in two goals, Gary Sice another and Damien Comer and Shane Walsh hit three points apiece. I was really pleased that Gary O'Donnell was the man to be receiving the cup. He was a real leader, with the right attitude, a warrior to his toes.

One of the best aspects of being involved in such a momentous victory was bringing the Nestor Cup to Paddy Coleman's house. Paddy was a Dunmore man and the MacHales were inexorably linked with the prosperity of Galway football. We have never won an All-Ireland without a Dunmore representative. They provided the likes of the Donnellans and the Keenans.

Paddy's brother, Bertie was a selector on the three in-a-row team of the 1960s and a long-time member of the county board. It was Bertie who formally proposed the Dunmore and Galway motion recommending the formulation of provincial and All-Ireland club championships at GAA Congress in 1970. All GAA people owe Bertie Coleman a debt of gratitude, not just Galway.

I played for Galway with Paddy's son John but had never met Paddy himself. He was a close friend of Bosco McDermott's however, so when Bosco asked if we could bring the cup to the house, because Paddy had actually married into the Nestor family, I couldn't refuse. It was the only house I brought the trophy to, and it was my great honour to do so.

We called down and met Paddy and his family. They were all football mad. It did us good to see the impact winning a match had on other people.

Paddy travelled around the country with Bosco to see Galway play, regardless of distance or weather. Having gotten to know him now, I would always talk to the pair of them before and after matches.

Sadly, Paddy died early in 2020 at the age of 95. Thankfully, he had been healthy most of his life and was cycling up to six weeks before he passed away. According to John, he considered the day we arrived with the Nestor Cup as one of the greatest of his life.

◆ ◆ ◆ ◆ ◆

LOSING TO TIPPERARY by nine points in the All-Ireland quarter-final ranks up there with the two Connacht final defeats by Roscommon as the most disenchanting of my term, and it can be attributed to a basic lack of workrate.

The industry levels were very high in the first 12 minutes, but we missed lots of chances. The response to spurning those opportunities was alarming. Instead of redoubling their efforts, the players dropped their levels and let the game get away from them.

It is hard to know but you would suspect that the natural Galway arrogance might have seeped in slightly and that some of the players just could not see themselves losing to Tipp. It would explain the flatness that existed for most of the hour, though Liam Kearns' side clearly deserve credit for the way they put us away.

Afterwards, I was able to look back on it as a bump on the road that could be expected given the extent of the repair job that had been required but at the time, it hurt.

The Mayo team we had beaten and would beat in the next two Connacht Championships, awaited in the semi-final. They would lose a replayed All-Ireland final to Dublin by a point, despite conceding two own goals in the drawn affair.

All the pieces were not in place yet.

CHAPTER 18

GIANT STRIDES

It's very hard to show character when everything's going your way. You can only show it when it's not, when it's going against you… when you're low on the ground.
– Kieran McGeeney, July 13, 2013

INCONSISTENCY IS A common characteristic of youth and as a team, we were still feeling our way. I felt we were gaining ground so there was a touch of frustration about not retaining our provincial crown.

We would have been the first Galway team to do that since I was captain in 2003. I wanted to move that on, just like I wanted to pass on the mantle of being Galway's last All Star the same year.

Losing to Roscommon in the Connacht final was one of the bitterest defeats. We had done so much work by overcoming Mayo again and were on an exceptionally good run, winning six games in-a-row and securing promotion to Division 1 of the league, as Division 2 champions.

Bouncing back from the devastation of that loss, and the over-the-top criticism that followed to beat Donegal, with close to a complete performance was testament to the character of the players.

They had been questioned and some of that was legitimate, but they were a steely outfit now. They didn't take being bullied lying down and the display against Donegal was the perfect riposte to the naysayers.

In Japanese business management, they rejoice when they find mistakes. The philosophy is that once a mistake or weakness has been identified it can be rectified and eliminated, thereby making the organisation stronger.

With that in mind, giving best to Kerry in the All-Ireland quarter-final did not keep me awake at night. You'd prefer to win but it was another new experience for the players. Kerry had a history of beating Galway at Croke Park, but we had troubled them.

I felt sure the experience would stand to us because the players now knew the mythical green and gold jersey was not a shield to human frailty.

As we had shown, we tended to pay attention at lesson time.

♦ ♦ ♦ ♦ ♦

AS WE MADE improvements in our physical and mental conditioning, we became more competitive in the heavy going that Galway weren't renowned for flourishing on.

The league had been good to us in terms of trying out a clatter of players, but if we were to continue our upward trajectory, we would need to be operating in Division 1 against the best teams in the country over a period of time. In 2017, we made the leap, topping the table and defeating Kildare in the final.

We had drawn our opening tie with Cork at the beginning of February and after wins over Fermanagh and Clare, got caught by a 66th minute goal from Donal Lenihan in Navan to lose by a point to Meath.

At that juncture, it could have gone either way, but we got just the answer we were looking for by blitzing Derry in Tuam by 5-15 to 2-15. It showed that we were developing different styles of play depending on the opposition.

You needed Plans A, B and C to have any chance of succeeding.

It is easy to counteract one plan and if you are relying on a sole approach, you are in trouble. Jim Gavin learned that when he abandoned his gung-ho approach – playing the 'right way' he called it when he took the job. Donegal put paid to that fantasy in 2014 and Dublin became far more pragmatic.

They became far more versatile but always paid every bit as much attention to defending properly, as they did to attack.

We did the same, but it is important to point out that we paid every bit as much attention to attacking effectively as we did to defence. We racked up 3-15 to account for Down, leaving it all to play for against Kildare. The Lilywhites were already qualified and made 14 changes from their regular lineout for the trip to Salthill.

There was pressure on anyway, because Galway were trying to get to Division 1 for the first time since being relegated in 2011. Now, that expectation was ramped up with an understrength team coming, laced with players that had a lot to play for with a final to come the following week.

The common consensus was that we had to be wary of complacency but of greater concern to me was the potential paralysis brought by fear; that some players would visualise the public reaction to losing.

It turned into an arm wrestle and the pressure told as we made errors and were cautious. But the players dug out a one-point win.

Seven days later, the margin was two, and we had 10 different scorers in the 0-18 to 0-16 success at Croke Park. That was such a vital win, because Galway hadn't enjoyed a good day at HQ in far too long. It was a national title, the first since the 2001 All-Ireland. Getting to the top tier was essential too in terms of moving to the next stage of development.

ON A PERSONAL level, it was nice to add the Division 2 title to the third and fourth division crowns won with Sligo. I always trusted myself and believed in my coaching methods, but managers aren't any different to players in terms of the positive effects of winning football matches.

We were in a good position moving into the Connacht Championship, though the nine-week gap until the semi-final was a substantial disadvantage, given that Mayo had had the benefit of nice examination by Sligo three weeks before.

We let Mayo back into it in the second-half, which we never should have given that Keith Higgins had been sent off in the 26th minute, but one point is as good as 10 in knockout fare. The lads were brilliant defensively once more. Kevin McLoughlin's first-half goal came from an unlucky break, as Lee Keegan's shot hit the post. Damien was getting treatment for a head injury at the time. That meant we only led by a point, after playing with a strong wind.

The intensity stepped up another level after the restart and we really imposed ourselves on our neighbours. Damien's mammoth shoulder on Diarmuid O'Connor was just one example but it really lifted the Galway supporters.

Seán Armstrong was kicking beautifully from placed balls and his sixth point, from a '45' into the elements, told of immense confidence. That put us four ahead and though Cillian O'Connor brought it back to the minimum from frees, we held on for another outstanding win.

Unfortunately, we couldn't follow it up.

The first 15 or 20 minutes of the decider are hard to explain. Fear or complacency? I'm still not sure which it was but there was a distinct lack of energy that left us trailing by seven points after just 14 minutes. Even playing into the wind, that was unacceptable.

When Brian Stack goaled early in the second-half, the margin was nine, but this wasn't to be another Tipp, when players folded early. Illustrating the extensive progress they were continuing to make, the lads worked themselves back into the game with six consecutive points, despite kicking a lot of wides.

We were building momentum, but David Gough took it away with some bizarre frees against us at either end of the field that stopped us in our tracks. Two of these in a matter of seconds provided a two-point swing, the difference of being within two and falling four behind.

Roscommon deserve great credit for some spectacular scoring in the last 10 minutes, when they threw over points from everywhere. The final margin of nine points wasn't a reflection of the game.

Losing hurt badly. You cannot take on Roscommon half-cocked and for whatever reason, the players were nowhere near the level of intensity they needed to deal with Kevin McStay's crew.

I wasn't impressed when Kevin came up to shake hands with me and left the pitch before the final whistle. It smacked of arrogance and was very dismissive. I said nothing but I wouldn't forget.

♦ ♦ ♦ ♦ ♦

THE KICKING CAME hard and heavy.

Players got it, I got it.

Some of it was poisonous and it was the kids you'd worry about most because both Mary and my mother took no more notice than I did. We just had to store it in the hurt locker and focus on the job at hand, which was to lift ourselves.

I get so much satisfaction when I look back on the 4-17 to 0-14 defeat of Donegal in Sligo. Johnny Heaney kicked 2-2, Liam Silke and Danny added goals, Seán kicked six points and the defensive unit excelled.

It spoke volumes for the players that they could drag themselves out of the absolute pit of desolation they had wallowed in for a few days after being dumped on their arses.

As a management team, we made it massively personal. Yes, we had game plans, but the focus was on lifting devastated players and getting the emotional levels right. There were several aspects to that.

We pointed out the positives of the Connacht final, breaking it into 12-minute blocks which we liked to do. Even in the horrible start, we put together some good elements. And of course, the fightback was extremely positive.

Then there were Gough's few tough decisions and the stunning scores at the end that all contributed to the margin. We weren't nine points inferior to Roscommon.

You couldn't just point fingers though, and attribute it to a bad day. We had to acknowledge the low levels of aggression from the throw-in. Attitude is a non-negotiable and Roscommon, who were always frenzied in the face of a maroon jersey, fed on our early passiveness.

If the fall-off was because they didn't value the Roscommon threat as highly as Mayo's, that was disappointing. But they would have to get those levels back up against Donegal, or the same would occur.

So, it wasn't that they had suddenly deteriorated. They just had to make sure they were at the right pitch of intensity against a team that would look to bully them, if they let them.

The carrot and stick were used. You don't lift people by lambasting them, but you had to point out where the deficits were, while shining a light on what they had done well. This was an opportunity for redemption.

We brought the lads up to Markievicz Park the Saturday before. It was just management and players, with us emphasising repeatedly how much we believed in them.

Did we know we had them in the right place? If you asked me that question five years ago, I'd answer it very easily. Looking at it now, I have no idea. I have been convinced before games that we are flying and will bury the opposition, but it hasn't manifested itself in battle.

And then there was the Kerry game with Sligo, when we nearly didn't make it to the pitch after our flight was delayed. We were completely rushed, had an awful warm-up and played brilliantly to almost topple the subsequent All-Ireland champions.

It is the mind that counts.

Mentally, we got it right and Donegal were blown away. It was exhilarating, a supreme performance. The hurt shone through. Hurt at being dismissed and hauled through the coals like they had kidnapped everyone's grannies. More than that, hurt at dropping their own standards.

KERRY BEAT US by eight points in the All-Ireland quarter-final. That was a lacklustre game, slow and ponderous.

The perception afterwards was that we had been too cautious but that wasn't meant to be the approach. The intensity levels weren't high enough again. I'm fairly sure that was fear, playing in Croke Park against Kerry, who Galway hadn't beaten in a big game for donkey's years. You need days like this to learn.

Some media people didn't like hearing this line from me but it's the truth and it takes that long when you are coming from as low as Galway were.

The analysis ignored that we created five goal chances and took none. Overall, the process had stood up well, but we were always playing catch-up once we started so sleepily to be seven behind just before half-time.

That we scored three of the next four points testified to the vast improvement in mental courage and we were still within four points at the three-quarter mark, with Seán and Ian Burke causing a lot of problems.

Kerry finished strongly but I could not be too disheartened. You always want to win but I felt it had been a good year, that our systems had flourished. We had enough chances to beat Kerry, though I'm not saying we should have won.

We could take plenty from it, from the league, from Mayo and Donegal.

We were almost there.

CHAPTER 19

POOR PADDY

He was always very tactically aware. He had brilliant vision on the pitch and trying to create that spatial awareness in players is difficult. But you can see improvements in them as they go along – he really is trying to coach them. You can spot his traits coming through on lads. The current Galway boys, although they're coming to the fore, they were clearly in need of a bit of steeliness to bring them up to where the top teams are. What Kevin has done is he has imposed that bit of steel on them again. You can see it. They're very purposeful now. There's a difference between playing for the jersey and playing to get a jersey.

— John Divilly, *The Irish Times*, July 9, 2017

I really enjoyed my time coaching with Kevin and the lads in Galway. I gained a new perspective on specific areas of coaching and team preparation. Aspects of their coaching philosophy, especially spatial awareness and footwork techniques, and technical skills, I have brought with me to add to my own coaching experience.

— Paddy Tally, GrowCoach.ie, 2020

WORD MADE ITS way to me that Galway had been top of the agenda at a referees' meeting on Tuesday night and as a result, without going overboard, I mentioned to the likes of Eoghan Kerin and Seán Andy Ó Ceallaigh that they needed to be extra careful as they risked suspension on an accumulation of cards.

We had already qualified for an All-Ireland semi-final and nobody wanted to miss out on that. It probably took just a little edge off some of them, as they were erring on the side of caution. The result was a flat, over-cautious performance and we lost by eight points in Monaghan.

What really angered me was that the topic reared its head again on Sunday morning and I asked a county board official to go to the referee Conor Lane, to seek assurances there was no extra focus being placed on us.

It was evident that the media commentary, particularly that from the TV studios, had set an agenda, as it seems to a lot in GAA. The pundits had put us in the referees' crosshairs.

Public Enemy No 1.

♦ ♦ ♦ ♦ ♦

GOAL-SETTING IS driven by what you have. By 2018, our goal was to win the All-Ireland. We were now operating in that sort of arena.

We gave it a good go. We got to a Division 1 league final undefeated, regained the Connacht title, beat Kerry in Tralee and Croke Park, and pushed Dublin to the pin of their collars in the All-Ireland semi-final, though the nine-point margin meant we would get little recognition or indeed acknowledgement of that.

We had played all of the top teams and Dublin were the only team to have beaten us in a meaningful game.

The stats show that we created far more chances than the Dubs in the first-half but an absence of economy proved costly again. It was a pity, but we ended the season the second-ranked team in the country in my opinion.

I was over the moon that Ian would bridge the gap back to me as the last Galway All Star in 2003 but absolutely appalled that Shane didn't get the nod. Maybe it wouldn't fit with the narrative that had been established, that we had constrained him in an inflexible system.

Through the course of the entire season, Shane was magnificent.

He had developed his game so much and worked hard in doing so. All Star 'forwards' aren't selected on workrate and invisible influence. Few saw what Shane was doing in that regard. However, even in terms of just his scoring impact and creativity, he excelled. He was one of our driving forces in all our major wins.

It was funny how Bernard Brogan's reinvention under the tutelage of Pat Gilroy was celebrated. But in the case of Shane, he was being 'blackguarded' by management. But we were accustomed by now, sadly, to the lack of balance.

The critics were piling up, and whatever about the lazy descriptions of us being over-defensive – an astounding departure from the reality of the situation – once the pundits started labelling us as ugly, nasty, purveyors of the 'Dark Arts', it began to have an impact on the team in a very real way.

In a sense, I took the 'Dark Arts' thing as a compliment. For years Galway were dismissed as soft, a pushover. This team didn't take a backward step

We were buoyant as a group now, having slogged through three years of painstaking learning. We were a serious outfit, and everyone knew it. Mayo's continuing competitiveness in All-Ireland finals was a boost, given we were beating them.

And we felt, even in defeat to Kerry, that there was no cause to fear them.

After three years, I felt it was time to freshen things up a bit. It was always on my mind and over the years I approached Ja Fallon, John Divilly, Pádraic Joyce, Declan Meehan, Martin McNamara and Derek Savage to come in, but none of them were in a position to accept for one reason or another, although John did train our Dublin-based players for us.

I had been aware of Paddy Tally from his involvement with St Mary's when they won the Sigerson Cup the previous year. They would not have been among the fancies, but he set them up very well. He had been part of Mickey Harte's backroom set-up when his native Tyrone won their first All-Ireland in 2003.

That he was from a different geographical area and mindset became an increasing attraction the more I mulled it over. That would challenge us all and that would be something to look forward to; someone from 'outside' coming 'in'.

He joined up in January and proved popular with everyone. He was a tremendous addition and brought a lot to us in what would be a year to remember.

◆ ◆ ◆ ◆ ◆

DIVISION 1 FOOTBALL was just what we needed at that stage in our development. It is a dog-eat-dog environment and the days of the elite paying scant attention to spring fare are long gone. You would be under duress every week. This would test our mettle individually and the viability of our process.

We astounded most observers by topping the table undefeated, despite being without our Corofin contingent for much of the season and we did it exhibiting different traits and styles of play, depending on the opposition. We were introducing more variety all the time and it made us a dangerous outfit.

We showed grit in awful weather against the masters of trench warfare, Tyrone in Tuam. A week later, there was a real dash about our play as we defeated Donegal in Letterkenny. We relished playing Mayo by now, dishing out the type of medicine they had been delivering to us for long enough.

It was when we beat Kerry by a goal in Tralee that people took note. Some didn't like what they saw.

At least Colm O'Rourke was being consistent in having a go at Galway. But whereas 20 years before, he was saying we lacked substance, had a midfield with no legs and could not be considered All-Ireland champions worth lauding for 'only' beating Kildare... now we were 'a little bit ugly'.

We continued to adapt, happy to concede more in games where we felt we could really get at the opposition, but closing off the gaps against sides that could hurt us if we left ourselves open.

Comfortable wins over Monaghan and Kildare bookended a 0-13 apiece draw with Dublin at Pearse Stadium. This was an excellent result, achieved while continuing to experiment with personnel. Barry McHugh was our leading scorer that day with five points and Peter Cooke shone as well.

That left us top of the table, an achievement to be proud of in our first season back in the top flight.

Dublin found a little bit more improvement than us in the final, prevailing by 0-18 to 0-14 to bag their fifth title in six years. It would have been fantastic for Galway to win a first Division 1 crown in 37 years and personally, I would have loved to have completed the clean sweep of four divisions.

We weren't far away though.

◆ ◆ ◆ ◆ ◆

'I'M GETTING BLAMED for everything!'

It became a standing joke after the latest excoriation of Galway and the statement of fact that it was all Paddy Tally's doing.

Those dastardly Ulster coaches! What are they doing to our lovely Galway?

Poor puzzled Paddy would come into training bemoaning his fate.

'Why is it always my fault?'

We got a good laugh from it. Initially, his influence in this regard was being hailed. This was what Galway needed. But it turned, possibly as soon as we beat Kerry. Kerry and Mayo loved to clap Galway on the back for the traditional all-guns-blazing style – while they were raiding our larder at the other end and sending us home on the back of another beating.

We weren't focusing on defence over attack. We set up well, absolutely.

We coached defending, on what all the players did when the opposition had possession. We did the same for what the other 14 players did when one of ours had possession.

The truth is that Paddy had nothing to do with our defensive systems because they had been a work in progress for three years before his arrival. Such painstakingly detailed walk-throughs, the monotonous nights growing understanding of space, teaching better footwork and how to tackle without even laying a hand on an opponent. I wasn't throwing that in the bin.

Paddy was excellent for us and the players loved him. It's just that he wasn't involved in our 'defensive system' even in the minutest way! His work was on other areas, on and off the field.

The other thing was that our defensive processes bore absolutely no resemblance to what is utilised by Ulster teams. Suggestions to the contrary exposed the lack of understanding of coaching and systems at that level.

Ulster defence is primarily about getting bodies back and filling the space, working hard. But it's mostly straight lines. We'd be back in the arc, falling off in blindsides and covering lanes two, three and four up the middle of the pitch. It was constant movement, blocking angles, shepherding towards specific routes.

We did ramp up the physical side in 2018 but we had been working on moving chess pieces, moving and replacing, making angled runs, imposing other pressures apart from physical, such as the coaxing pressure that worked so well against Mayo.

Adding the physicality was the next step.

I couldn't introduce it until the footwork was right and all the other pressures were in place. If you go physical too early, you end up lunging into a tackle. If you don't make an impact, you expose your team and you're out of the game. That's why I would rather a system first and foremost.

I had another system, that involved players being numbered 1 to 5. We weren't shouting numbers out on a pitch or anything like that – they were just specifics that had to be covered.

If I'm a No 1, I'm closest to the ball and I put pressure on the ball, whatever the pressure is. If there are two players coming at me, I stand off. If there are two with me, physical pressure. So as No 1, I am the man responsible for that ball.

No 2 has to get close enough to help on whichever side I might be in trouble. If I'm beaten, then he can move off his man and step in. So, the next nearest player has to recognise that situation and get to that point.

No 3 means that you need to get to No 2, because No 2 might be called into action at any second.

No 4 is away from the ball, isn't involved in contact at all but is in the right place that if someone comes from the opposite side, he'd physically get in front of them. So, 4 has nothing to do but running or pressure on ball.

Then you have a Red 5. That's high alert, with somebody coming into the scoring arc. This is where the 'Dark Arts' come in. It is a physical contact all over. He is not being left within an inch of the goal.

He's in your house, get him out of your house quickly.

Pulling, dragging, physical contact… whatever it takes.

Finally, there is a Black 0. If you're a Black 0, you're a lazy player and you're a detriment to the team, with nothing to offer. When you analyse games and the same guy is being a Black 0, he has to go. It's one thing asking someone to do something they can't do. There are ways of putting people in positions where their deficiencies might not be as exposed. But when it's laziness, it has to be hit.

You cannot have a Black 0 anywhere near your squad.

THIS GOES BACK to *79:1*.

To be impacting the game when the opposition had the ball, you had to be one of the five points. If you're a 0, you're not impacting the game and are worthless to your teammates.

This was all a planned evolution, but I couldn't talk about that at the start. The way it was in Galway at the time, there was a good chance I'd be sacked after 18 months. But it was where I planned to be, three and a half years down the line.

Our offence was far more imaginative than given credit for too but, just like the defence, it was misunderstood. We went after a lot of teams. But you obviously couldn't go bald-headed against Dublin. You went at it another way and as we proved, you could still be creative.

And remember, you had a packed defence to break down with them too.

We were about movement, using the width of the field, the five lanes from right to left, filling space and emptying it, constant rotations. People give out about sideways passing but you don't just run into a slew of bodies. You have to move them around.

In a zone defence for example, you really cause a problem by sending three players down the same channel. Because in a zone, a defender isn't picking up a man, he's just taking a space but if three players hit his zone, he is in a dilemma then.

And if he moves out of his zone, as he will be sorely tempted to do, you have created a priceless bit of space.

From there, it comes down to finishing and that is where we were found wanting in the really big games.

◆ ◆ ◆ ◆ ◆

ED SHEERAN ENTERTAINED thousands at Pearse Stadium and we did the same for our supporters in MacHale Park, overcoming Mayo in a third successive Connacht Championship.

We left it late, a Johnny Heaney goal in injury time snatching it after the teams had been level five times during a fiercely contested second-half.

It looked to be going to a replay with the teams deadlocked on 0-11 apiece, but the goal was another illustration of our attacking intent and ability.

Adrian Varley found Ian with a perfectly weighted 25-metre kick pass straight into the chest. Seán Kelly timed his run to the millisecond to take the pop pass. He was moving before Ian had gathered possession. The transfer was seamless.

A bit of twinkle toes footwork by Seán bamboozled three Mayo defenders. Johnny was bursting to get in support, the angle of his run sure to get him into space and into the scoring arc if the last offload was executed properly. The weight and timing were ideal. Johnny took the ball in his stride, moved into space and unleashed a rocket to the roof of the net.

Mayo responded with a pointed free by Cillian O'Connor, but we were mentally as well as physically strong now and a Tom Flynn point immediately after told a lot.

It was a magnificent victory albeit that Mayo had played with 14 men for 40 minutes and lost Tom Parsons to an horrific injury. Every GAA person was delighted that Tom made it back to play, a testament to his fortitude.

But Mayo had shown their resilience over many years. They weren't rolling over and making it easy for us. We had to take it, and we did.

The impact of our bench showed the benefit of exposing so many players to the fray over the years. Adrian, Ian and Seán all did well as subs, along with Eamonn Brannigan and Peter.

We were full of confidence after that and opened up on Sligo in the semi-final, 11 individual scorers registering 4-24.

Roscommon awaited and for a while, it looked like they might be going to break our hearts again. We turned the ball over 12 times from misplaced passes, apparently intent on shooting ourselves in the foot... knee, chest and head. It was horrendous inaccuracy for that level of competition.

Five points down after 22 minutes, we were doing well to get it to three at half-time. It was time for cool heads in the dressing-room, to reset. We spoke about 12 months earlier, the hurt of the criticism, of Kevin McStay's 'early' handshake before the final whistle, and that the future for a lot of us, players and management, depended on the next 40 minutes.

From there, we focused on the process.

Stop, start and continue.

Stop doing 'A' ... start doing 'B'... continue doing 'C'. If we got back to our game, and kept the levels high, we would win.

The maturity and resilience stood out. The accuracy improved markedly, and we took our chances. Shane shone again, kicking eight points from 10 shots into the wind and was involved in countless transitions from defence to attack. He also forced two turnovers from his three physical tackles and got himself in the right place to exert a different type of pressure when Roscommon had the ball.

Tom also stood out at midfield after an iffy first-half. We scored four points pushing up on Roscommon kickouts. Eoghan, Ciaran Duggan, Seán, Adrian and Peter also played roles off the bench again and we were easier winners than the 0-14 to 2-6 scoreline would suggest.

I didn't say anything when I shook hands with Kevin after. I didn't go early, but I can guarantee you it was the first place I was going after the final whistle and it wouldn't always be.

Now I must be clear on one thing. I have tremendous admiration for Kevin, for leaving the studio to put his head on the chopping block of county management for three years with Roscommon. He had already enjoyed All-Ireland success at club level with St Brigid's. Kevin walked the walk and that experience gives him credibility in his media commentary down the line.

But whether by accident or design, he had shown disrespect to Galway 12 months previously in doing something you never see in the GAA, shaking hands before the final whistle and leaving early. So yeah, we used it as motivation and I enjoyed it when it was my turn. But I hold no grudge against Kevin. I respect him for taking on the Roscommon job and for what he did with it.

♦ ♦ ♦ ♦ ♦

THIS WAS THE first season of the Super 8s, a new challenge for everyone. You could not be sure what impact it would have but we were confident in our fitness and conditioning. We just had to take each game on its merits.

First up was Kerry in Croke Park.

It was ideal in terms of measuring our progress given our defeat to them at HQ 12 months earlier. The result was one of our best wins in my time as manager, the first over Kerry in the championship since 1965. It was the first championship win at Croke Park since 2001.

This was a top-class performance. Not enough note was taken of what we had done in Tralee, when we imposed ourselves physically on Kerry. The expectation was that it would be different in knockout fare at Croke Park. Kerry would do to Galway what Kerry always did to Galway.

But you can be sure the players on both sides hadn't forgotten Tralee.

There was so much more to our performance than physicality though. We kept it tight and ground Kerry down, leading 6-5 at half-time and edging further ahead in the second-half.

Our transition for Patrick Sweeney's match-sealing goal was marvellous; from Eamonn to Shane, who had the energy to burn the Kerry defence after another huge game, and then Patrick, who finished at the second attempt.

Look at the clip and you can see that we are filling the five channels. There are runners everywhere. In the commentary, when Eamonn picks up the ball, Marty Morrissey says there's nobody except Adrian Varley up front.

But there are four forwards inside the '20' spread across the channels when Patrick is finishing. That's selfless running but not of the headless chicken variety. It gave Shane the opportunity to access the weak point that had been exposed by the others.

It was powerful football. It was a statement.

Whatever happened now, this little team had left a legacy. Think about it – nobody my age had ever seen Galway beat Kerry in the championship.

They had now.

But, of course, the credit didn't flow afterwards. It was about how Kerry hadn't played well.

Go figure.

The players were in box four now of the competence pyramid... unconscious competence.

A couple of years earlier, when losing to Cavan with promotion up for grabs, they were probably in box two or three, of conscious incompetence or conscious competence. Now it was flowing, happening organically, naturally. Unconsciously.

As a coach, there is no greater pleasure than that, over and above a result.

Kildare were a danger, buoyed by their 'Newbridge Or Nowhere' triumph over Mayo but though we couldn't shake them off, we always felt we could do damage to them offensively and prevailed in high-scoring affair, 0-19 to 0-16, with 13 individuals in maroon getting on the scoresheet.

The combination of other results meant we were qualified along with Monaghan, who would be our final opposition in Salthill. The fall-off in intensity came as a huge surprise and there could be no arguments about the result, as we only scored eight points and the visitors doubled that tally. We provided far too much space and offered little in attacking intent. We were very flat indeed.

Maybe it was the combination of big games against Mayo, Roscommon,

Kerry and then a game in Newbridge against Kildare where we could secure an All-Ireland semi-final spot for the first time in 17 years. And maybe it was actually breaking new ground. Maybe there were one or two that took Monaghan for granted, especially on home turf.

Then there was me giving the message about avoiding cards. So, I took a little bit of the blame for that.

Monaghan won and we had to wipe it from the memory. It didn't affect us in a negative sense in terms of mindset though and our performance against Dublin showed that. Even without Paul Conroy and with Ciaran making his first start after being eased back from injury, we were excellent.

IT WAS TRULY staggering that the post-match analysis centred on Galway being negative and blown away. I can't understand how they would not have the stats that we have – the packages are available to everyone. Surely if they knew we had created 50 percent more chances in the first-half than Dublin, they might ascertain that we were doing something right in an offensive sense.

What we were doing wrong was not capitalising. We had them on the rack. Damien had a goal and should have had a second almost straight after, when Stephen Cluxton saved. Instead, Con O'Callaghan got a goal just before half-time and we trailed by two points when we should have led by five or six.

That is not just my opinion. That is according to the formula for expected return, based on percentage success rates from the areas in which we created our opportunities. The figure is actually five and a half points.

That's a completely different ball game mentally and in terms of how you go at the second-half. It's the difference between having something to hold on to and at some stage, having to leave some gaps to chase it. Dublin thrive on space with their athletes. It's why you can't push up to force turnovers against them high up the pitch.

Nine points was no reflection on that game, though it would have been 12 but for Shane's late goal. But if you read the reports, we had been pummelled from start to finish.

Incidentally, even by the 59th minute – though the dynamic of the game is altered because of the seven-point differential between the interval advantage we should have had and reality – the expected return on both teams' chances created would have had the sides level.

All the invisible percentages we were working on were with a view to being a team that consistently competed to win. That was our mission.

It wasn't to actually win because once you hit the elite level, it is about fine margins. Mayo are the obvious example of that. They had some deficiencies that were exposed but with just a little bit of luck they might have won a few All-Irelands in the last 25 years.

That's the one big criticism of the squad to this day.

Our process stood up, our transitions were excellent, but we didn't take our chances. The All-Ireland goal was achievable, had we been more clinical. But we would work on that for 2019 and continue our improvements.

◆◆◆◆◆

IN INTERVIEWS BEFORE the league final, I talked about going up to The Coliseum. The skewed system that gives Dublin the huge advantage of playing all their games in Croke Park is an issue that needs to be dealt with.

They play every game there.

EVERY GAME.

It beggars belief that you would hand such an advantage to a team in the marquee competition.

I would categorise it as a six-to-eight-point advantage. Travel is part of it, being in your own bed the night before the game. Your home dressing-room, understanding the goal posts and the vagaries of the wind and other conditions. The few momentum changers and decisions that go your way because of the crowds.

Croke Park is the national stadium for all the counties, paid for by the members in a variety of ways and by the taxpayers of the country through State funding. It is scandalous that it is used to give one county a massive advantage.

Dublin have so many spectators. We see the amount of sponsorship and revenue they can generate. For all their good planning, are you telling me that they could not build a 30,000-seater stadium like Galway, Mayo, Limerick and countless other counties?

They didn't do it because they knew they wouldn't have to. It is a complete lack of fairness that has to be factored into their status as a six in-a-row team.

There's no disputing the fact that they have excellent players, who are very consistent and extraordinarily strong psychologically. They prevail when taken to the line, and have shown all the traits of a brilliant team. They *are* a brilliant team.

But think of the clutch points they have scored, and the ones missed by their opposition in tight games – would Cillian O'Connor stick them if he were in MacHale Park?

There has been some discussion about Dublin forfeiting one of their Super 8 games at Croke Park, in the event of this structure being retained in a post-Covid championship. While they are being given an obvious leg up by getting an extra home game and their opponents an extra away game, I see having the All-Ireland semi-final and final on home turf as a greater issue.

I acknowledge that the final will always be in Croke Park, but if Dublin didn't play as often there, the advantage could be reduced to some extent. I certainly think they could play a semi-final in Páirc Uí Chaoimh, for example.

If the GAA cares about equity, it is something they will look at.

Look at the bookies' odds. Why are they different, depending on if you're playing home or away? Because playing at home is an advantage.

For the purpose of this exercise, I asked a Boylesports executive to price up Galway v Dublin at Croke Park and Pearse Stadium, with full attendances in pre-Covid times. His team came up with Dublin at 1/3 in Croker and 4/7 in Salthill. That would have Galway at around 11/4 and 7/4 respectively.

I am not a bookie but they are surrounded by actuaries. Actuaries are telling us that the stats decree playing at home is an advantage.

I can't put it any simpler than that.

CHAPTER 20

TIME TO SAY GOODBYE

I think by taking me out of the equation, it can remove some of the over-the-top negativity that was coming at the team, which I feel was unfair. When you are preaching patience about a young group, we didn't carry that through as a county at all this summer. I think, part of that, was down to the fact that I was there for so long and that, maybe, I was a lightning rod for that negativity and criticism, which, if you are 19 as David (Clifford) is or Seán (O'Shea)…is not a nice environment to try and develop yourself.
— Eamonn Fitzmaurice, August 4, 2018

The state of Galway football when Kevin got involved, he really steadied the ship for us. We were getting places. We'd a good structure in there… Kevin seems to have taken a lot of the flak. When I came in first in '09, the first five years of my inter-county career had four different managers. So you'll appreciate, Kevin being in there for five years, what structures he got in place. That will be very important to whoever takes over… a lot of our core players are in their prime or coming to their prime.
— Danny Cummins, Off The Ball, September 3, 2019

I WAS FULL of energy, looking forward to 2019, even with the increasing onslaught from the TV studios and columnists' pages, and Paddy Tally moving on to become Down manager.

Confidence and belief in our processes was fortified by 2018. We had to work on being more ruthless.

The optimism did not translate to trophies, which was the currency we were trading in at this juncture. The primary reason was simple.

Injuries.

We were ravaged.

This always sounds like an excuse. Maybe sometimes it is. In this instance, it is a very legitimate reason. We were missing nine or 10 players almost all the time, all players that would be regularly involved on the pitch in the height of summer. Some were just coming back at the end of our campaign but were nowhere near top condition. Even then, as we welcomed those, we lost others.

By now, nobody within the camp was surprised the injury blight did not come up in analysis, though it was clearly a critical element in gauging the body of work. I couldn't make a big deal of it at the time because you don't want to be delivering a negative message to the group and the players that are coming in. You don't want to put an excuse in their minds.

They must believe they can win.

But you would think professional analysts would refer to it.

We had qualified professionals in a variety of roles and their binoculars were trained on their areas of expertise. It was my job to ensure that the binoculars weren't always aimed in the one direction. We looked at our medical and conditioning departments.

Was there something we needed to change? Was the training or rehab contributing to our issues?

The evidence did not support that possibility. We certainly would have changed it, had it done so. It would have been almost desirable to be honest, because then we would have had a solution.

But the majority of the injuries were ankle, knee, shoulder – they weren't soft tissue. Most of them were down to a contact or a twist, which is bad luck and that is out of your control. Damien fractured a bone in his ankle playing in a charity soccer game on St Stephen's Day. Paul suffered two broken legs.

We just had to soldier on.

MAINTAINING DIVISION ONE status in those circumstances was a fantastic achievement and vital to the future. Incredibly, we were still in contention for a third league final on the trot going into the last round of games, but defeat to Tyrone in Omagh put paid to that.

By then, we were minus the services of Damien, Paul, Declan, Ciaran, Peter, Adrian and Cillian McDaid, who had returned from a stint in the AFL with Carlton the previous year. We had also gone through the league without the Corofin contingent, as they advanced to the middle leg of their fabulous All-Ireland senior club championship three-in-row.

As the year progressed, Eamonn, Seán, Kieran Molloy, Tom, Fiontán Ó Curraoin, David and Gareth picked up knocks that ruled them out for sustained periods. It was an epidemic.

The advantages were exposure for a number of less experienced players to high-performance preparation and play, which would be beneficial in terms of unearthing talent, fostering increased competition, raising standards and ultimately, creating a stronger squad down the line.

We were poor against London in the championship opener at Ruislip, stuttering to a four-point win. There was never a threat of getting caught but squandermania in front of the posts and some terrible passing turnovers kept the exiles involved, the home crowd invested and inevitably increased anxiety in our ranks.

The control was much improved in the second-half, and London were always capable of making it difficult but even in our weakened state, the overall manner of the 0-16 to 1-9 victory was not what we would have liked.

The players knew that it wasn't good enough and responded in real style by blitzing Sligo. Again, despite registering 3-11, our finishing left a little to be desired, while we lost Kieran to a dislocated shoulder. At least Cillian was able to come back into the line-up.

Martin Farragher and John Daly were two players who had benefited from the injuries to get more game time and they did well, while Liam Silke, who had been unavailable 12 months earlier, shone with a high-energy performance.

We lost the Connacht final to Roscommon by four points. Two years before that, they had beaten us when we had everyone available, but this was still a bitter blow because we had dominated the first-half to lead by six points.

Only two points were recorded in the second-half however, following a terrible fall-off in intensity and workrate. It was at times like this you wish you were back in basketball and could call a timeout. It is extremely difficult to get messages onto a GAA pitch in that scenario.

You just need someone to take it by the scruff of the neck and to emphasise the need to refocus. You need leadership and too many of our leaders were unavailable for selection.

We had the players on the pitch to win the game. The first-half showed that.

But we didn't get our hands on enough dirty ball in the second-half. The malaise set in early with a couple of horrendous misplaced hand-passes and the lads couldn't drag themselves out of it.

Getting Mayo after a round of club championships was probably an ideal draw in the qualifiers in terms of a pick-me-up.

PETTILY, THEY REFUSED a coin toss to determine home advantage, forcing supporters from both counties down to Limerick. I suppose they got the win, so they didn't mind, but they weren't thinking of their followers, that's for sure.

They were coming through the qualifier route they were so familiar with and had used to such good effect to build momentum but there was nothing missing in our aggression level or will to win.

We got Peter back and he excelled at midfield, despite such a lengthy lay-off, scoring four spectacular points in the first-half. We were so hobbled in that area that we had to push Cillian, a natural half-back, in alongside him. We were able to bring on Damien, Tom, Kieran and Adrian as subs and they all added to our endeavours considerably.

Unfortunately, we had given ourselves too much to do by conceding two goals to James Carr in the first eight minutes and falling eight points behind after 23. One of those goals was a poor error as Bernie fumbled a high ball. The second was an exceptionally good goal.

The courage, tenacity and spirit exhibited thereafter was phenomenal and I could have nothing but praise for the players' efforts. Mayo are just too good a team to give that sort of a head start.

That said, we nearly did turn it around.

We got it back to a goal at the end, 2-13 to 1-13, despite finishing with 12 on the pitch, Ian having been sent off on a second yellow, and the two Dalys being shown black cards after we had emptied the bench.

The galling aspect of it all is that we managed to carve out the opportunities to record what would have gone down as one of our most famous victories had we been able to fashion it against our old rivals.

Liam had a penalty saved by David Clarke in the 53rd minute when a goal would have brought us to within three and rolling with loads of time left. We also failed to hit the mark with a couple of more frees, and struck the post from another.

In addition, the referee Joe McQuillan made a couple of bizarre decisions that were critical in a game of that nature and stature. We could not fault the players in application or bravery. They stuck to the plan and died with their boots on.

♦ ♦ ♦ ♦ ♦

THERE WAS ANOTHER year to go in my arrangement with the county board but the atmosphere surrounding us had become toxic.

It was not an enjoyable environment anymore. The commentary surrounding the team had become so vindictive and lacked any balance.

As the CEO of the brand, I was the figurehead.

It did take its toll on me, though I could put up with it if that were the only negative. I had to consider if the criticism would continue as long as I was there and the impact it was having on the players personally and on how we were being refereed. Would the group get some slack with a new man in?

It was a dilemma and one it took me a while to resolve. I got out my notebook. On one side I wrote a list of pros for staying.

On the other, the cons.

I had put a lot into bringing Galway from the depths of despair to being real contenders for honours, to be competing consistently to win. We were an established Division 1 side now and had a plethora of injured players to return. We would have our strongest ever panel. An All-Ireland was on the horizon.

Sadly, the list of cons dwarfed the reasons for staying. Five years was a long time and with the likes of John Daly, Peter Cooke, Antaine Ó Laoi and his brother Finian now coming through, you would probably need a three-year term.

Did I have the energy for that? Did my selectors?

I had approached a number of my former teammates to get involved to freshen it up, but they were unwilling or unable to get involved.

I was losing out financially in terms of compromising on my work. Having been involved at county level for more than 30 years, it was perhaps time to just slow down a bit for myself and spend more time with the family.

They had been exposed to a lot of horrible stuff, in person and online: the vitriol, the hate, the poison, and a lot of it from so-called Galway supporters. I say so-called because real supporters don't indulge in that stuff. They would never be interested in wounding individuals, in putting them through the emotional ringer. They back the team.

THERE HAD BEEN two occasions when I deemed the threat of assault to be real, where I thought I was going to be hit.

Anyone who thinks this is an acceptable situation for a man to be in, giving his heart and soul for his county, like he had always done, is unhinged.

I felt I couldn't win in my dealings with the media.

When I answered questions, I was portrayed as narky and defensive, so that's what the public believed. In management, if you're trying to explain, even when the facts speak in your favour, you are wrong. So I stopped explaining.

Unfortunately, some elements of the media kept peddling their inaccuracies, either through laziness or ignorance. That seeped into the public and would then seep into players. It seeped into referees too, to the stage where it might cost us two or three points a game. The team might benefit from the head being cut off.

As Eamonn Fitzmaurice had hoped with Kerry, with a new appointment, there was invariably a year's grace anyway. The players deserved that.

Then there was the refusal of the county board to consider constant recommendations in annual reports I provided them at the end of every season with regards to long-term planning in a range of areas including coaching, finance and medical. This was high-performance sport.

Unfortunately, the county board did not match that.

We were never going to be Dublin in terms of the money they could generate but we could be every bit as organised, professional and ambitious in terms of vision and approach. Galway weren't.

There was only one decision to make.

I said goodbye, every bit as proud of my time as manager as I was with what I had done as a player, espousing and applying the exact same principles. It was funny that those principles earned me praise as a player, and abuse as a manager.

Galway were in a far better place by every measurement you could care to think of, with a team with an average age of 24 and a half lining out against Mayo prepared to claim the ultimate success.

I could walk away with my head held high.

It was a massive honour for me to lead the Galway senior team for five years. I am thankful to the powers-that-be for affording me that opportunity. In my time, I also got loads of support from the county board and I will always remain thankful for that, and for being treated with courtesy and kindness.

CHAPTER 21

LEGACY

It's a terrible thing to see and have no vision.
— Helen Keller

The pieces that usually fit best are those you have carved yourself,
to your own design.
— Matt Busby

FOR THE FIRST three years, I had a great relationship with the Sligo County Board until a change of personnel made it more difficult. It was not quite the same in Galway, however, although there were some good people I got on well with.

I would love to have received a phone call every second week asking, 'What do you want?'

'What can we do for you?'

More often than not, it was me making the call and hearing, 'I'll do my best.'

County boards are running huge operations with vast sums of money generated and spent annually, and it is time for people of the requisite knowledge and experience to be appointed in a variety of sectors to ensure the best is being done for GAA people.

Most people are in jobs within boards for the best reasons.

The majority are volunteers, with a passion for the promotion of the games. No longer though, should years of loyalty and service determine a position.

You need the best qualified men and women, people that are comfortable in the elite performance environment, and are held accountable.

What I found terribly frustrating in Galway was that there was a reluctance to address many of the key areas in which we were found wanting; to secure a long-term legacy, no matter how often I or anyone else highlighted the urgency in addressing the situation.

WHEN PAT LAM was Connacht Rugby's head coach, we got him in to talk to the players. He would speak superbly about the power train and the people within an organisation that inhabited the different carriages.

Those in the front carriage had clarity of vision and knew exactly where they wanted to go. The next carriage after that was communication. Then there was body language. Then there were people's thoughts.

You also had a carriage of actions. These were important elements of the train but it was being driven by the vision.

The last carriage was the baggage. This carriage got bigger as the journey progressed unless the clarity of vision and people's roles within that remained defined and well communicated, not just verbally, but in terms of body language and listening.

A county board needs to be on that carriage, to help drive that train faster to its destination. I have long requested that a vision for the under-12s, the under-14s and under-16s, be written down on paper and acted upon.

What are the targets? What skills should be acquired and by when?

Be clear on the technically advanced nature of the coaching and appoint top class coaches, adhering to the vision rather than an *ad hoc* scenario dependent on who is in the job in any given year. There should be a Director of Football in every county that wishes to dine at the top table and be in a position to win top honours.

Galway do not have a defined playing and coaching philosophy and it is stunting progress. Around the time I retired, Galway won two All-Ireland under-21 championships in 2002 and '05. The youngsters of 1998 were now at the age I was when they came into the team and should have been combining with the best of these young players to maintain Galway's position at the top table but instead, the county hit the skids and could barely be competitive in Connacht until we came on board and resolved to address the glaring deficiencies.

When I began working with players from the 2011 and '13 All-Ireland under-21 successes, I could not believe how unprepared they were for senior football. Is it success to win an underage All-Ireland... but not have the tools to step up?

There were huge flaws in footwork, lunging into tackles, poor peripheral vision on the field, body positions receiving the ball, understanding of positions to take up on the field, and so much more. These bad habits were never addressed through the academies and the older players are, the harder it is to start from scratch.

Brian Silke often talks about the culture at Corofin that began with Frank Morris setting up an underage coaching structure that emphasised learning the basic skills above winning games.

Being able to kick with two feet was non-negotiable and yet, I wouldn't be sure that even half of county players can do that well. You would never see a basketball player that couldn't pass off either hand.

Many county players can't give a hand-pass off one of their hands, not to mention kicking the ball with their 'wrong' foot.

Imagine what you could do at senior level if by the time a player steps out of under-21, he is coached to be ready – that he could immediately move to the next level? Instead, it took us three years hard labour before we could consider ourselves All-Ireland contenders.

I PRODUCED AN end-of-season report for the first few years while manager of Galway and from the outset had a vision of establishing a structure whereby best practice would be the order of the day, with a professional in place to generate revenue, have the best medical support for all our teams, and a coaching structure adhered to by all participating coaches rather than dependent on who is appointed to various underage roles in a given year.

Time and again I stressed how important it was to appoint a Director of Football and the obvious benefits it would bring.

It was frustrating that the board executive seemed to take little or none of this on board. I was trying to be proactive to get them to at least be reactive but so often, inactivity was their default setting.

One thing we did achieve from our report was the construction of another full-size grass pitch at the Loughgeorge facility in Claregalway. This had been built by the Football Board in 1999, after our All-Ireland success the previous year, but it still only consisted of one full-size pitch, a small astro-turf pitch, dressing-rooms and an eating area, when I was appointed manager.

The development of a second full-size pitch, which we lobbied hard for, was very welcome but the problem was that Loughgeorge was now a so-called Centre of Excellence for all county teams... football, hurling, ladies football and camogie, and all underage squads. Is this really sufficient? Is this fit for purpose, for a county that wishes to consistently fight for All-Ireland titles?

I was delighted when they appointed a finance and operations manager in 2019. The job went to Mark Gottsche, the former Galway player who served London for many years but has now returned west. Hopefully, he gets the support and can have an impact.

I brought a commercial manager to the table because of the absence of financial vision outside the historical practices and centralised grants. Joe Gorham had more than 30 years of experience in the banking sector, so he had the know-how to go with his passion for the GAA from his years with Galway, Mayo and Sligo.

It took a while to get the board to acknowledge the necessity of such an appointment, but they accepted Joe as the perfect candidate. He was in the post for two years but got no support. He was so committed that he turned down an approach from Connacht Rugby after the first year. When they came back a year later offering him the job of domestic rugby manager, it was a wonderful opportunity he could not spurn while we were banging our heads against a brick wall with the county board. I hope Mark fares better.

Dr Enda Devitt has been the Galway senior team doctor since 2011 and is with Connacht Rugby since 2018. He is an expert in the area of concussion but most importantly, he is a man of vision and passion for Galway. With my encouragement after a number of discussions, he submitted a performance health management proposal to the county board in November 2015 revolving around providing the best care for players from the moment they enter the county system.

It was a very impressive document, proposing the establishment of a definitive pathway for all age grades that would improve detection, treatment and long-term welfare. He established a relationship with Cathal Moran, professor of orthopaedics and sports medicine at Santry Sports Clinic, with a view to providing rapid access to the experts in the field of sports medicine at SSC when players had long-term injuries. This would work in tandem with the local hospitals and medical specialists providing their valued expertise.

Enda offered to take the lead administration role with his proposed pathway of injury management, being the point of contact if a physio with an underage team needed access to imaging and further consultancy.

He proposed the creation of an intermediary role for a physio intern, collecting and reporting all injuries to better analyse how injuries were occurring and to change habits if required to prevent longer-term issues occurring.

It would not cost the board more money due to the GAA insurance scheme and neither would it impact on existing relationships with local hospitals and specialists, but work in tandem with them to ensure all grades within Galway football/GAA got rapid access to the high standards of care.

Nobody ever came back to either of us on the proposal, which is staggering, but you need professional people in place to think in elite terms and act out on that thinking. That was why Enda went ahead and formulated a relationship with Santry. Rapid access imaging is now available.

I would have made similar proposals in my reports. I always felt that with Galway such a hub for the production of medical products, the likes of Medtronic, Creganna and Boston Scientific, should be approached about establishing some sort of sponsorship arrangement akin to what exists for drinks or boot companies. Not a financial package, but the provision of medical supplies or testing equipment for teams.

In his submission, Enda proposed the immediate rollout of a screening programme for all underage players. The senior team had cardiac screening funded by the GPA and he urged that it should be best practice – and indeed this was a GAA recommendation - that all players be screened at 14 and again before they reached 25.

Enda wanted to establish a system for musculoskeletal screening of all underage squads also, with support provided with S and C and physiotherapy staff oversight.

I followed up on this when it wasn't in place, even though as senior manager it wasn't my specific job. But it was a glaring omission. Cardiac screening could be done by an Irish company at €65 a player. Yet it is not happening, despite GAA recommendations and what should be a desire for best practice and player welfare.

That our underage squads are denied this screening is a major concern.

We wanted to put something in place, not just for our senior team but for Galway GAA, to leave some sort of a far-reaching legacy, where the entire situation would be better. You get the foundations right and the rest will prosper. If we did that, Galway could be producing good, fit players that were happy, well looked after and were people of character.

That would mean we were competing more consistently for All-Irelands.

In one of my reports, I noted how former Manchester United manager Alex Ferguson described the Premier League/Champions League/FA Cup treble of 1999 as, 'years in the making', based on the development pathways established for players to grow, learn and develop both in relation to the game and the desired culture.

Other topics addressed in the report included facilities, communications, players' personal development off the field – all coming back to an overall environment conducive to elite sport and the care of those operating within it.

The silence was deafening on many of my questions and recommendations about long-term ambitions and goals. On countless occasions I revisited the desire for a defined vision and ethos. After I left, I was asked by a few officials about my reports – they had never seen them, which I found most disappointing to hear.

I feel Galway has huge potential but I don't think enough is being done to attract, retain and develop enough stars of the future. There are challenges down the line, for all of us, but running the games within a county is no longer a part-time affair and should not be viewed in that manner.

Until these limitations are addressed, Galway will always lag and any success achieved will be in spite of, and not because of the structures.

CHAPTER 22

SUCCESS

The manager that achieves the most this season won't necessarily be the All-Ireland winner.
– Conor Counihan, *Irish Examiner*, May 29, 2010

The deep coaching we got from Kevin and the lads improved me and all the players significantly with critical skills that we had never been coached on before.
– Shane Walsh, GrowCoach.ie, 2020

ALL MANAGERS KNOW the truth of what Conor Counihan said a few months before he became an All-Ireland-winning manager.

There can be the odd back-handed patronising compliment for a manager of a Division 4 team but that doesn't last long either, as someone like Turlough O'Brien found out at Carlow, where his methods and results after an historic league promotion and championship victory over Kildare were analysed as if he had the playing and financial resources of a top eight outfit.

Ultimately, it is the boss of the champions who is rated the best, the difference of a point or two apparently separating a buffoon from a genius.

Patently, this is idiotic.

IN MY ANNUAL reports to the Galway County Board I described success as a relative term due primarily to how it was measured and who was doing the measuring. Often the factors or indicators used to measure success are quite arbitrary and, as a result, differences in opinion can be wide-ranging.

I went to great lengths to assess the reality of the players' abilities, the team's potential and the organisation around them when setting goals. Therefore, I was unambiguous about the first two years at Galway being about the improvement of skills, creation of culture and establishment of building blocks, and building relationships. Year three was moving year, as we developed our attacking and defending systems and game plans, and earned promotion to Division 1, which was a key target.

It was only in the fourth season that we spoke about winning an All-Ireland. But we didn't shy away from that being a target once we had the tools to pursue it.

Realistic goals are imperative.

Supporters often have idealistic expectations and their judgements are invariably based on the scoreboard. County executives can be driven by conflicting priorities required to run the organisation versus performance outcomes.

Few understand the necessary technical, tactical, physical and mental aspects that must be developed in order for teams to compete at the highest level of any sport. The same can be said for many of those working in the media.

Because no Long Term Development Plan (LTDP) is in place with Galway – as far as I am aware of anyway – it left us as a senior management having to pick up a significant amount of slack, doing work that should already have been done to tackle substantial individual and collective deficits.

And obviously, that would have applied to every manager before me. Success should be viewed within that prism.

I always liked to deal in blocks, rather than something short term. A game, a month or even a season isn't a lot. With Sligo and Galway, I had five years and that is sufficient to paint an overall picture that is more accurate than one season that might not have hit the heights we would have hoped for.

In terms of pure results, Sligo won Division 4 and Division 3 National League finals in consecutive seasons to be promoted to Division 2 and appeared in two Connacht finals.

In 2009, a Diarmuid Murphy penalty save from David Kelly denied us a famous qualifier win in Tralee, and Kerry went on to win the All-Ireland. The following year, we defeated Mayo and Galway in the Connacht Championship, making it the first time in 63 years one of them was not in the decider.

It was the first time Galway had lost in Markievicz Park in 25 years, and it was Sligo's first ever replay win over Galway – and Joe Kernan's first ever replay defeat as a manager. We lost the decider by a point to Roscommon.

In 2012, we recorded the county's first ever championship win on Galway soil – Sligo had beaten Galway in the 1922 championship but had to replay the game after an appeal and lost. Two points was the margin in the provincial final, this time against Mayo, who would reach the All-Ireland final.

Charlie Harrison was awarded what was only Sligo's fourth ever All Star in 2010 and first since Eamonn O'Hara eight years earlier. This is an individual award, but you need to be on a winning team to get an All Star. It does also attest to a player's response to the coaching he is receiving.

My three selectors all progressed from their time working with me. Paul Taylor became Sligo senior manager, Dessie Sloyan the county under-20 manager and Paul Durcan took over as boss of the ladies' footballers.

ONLY JOHN O'MAHONY has had a more successful tenure as Galway manager since the legendary Mattie McDonagh oversaw the annexation of two provincial titles in 1982-83.

Having not won a Connacht title for eight years and only garnered two in 13 seasons, Galway were provincial kingpins twice during my time and appeared in five finals, including a replay. We were consistently competing to win silverware.

In 2018, we secured our first championship win at Croke Park since the 2001 All-Ireland. That was also our first championship win over Kerry since 1965. We reached our first All-Ireland semi-final in 17 years, through the far more difficult route of the inaugural Super 8s into the bargain. Kerry did not make it out of our group.

In the league, we returned to Division 1 in 2018 for the first time in eight seasons and reached the final, 12 months after claiming second-tier honours. Maintaining Division 1 status the following season with such an horrendous injury catalogue and minus the services of the Corofin players for the majority of the campaign, was one of the great successes of my spell.

We ended Mayo's stranglehold on Connacht. In my first season, they won their fifth title in-a-row and sixth in seven seasons. They beat Galway regularly in the course of that run, the previous three by margins of six, 17 and seven points. We got it down to four – which flattered them – in my first year and beat them the next three.

When Mayo defeated us in the 2019 qualifiers, they were ending a run of seven consecutive wins for Galway over our great rivals in all competitions.

Overall, Galway's winning percentage in my five years in league and championship rose from 33 percent to 67. The turnaround included a winning record against Mayo (five wins and two losses, compared to five out of five losses from the previous five years). The two Connacht final defeats to Roscommon hurt but overall, Galway's record against them in my time was four wins, two losses and a draw. We were back as 'Kings of Connacht', and that's a fact.

I was 2-0 against Sligo, having been with the Yeatsmen when we inflicted a couple of defeats on my native county.

The only counties with winning records over us were Tyrone (1-2), Cavan (1-2), Tipperary (0-1) and Dublin (0-3-1). That compares very favourably to the five seasons prior to that, when Mayo, Sligo, Meath, Westmeath, Laois, Cork, Donegal, Kerry, Antrim and Louth all had winning records over Galway. We were 2-1 up on Donegal, shared the spoils from four clashes with Kerry having been 0-3 in the previous period and held a 2-1 advantage over the ultra-competitive Monaghan.

In 2018, Ian Burke became Galway's first All Star since I was honoured 15 years before.

We spread the net wide as we committed to increasing the depth of the squad and looking beyond just the obvious graduates from the underage system. In all, we invited 144 players into the squad from 38 clubs: Annaghdown (7), Athenry (3), Aran Islands (3), An Spidéal (5), An Cheathrú Rua (3), Ballinasloe (5), Barna (4), Caherlistrane (5), Caltra (2), Carna (2), Claregalway (3), Clifden (1), Clonbur (2), Corofin (16), Cortoon Shamrocks (3), Glenamaddy (1), Dunmore (2), Headford (4), Kilconly (2), Killannin (6), Killererin (3), Kilkerrin Clonberne (4), Menlough (1), Micheál Breathnach (4), Milltown 3), Monivea (3), Mountbellew (9), Moycullen (6), Leitir Móir (3), Oranmore (2), Oughterard (2), Renvyle (1), Salthill Knocknacarra (8), St James' (4), St Michael's (4), Tuam Stars (4), Williamston (2), Sarsfields (1). More than 25 players made their championship debuts.

In our first couple of seasons, 52 players turned down the invitation to come in. By year five, not one player turned down the call because playing for Galway was a far more attractive proposition.

Attract, retain, develop is the foundation of underage academies but applies at senior level too and pride was restored in the football jersey.

WATCHING BARNA WIN their first club championship matches since 2013 was a thrill as Seán Conlon had taken over, bringing the Galway principles with him. Brian Silke had a strong CV already with St Sylvester's and Corofin and is back with the Corofin under-20s now.

My former minor and under-21 colleague, Tommy Finnerty was our free-taking coach – Shane Walsh used to call him Tommy Perfection – and one of our kitmen with Galway. He was manager of the Oughterard team that won the All-Ireland intermediate club title in January 2020. He spoke in interviews about how he learned from watching us and by picking my brain when I collected him on the way to training for five years.

I smiled when he referenced, 'Run 5, Save 50', in his interview after the final, in reference to playing smart and nipping potential trouble in the bud by making the first run. I was ecstatic when they won the All-Ireland and was there along with all of Killannin cheering them on.

We had to support from afar due to Covid, but were just as delighted when our other neighbours, Moycullen were crowned senior champions for the first time, in October 2020. I work in the town and have a lot of friends there, so I was delighted for them, as I was for the likes of Gareth Bradshaw, David Wynne, Peter Cooke and Seán Kelly, men of good character who had represented themselves so well in their time with me at Galway.

Interestingly, Gareth and David were responsible for the tactical analysis and both also offered the group a technical coaching element during post-game video reviews. Gareth told me that they utilised the methods learned under our tutelage in going through footage and it was brilliant that they played a role in such an historic achievement.

It would be lovely to think that some of the players with real leadership qualities and ambitions to be coaches, might be able to draw on some of the things they picked up in their time with us. Gareth himself has just announced his retirement – he was a fantastic servant to Galway. I certainly could see him becoming a very good manager if it is a path he considers taking. Gary O'Donnell is another with that obvious potential.

Another kitman with us, Conor Carey is managing Headford.

Paddy Tally, who was coach in 2018, is now manager of Down.

I take tremendous satisfaction in my former colleagues moving on and doing well, just as occurred in Sligo, and in some of the players becoming involved in the analytical and coaching side of it. It speaks to a culture of learning and the inclusive nature of our environment. Delving a little deeper, I look at the improvements we brought about in players as a result of our coaching, giving them the tools to perform at a consistently higher level.

Tom Flynn was one of the most improved players in the squad on the back of physical coaching, as we worked on his body position, helping him to decide when to jump for the ball and when it was better to hold his ground. He became very consistent at this and grew into a leader on the field because of it. It was similar with Peter Cooke.

Paul Conroy had to learn about the percentages when it came to his kicking ratio. He is a particularly good kick passer, but the situation wasn't always right, or the pass wasn't always on. When he pulled off the 'Hollywood' kick, it looked extraordinary, but his percentages were low. Every time he turned the ball over, he was setting up an opposition attack and putting us under pressure on the counter.

It was about risk-versus-reward and Paul learned that.

We worked with Alan Costello on his fitness but also his decision-making. He tended to carry the ball into contact, and had a predilection for the cross-field kick pass. Once he improved on his decision-making, his skills made him a huge player for Sligo. David Kelly and Seán Armstrong were similar types of players who tended to win possession running out towards the sideline. After he was Man of the Match against Sligo in my first year, I encouraged our defenders to let Seán win the ball in those areas and to just shadow him in that direction, where he could have no impact.

We worked on screens and V-cuts with the two lads and they really took it on board, the result being that their scoring and assist rate improved considerably as they were winning the ball in the scoring zone. David became one of the most dangerous forwards in the country for a few years.

Shane McManus and Eugene Mullen were the type of players you loved in your squad. Gary O'Donnell, Declan Kyne, Gareth Bradshaw and Johnny Heaney were similar. They lived for working hard and getting better. They looked after the nuts and bolts. We could rely on them. They didn't have the high profile but were voracious in their appetite for coaching as long as we continued to challenge them.

The gunslinger always gets the praise from the pundits over these guys because of the one extraordinary feat, or the injury-time winner, but it is all the right things the O'Donnells and Mullens of this world do that kept us in the game for it to be won. They are the real difference-makers.

Shane Walsh was always a supremely talented footballer, but he needed to improve his consistency and workrate, to contribute more to the team and thus be a better player. It is peculiar that people view such traits negatively, but Shane was such an influence in 2018 that he was one of the first players on my team-sheet and should have been one of the first players on the list when the 2018 All Stars were selected.

Ian Burke becoming much more of a *triple threat* really stood out in the big games for Corofin as they won their third All-Ireland. He put a lot into that, to placing doubt in a defender's mind and not being one-dimensional.

He is lightning quick but having that sort of advantage can turn forwards into one-trick ponies, where other parts of the game remain undeveloped. Smart defenders or defensive systems will ask different questions once they learn about players, so unpredictability is imperative to ensure you get to utilise your greatest strengths more often. You need to have other strings to your bow.

MY GOAL WHEN becoming manager of both Sligo and Galway was to be competing consistently to win and to leave them in a better place than I found them, so that the next manager would have a higher base from which to operate than I had inherited. I am deeply satisfied that we succeeded in this regard, thanks to the efforts of the players and my backroom staffs.

In Sligo, apart from my selectors, the two Pauls and Dessie already referred to, I had Brian Henry, Pádraic Langton, Brendan Murphy (analysis), Tommy Craddock (fitness coach), Declan Clinton (doctor), John Coyle, Therese Devaney (physiotherapy), Mick Toland (S and C), Gerry Hussey (sports psychology), Peter Greene (logistics), John Murphy (chairman/liaison officer), Ray Kilcoyne,

Reggie McNulty (kitmen) and Niall Gallogly (catering).

In Galway I had Paddy Tally, Kevin Stretch (coaches), Aofáine Walshe, Dave Mullally, Niamh Francis (physiotherapy), Gerry Hussey, Tony Óg Regan, Cathal Sheridan (sports psychology), Enda Devitt (doctor), Joe Gorham (commercial manager/logistics), Paul Harty (logistics), Tommy Finnerty (free-taking coach), Damien Sheridan (goalkeeping coach), Peter Lee, Conor Carey, Cathal Walsh, Dara Walsh (kitmen), Cathal Walsh, Noel O'Reilly, Dennis Carr (video analysis), Simon Kavanagh, Stephen O'Meara, Paddy Griffin (video work), Sophie Conroy (nutritionist), Owen McArdle (catering), Greg Muller (S and C/Culture), Keith Carr, Ronan Heffernan, Kevin D'Arcy (S and C), Seán Silke (backroom support), Pádraig Ó Neachtain (PRO) and John Divilly (trainer of Dublin-based players), while Brian and Seán were my right-hand men. You do nothing on your own.

That message was never more important than when I think back on the roles played by our spiritual advisors (and great Galway supporters) Fr Pat Donnellan and Fr Dermot Moloney, who celebrated Mass with us all over the country. The nuggets of advice in their sermons guided us through sport and life.

It doesn't matter who you are, or who you think you are. It will always and ever be about the team. It has to be in order to succeed.

The Invisible Game

CHAPTER 23

THE NO-STATS ALL STAR

Champions are champions not because they do anything extraordinary but because they do the ordinary things better than anyone else.
– Chuck Noll

The type of game we play at the moment, we are inclined to do a lot of work that nobody sees. But, as the fella says, you are better off playing well for the team than playing well for yourself. I'm not out there for a massive game against Kildare. If I can stop two or three of their men coming forward, then it doesn't matter if I'm noticed or not. If I can come off the pitch with a medal in my pocket at the end, I'll be happy.
– Kevin Walsh, *Sunday Independent*, September 27, 1998

ASK A RANDOM person on the street to name a basketballer and they might struggle to go too far beyond Michael Jordan.

Give those with a passion for the sport an opportunity to list the best players and it would take some time for Shane Battier to be listed. The chances are he would never be.

The natural inclination is to be drawn to showreel operators and that is understandable. But each sport has a set of skills and disciplines that are considerable in number, and you need far more than a highlights package to win games.

The problem with commentary surrounding football is that a higher value is placed on 'Hollywood' skills but you should try to coach every skill and learn every skill, for each has equal value and its acquisition improves a player.

If ever a sportsperson encapsulated my philosophy as a coach and my belief of what a team player should be, it was Shane Battier.

'HE'S AT BEST, a marginal NBA athlete,' is how Rockets general manager Daryl Morey described him. That was all his first team, the Memphis Grizzlies could see and he was never rated there, despite being on the NBA Rookie Team of the Year in 2002.

They finally succeeded in offloading him four years later.

He carved out his reputation as an effective defensive guard in five years with the Rockets, where they looked beyond the shortfalls and saw how Battier used his intelligence to influence games. It took a long time for others to notice but once everyone in the dressing-room understood, it suited Battier just fine not to be constantly fielding calls for interviews.

Even when he neutralised the threat of the greats, such as the late Kobe Bryant, it was attributed to the LA Lakers legend playing poorly. Battier was so underestimated that nobody believed he could have been responsible.

Those who lined up with him did and in time, the fans in the bleachers did.

When the victims piled up – Bryant, LeBron James, Chris Paul *et al* – the intersection in the Venn diagram of all occurrences contained one name... Shane Battier.

The wider basketball community began to put two and two together. There was a brilliant article in *The New York Times* in 2009 that captured his process well, written after his second selection on the NBA All-Defensive Team. The headline said it all...

The No-Stats All Star.

Battier was not a scoring threat and didn't provide too many direct assists. He didn't claim many rebounds or steals. There were few blocks.

He wasn't much of a dribbler and was slow.

But the trends told a story. In his rookie season, the Grizzlies had a win-loss record of 23-59. By his third, that was 50-32, a record for the franchise, and they made the play-offs, a feat repeated the next two years.

Their first season after his departure was a league-worst 22-60.

The Rockets team Battier moved to had just come off a 34-48 campaign. In his first term at the Toyota Center, Battier helped transform the record to 52-30.

In 2011, Miami Heat moved for the then 33-year-old. They had acquired James' services 12 months earlier but the expected championship had not resulted. The recruitment department recognised Battier as the missing link, the final piece of the jigsaw, and the Heat got their rings in his first two seasons.

James was named MVP but he hadn't been able to do it without a team.

James was an all-singing, all-dancing player, a franchise maker, a genius. But he needed the man doing one thousand unseen things that make an impact to get the team over the line.

In the aforementioned feature, the author Michael Lewis described it thus:

Battier's game is a weird combination of obvious weakness and nearly invisible strengths. When he is on court, his teammates get better, often a lot better, and his opponents get worse – often a lot worse...

Here we have a basketball mystery: a player is widely regarded inside the NBA as, at best, a replaceable cog in a machine driven by superstars. And yet every team he has ever played on has acquired some magical ability to win.

Morey abhorred the notion that the leading scorer was the primary contributor to his team's performance. He wasn't interested in the individual with the most rebounds but what the team's overall chances were of winning them.

Though rarely picking up rebounds himself, the team's success rate in this department, like many others, increased when Battier was on the court. He tipped the airborne ball to a teammate rather than risk not being able to get a clean catch.

Or he stood in front of the opposition's best rebounder.

Positional sense, spatial awareness, footwork and strong hips were all in play here, and he wasn't even touching the ball.

Battier was brilliant at knocking a ball out of an opponent's hands but there was no stat for that. It wasn't a block as the dispossession occurred prior to an attempted shot. Yet it turned the ball over for his team on countless occasions and frustrated the absolute daylights out of a star unaccustomed to losing control so easily and feeling embarrassed that a 'no-name' was the cause of it.

Little wonder Morey took to calling Battier 'Lego'.

When he was out there, all the pieces fit.

What he did to Bryant was reduce his efficiency, make him shoot from places he was just a little less comfortable in. To do that, he had to corral him into those areas, against his will. There is no measurement that credits Battier as Bryant misfires.

It just looks as if Bryant is off his game.

Battier's high school coach Chris Keener recalled trying to add some flair to his protégé's game. It didn't' work.

'I came to the conclusion he didn't have the ego for it', noted Keener.

◆ ◆ ◆ ◆ ◆

THE CLUES IN my coaching philosophy were there for all to see in my playing days. Everything I held dear when on the pitch myself, I emphasised as a coach.

Anyone watching closely, who understood the game of football, would not have been surprised that I valued workrate, selflessness, a team ethic and those thousand unseen things above all else.

If you are only on the ball for a minute in around 80, you have to be able to influence a game in the 79 that you are not. It is common sense.

The Barcelona team regarded by many as the best club soccer team there has been had a very high workrate, starting their defensive work by pressing from the front. Lionel Messi was not absolved of those responsibilities. Liverpool do the same now.

That is all planned. It is very technical and very tactical.

It is more than just putting pressure on the opposition. It is about getting them to kick the ball in a particular direction, away from their strengths, towards your own.

I probably got more credit than Shane Battier did, though like him, the rewards came late in my career. I didn't care for the headlines or who got them. It was about doing what was best for the team, so that the team could prosper.

Now I didn't think it through as deeply in my playing days as I would subsequently. Much of it came naturally. Mary Nihill sowed some seeds and playing basketball was undoubtedly an influence in countless ways.

Fast, secure and sympathetic hands were clearly a by-product of basketball, while I developed considerable spatial awareness, which is imperative in attack and defence. I could influence an opponent's next play by taking two steps to the left or right.

Vision was a strength too, again, with and without the ball. The 360-degree mentality of basketball undoubtedly accentuated that trait.

Sometimes, if I wasn't soaring high to catch skyscrapers – and due to my knees I had to pick my moments in that regard – people might say I had a bad game. Or that I wasn't influential. That's because people remember the spectacular or dramatic more easily.

Yet they might also be saying your direct opponent played poorly. Maybe there was a reason for that.

You didn't have to win the ball yourself but could ensure that your team did.

You could make sure the opposition danger man wasn't a threat with a subtle move into his run as he was launching himself for a kickout, or just holding your ground with strong hips, taking control of the area you expected the ball to land in.

You used your intellect, you positioned yourself correctly, you influenced what was happening on the pitch... without ever touching the ball at times.

Basically, I thought my way around the pitch. My goal was to be in the right place all the time, for every play of the ball. And obviously, for all bar a minute of the game, I wasn't on the ball. But I knew I could make something happen, make a difference, often just by taking up the correct spot. By playing the invisible game.

NOW I WAS far less under-appreciated than Battier, and three All Stars came my way, but what I could never comprehend was that the type of skills I possessed are still not really coached in the GAA.

If a person had them, fantastic, but if it wasn't innate, it wasn't taught.

That is ridiculous.

If it can be taught to basketball players, and I would start basic work on footwork with six and seven year-olds, it can be done in football. And you create better players, with a more rounded ability to impact a game.

In his last campaign, Shane Battier was named NBA Teammate Of The Year. If you were to aspire to individual accolades, I can think of none better.

CHAPTER 24

SPACE JAM

I spend the entire 90 minutes looking for space on the pitch.
– Xavi Hernandez, *Daily Mail*, **February 10, 2011**

He cuts an incongruous figure on the field sometimes, his hulking frame slightly hunched, his long stride now a little clipped. But it is all that is ungainly about him. On countless days his ability in the air and his perception of the space and players around him have helped stabilise Galway. He is their metronome.
– Michael Foley, *The Sunday Times*, **May 19, 2002**

MY JOB AS a coach is to improve performance. The best way to do that is to trouble the comfortable and comfort the troubled.

There is always a danger when working to improve specific deficiencies in certain individuals, that you neglect others. It's the classic challenge for a teacher in a large classroom with disparate levels of ability.

You want to spend enough time with those towards the bottom of the ladder to bring them up to speed, but risk focussing so much on them that the more gifted stagnate because the lessons are too easy. Stagnation leads to boredom and hinders progression.

It can often lead to regression.

You must not neglect anyone. Everyone can and should improve.

Sometimes the more elite performers within a squad become so accustomed to getting their own way that they are a liability to overall team performance. They must be constantly challenged to prevent them lapsing into complacency. Once they take things for granted, they lose an edge.

The real champions know this and will test a coach by demanding to be discomfited in a learning environment. Those happy with the way things have always been will never find another level.

So you help those that are struggling to get a greater grasp of the game and take those that are finding it easy out of their comfort zones, so they can do the same. That leads to improvement in individuals and a better team.

ACCORDING TO AN International Olympic Committee document on the topic, 'A good coach has many traits. These include being positive, enthusiastic, supportive, trusting, focused, goal-oriented, knowledgeable, observant, respectful, patient and a clear communicator'.

The most important skill is to be a good listener.

After that, the coach must question, build relationships, have empathy, be open-minded and non-judgemental. You will not be able to reach players and help them eradicate their limiting beliefs without these abilities.

A coach cannot be dogmatic. There cannot be only one way.

That approach is not at odds with persisting with your philosophy. When you mine the detail, there are myriads of options within a broad belief system surrounding how you feel football should be played or what is required to get the best out of your players.

Take, for example, a Key Result Indicator (KRI) that illustrates the imperative of not carrying the ball into traffic. That is an overriding message to your team because you do not want to lose possession and get blitzed on the counter-attack.

But if you have one or two players who are tremendously powerful and capable of breaking that first line of defence, you will make exceptions for them. One size cannot fit all in any philosophy and game plan. It will surprise some people to read that line, thinking me a prescriptive coach, but that perception just comes from lazy, ill-informed analysis.

Defensive structure is by its very nature more rigidly configured but even within that, players are making decisions all the time. Once you are in possession, it is invariably more fluid, with many options, depending on how the opposition have set up.

So it is for instructions to players. There can be an overall team directive that doesn't apply to everyone. In a healthy environment centred on the unit, that will be accepted without question for the betterment of the team. You need a strong culture within the panel as part of that.

If you have lost seven of the last nine balls trying to take on an opponent, I am telling you to stop doing it in matches, all the while working on improving it. But if you have the ability to carry, I need you going down the throat of the opposition.

A really good sign of a coach is what he does with a smaller group. Operating with 15 All Stars makes management a lot easier. I have coached in all four divisions of the National League and it has provided me with a rounded experience.

THE COACHING ATMOSPHERE should be polymathic. It should be about there being a learning outcome from every session, in a wide and varied fashion, not just focusing on what is perceived as the normal or accepted styles of play.

The more you can take on board as a player, the more options you have and if all the players accept that, and ignore the external questioning that is unfortunately joined at the hip with innovation, you have a myriad of game plans and ways of taking on an opponent, thus leaving you better equipped to deal with whatever challenge you encounter.

To do the job properly, a coach must be willing to evolve. You need to coach ALL the skills, not just the sexy ones.

In 10 years of reviewing myriads of games – and that means thousands of players – I would be in the wrong game if I didn't pick up a few things.

In that time, I noticed a lot of the same frailties showing up. I would obviously tailor game plans to expose those weaknesses and look to upskill my own players so that they had what it takes to carry those plans out, and profit from the flaws.

So I can say with confidence that a lot of the skills that I consider vital to making space and reducing it are not being coached. Key elements of what should be part and parcel of a player's skillset are being left to the handful that have it naturally, either because they were born with the awareness or had a background in other sports that made it integral.

That's absolute madness.

SPATIAL AWARENESS IS at the epicentre of my coaching philosophy and Brian Silke and Sean Conlon are like-minded. That was why, after we finished with Galway – having seen the deficiency in coaching around this area from scouting opposition and looking at our own players coming through underage systems at club and county level – we came around to the idea of establishing a resource centre for inquisitive coaches and players, to provide answers to a lot of the questions being asked.

GrowCoach (www.growcoach.ie) gestated a little quicker than we had planned but the first coronavirus lockdown left us with more time on our hands than we had envisioned. We were conscious, too, that the same applied to inquisitive coaches readying themselves for a return to the fray.

When I decided to step down as Galway manager, it was the first time I wasn't involved in football as a player or coach since I was 12. That was strange but it was good for me.

I could step back a bit and reflect. This was something I wanted to do, to make what I have learned available and at least give coaches and players access to it, to allow them dip in and out, judge for themselves what might be useful to them.

We had done some workshops at various clubs around the country that were received well and have taken that to the next level now by producing webinars, illustrating a variety of skills that can help in offensive and defensive settings, ensuring that players can impact a game when they don't have the ball – which is, on average, 79 minutes of an 80-minute county match … 69 from 70 in a club game.

A lot of readers will recall the late Páidí Ó Sé's use of a well-known dictat during a rousing speech to his Westmeath players in the documentary *Marooned*, made of their remarkable Leinster Championship-winning season of 2004

'A grain of rice will tip the scale.'

In fiction, the equivalent is the 'Inches' speech delivered by Al Pacino's character, Tony D'Amato in the American football movie *Any Given Sunday*.

THAT'S WHERE SHANE Battier's thousand unseen things during a game come in. That's what I am enthused about in coaching. Not relying on stirring passions, or what players have within them, but instructing them so that they know what to do to grab that definitive inch, to carry out the unseen definitive action that tips the scale.

79:1 is not a defensive outlook.

It is a comprehensive one encompassing the entire vista of a game of football. All bar one player is without the ball when the team is attacking.

Are the other 14 not to contribute in any way?

Of course not. They can make a serious impact. So in attack, *79:1* is about having five channels versus three channels. It's off the shoulder runs causing chaos in a zone defence but understanding where the runs need to come from to break down the zone defence.

It's using screens and V-cuts, occupying a position with the predetermined intention of vacating it and bringing your marker away with you. It's width and depth. It's creating space, manipulating it and exploiting it.

Defensively, it's about taking that space away.

The mistake here is to always think of this as chasing around the place like a blue-arsed fly, putting in high-intensity tackles.

That looks great but is it always effective?

There are times when it is the right move but on a lot of occasions, it isn't. There are six kinds of pressures that include purposely not laying a glove on an opponent. You need to learn them and learn when to use them, but before that, you need to have good footwork, something that is rarely taught.

This is not to say that you don't do sessions on the more recognised skills – though you shouldn't have to be working on a player's weaker foot or hand at senior level. That work is an integral part of coaching from underage.

But there is a clear dearth of instruction surrounding impacting the game when you don't have the ball and that is pure folly when you only have it in your hands for a minute, on a very good day.

IT IS IMPORTANT to emphasise that this is not exclusive to county football.

All coaching should start at underage level. Forget about winning games. Teach the children. To do that, you have to teach the coaches.

Club underage coaches are often parents because they are the ones at the pitch. They must be trained and that training should be within an overall structure, so that there is uniformity to the messaging players get through the various age groups.

Then, when winning games is the priority, everyone has clarity. Your under-8s should be starting that process.

I see real value in this and encourage clubs and coaches to open their minds, have a look and take what they value from it. Let's have a look at just some of the key principles of making space and taking it away.

CHAPTER 25

FOOT PERFECT

You can't tell people anything, you've got to show 'em.
– Bruce Springsteen, Born To Run, 2016

Footwork is the foundation stone for every great athlete.
– Roger Federer

IF YOU HAND your son a chainsaw and ask him to cut back some trees at the end of the drive, there is no guarantee he will remove the right branches from the right trees, regardless of how detailed your instructions.

But if you go down to the location and point out which trees you want clipped back and the specific branches that need to be sawn off, the chances of the operation being completed as desired increase exponentially.

Show me, don't tell me.

That is integral to good coaching. You must be able to describe what you want and illustrate it. You must have reasons for why you are working on a particular discipline or strategy, be able to demonstrate them and back them up. If you are not able to show the players, you don't understand what it is you are trying to achieve.

Good footwork is the basis of any athletic achievement.

That sounds obvious and yet, it is evident that it isn't being taught. A recent research project from DCU surveying 2,000 schoolchildren on the island of Ireland revealed that one in two could not kick a ball properly. That was staggering but even more worrying was that one in four could not run properly.

The study found that the development of children's fundamental movement skills – running, jumping, catching and kicking – plateaued at the age of 10. This is a shocking failure, when existing research tells us that mastery of these skills is achievable by eight.

'If children don't have a solid foundation of basic movement skills, how can we expect them to do more complex skills as part of organised sport?' asked Dr Stephen Behan, head of the research team when the results were launched in January 2020.

'These findings highlight core issues that teachers, parents and coaches need to address,' added Behan's colleague, Dr Johann Issartel.

This stark trend is familiar to any underage coach but while they recognise it, not many are moved to address it, primarily because they are not equipped to do so, but also because they don't understand it as the best use of their limited time with players, when it is, in fact, the base of anything else they would ever hope to work on.

IF YOU ARE a manager of a senior county team and are presented with serious deficiencies in movement and footwork, it is a considerable job of work to bring about improvement. As proven from my 10 years with Sligo and Galway, it is not impossible and most assuredly worth doing but you would love to have had those hours to delve into finer detail.

You can teach an old dog new tricks but it's much more helpful to have it done at underage.

There are no shortcuts when teaching a new skill and creating new habits. Studies have shown that it takes 28 to 30 days to break a habit. That translates to between nine and 10 weeks if your team trains three times a week. It can be challenging to repeat the same move over and over again.

This is very much the case at county level, when players have more external noise to deal with. Having someone in their ear, metaphorically or literally, suggesting that the coach or manager has them doing mad stuff can sway players.

I understand not wanting to be made uncomfortable, of wanting to stick with what worked for me. I was only 12 but my first six months with Mary Nihill at St Paul's were not enjoyable. She was quite hard on me and wanted me to do new things. She did not relent.

She knew what she was teaching us in terms of footwork and team ethic would produce results on the basketball court and she was proven correct, irrefutably. I found it hard to change but the thing is to stick with it. If the coaches are good at portraying the message, it will come right but they must give you comfort too while breaking the old habit and creating a new one.

The habit curve starts with optimism at the prospect of doing something new but transitions quickly to hesitation and resistance as people struggle to adapt and the boredom of repetition kicks in along with disillusionment at the failure to grasp it. It is only as you move beyond day 20 – which is into a seventh week for most GAA teams – that you hit what is known as escape velocity, where the improvements begin to manifest themselves.

At the end of the process, a new habit is formed. The challenge for coaches and players is to get beyond that hump and that is where comfort, or empathy, is required.

The learning matrix of skill acquisition, which is central to the habit curve, begins with unconscious incompetence. You cannot do something and you aren't even aware of the fact. Then as you work on it in training, you know that this is something you cannot do. You are practising it, messing it up, practising some more.

That is conscious incompetence.

The third stage is conscious competence. This is the step-by-step stage, where you can do what you have been working on when thinking about it but it has not yet become instinctive. When that final stage is reached, where you fall into the learned skill or habit as a situation demands, without thinking about it, that is unconscious competence.

Some might say a player was doing that naturally now but there has been nothing natural about it. It has been taught and learned, though a painstaking process.

I ALWAYS INTRODUCED footwork drills to the under-8s at Corrib Basketball Club. They're sponges at that age. You cannot spend too long at it but you do it every day, for at least 10 minutes.

Start them off in a square, three lines of three, getting them to ape your movements – left, right, forwards, backwards or diagonally. The heads must be up, not looking down.

You advance that, throwing a ball to each person's left or right so that they have to move their feet to catch it. Then you throw it so they have to move diagonally, backwards or forwards. They start learning the steps naturally, not crossing their feet and losing their balance.

In time, you progress to shuttle sprints that demand the use of stutter steps to turn on a line.

You don't need to fill their heads with needless detail. Not alone are you not telling them *what* they are learning, you aren't even telling them that they *are* learning. You are certainly not explaining the technicalities of the stutter steps – those short little baby steps you put in before making that sharp change of direction.

What is happening though, is that they are learning movement and footwork, creating tools in their armoury that will facilitate more detailed coaching down the line. That is why when you are doing those shuttles, even with older players, the focus must always be on turning at the specific line rather than trying to win a race and cut corners. Remember what the objective of your session is, even if the kids don't have to know.

Footwork is at the heart of everything in football, going hand-in-hand with learning where you need to be at a given time in a game. It is an imperative in any athletic pursuit, and about far more than putting one foot in front of the other. There are so many different aspects to it – retrieval, cutting off angles, shadowing opponents, taking the quickest and shortest route from A to B.

ROGER FEDERER IS considered to have the best footwork on the professional tennis circuit and it is a major reason why he is still one of the best around at 39. Being economic with your movement saves energy.

Knowing where I was and needed to be on the pitch and having the variety of steps were vital for me as I continued to thrive in my mid-thirties.

Fiorentina midfielder, Gaetano Castrovilli studied classical dance for a year and has credited the footwork and co-ordination learned there for helping him become a breakout star in Serie A in the 2019-2020 campaign. Prior to lockdown, no player with more than 1,200 minutes on the field had managed more dribbles, not even wingers. No-one in his position had been fouled more.

Football is no different. Take, for example, the six defensive pressures you need to be able to apply when looking to take space away from an opponent. Footwork plays a large role in executing them. This is deeper coaching than ball skills.

These must be coached but at senior level, if players can kick a point off their left on the run, it is because they have learned to do it over the years. They will not lose that skill. We need to give them more in the areas where there are percentage gains. You have to understand that and identify those areas, so that in a tight match where teams match up pretty well in most departments, you might have the edge.

Often in close games, it is who can exert the most pressure that prevails.

The six pressures are:

1. Nil
2. Still
3. Coaxing
4. Closing
5. Chasing
6. Physical

Nil pressure won't win the ball back directly but it is ensuring that you are at least in a defensive position. It can impact the space you cover, not allowing a ball to be played into that area. So you're putting pressure on the kicker who can't deliver it there, and the runner, who can't run into that space. In the next chapter, I look at an example of a misguided attempt at physical pressure having a role in Michael Murphy's All-Ireland final goal in 2012. *Nil* pressure might well have prevented that score.

Still or standing pressure is providing a blockade without making any commitment. That pressure isn't necessarily in the vicinity of the player in possession. It might be closer to the intended target of his delivery. It might be closer to the player in possession, on your hunkers, not going in for the tackle, holding him up while your teammates get back. You are waving your hands to take space but not engaging. It's all about stifling the pass but not getting burned for pace.

Coaxing pressure is what I had to do with the cattle back home in the farming days. Your opponent has possession and may feel like the one in command, but you are shepherding him down a blind alley, or into an area where he can make no impact, or into a trap that has been set for him. At best, that forces a mistake and a turnover. At worst, it gives teammates an opportunity to take up good space-taking positions. You would always look to coax people down channels one or five – the outside channels. The inside channels of two, three and four are where you want to keep them out of.

Closing pressure is another mental pressure that can force a mistake. You aren't committing to a contact, but you're in the vicinity. You're in the opponent's head, preventing him moving the ball forward. You are closing the space between you and your opponent as quickly as you can, cutting out his passing or shooting options in the shortest time possible.

While doing this, you have to be mindful of what your next pressure is going to be depending on the situation. If you want *physical* pressure you continue to make contact with the player. If you want a *still* or a *nil* pressure, be ready to use your stutter step to stop at the right area with good balance.

If you want to put on a *coaxing* pressure then stop at a 45 degree angle on a high shoulder, preventing your opponent from going in one direction and more than likely taking him out of the middle three lanes of the pitch and towards lane one or five.

Chasing pressure isn't ideal in that you are running after someone who has a head start but it is still significant. You are still asking a question of the player in possession, hoping to force a mistake or be in a position to capitalise if they make one. It might not yield anything. Or it might prove invaluable. Sometimes you are just chasing a runner that doesn't have a ball. The chase might cause the supplier to think twice about giving the pass.

To be able to carry any of these pressures out, you need proper body positioning, proper foot positioning. We spend a lot of time in gyms horsing up weights, which is vital, but leg position and body position can be worth two stone if you get that right.

To force a player down a channel, you must have the ability to step and your body position has to be spot on.

Steps are imperative in taking space and carrying out all these pressures but they aren't exclusively about being defensive. You need very good movement to create space too, be it with sudden changes of acceleration or direction, V-cuts or utilising screens.

Too often, forwards run inside to out and take the easy option of winning ball moving away from goal, where they present absolutely no threat. They are retaining the ball, which is better than nothing, but they aren't offering an examination of the opposition if they do that all the time. Their possession stats might be through the roof but their markers are actually having a very comfortable day's work, happy to be shepherding them out towards the sideline.

THERE IS A defensive arc and the statistics are very clear about what is a low percentage area to shoot from and where the greatest yields are.

Clearly the latter comes closer to goal and a V-cut is a utilisation of a change of pace and direction to buy a yard so that you can get the ball in the scoring zone and have time to shoot. Ian Burke was very good at it. Seán Armstrong improved markedly in this area.

Forwards are always looking to deceive their markers and changes of pace and direction are primary tools in this regard. V-cuts are a combination of both, where you start by running outwards, then planting your outside foot to power off for the change of direction back inwards towards the middle, turning your lead foot in the way you want to move.

You need that movement and footwork for setting up screens too.

These are highly effective in a suffocating defence, with tight man-to-man marking and supplementary defenders ensuring space is at a premium. They are particularly suited for executing from set plays like sideline balls but the best coached teams can implement them from general play.

The player creating the screen must exhibit extreme patience. It is better to be late than early. You still have a chance of helping your partner if you are late. If you are early, you have made no impact at all. The aim is for your teammate to get free and score. So you cannot make your move until he has the ball.

Then, as he makes an arcing move, you step into the shadowing defender's line, blocking him. It is very surreptitious, and done well, looks accidental. The angle of your stance is important. If it is wrong, you don't block the defender. Get it right and your buddy is away. Then you give a little push and roll to provide support.

The screen and little push buys 10 yards, six or seven metres of space that represent acres in the modern game, created through footwork and body position.

Taking an opponent's running line is something I used to do under kickouts, particularly as I reduced my jumping due to the strain on my knees and groins. It was a go-to tactic if I was matched with someone who lived for the spectacular catch, like Roscommon's Seamie O'Neill. Like the screen, it was about patience and timing.

If I stepped across at the right time as he made his dramatic run before lift-off, his momentum might knock me over and the ref would often award a free. If that didn't happen, I had halted his run, he wasn't airborne and more often than not, the ball was landing into my chest.

Back in Chapter 10, when I was discussing what was required in battle against many of my midfield peers, I referred to the importance of claiming my ground, that square metre where I wanted the ball to land if my opponent was the type willing to compete on a standing jump. For that you needed strong hips, to be able to *take* that ground where the ball was landing, without pulling and dragging, without fouling.

I read Mark Keane's comments in *The Southern Star* after the Mitchelstown man, who is contracted to AFL side Collingwood, scored the dramatic injury-time winning goal for Cork in the championship against Kerry last November.

'It was more that I guarded the space so Tommy Walsh wouldn't be able to get into it. I judged that the ball would land there so I was guarding that space. From learning over in Australia, I just wanted to get in behind Tommy Walsh and use my body to work for me, and catch it for a mark.'

This is a skill that smart players will pick up but everyone can have it, if they are coached it, as they are in Australia.

Clearly, blocking is a defensive tool as well, as defenders take space from forwards, again with a good body position. This is particularly useful with a high ball dropping into the area. The principle here is to... *Find, Feel, Fetch.*

You *find* the forward, you *feel* them with good goal-side body contact, without committing a free – and the end result should be an easy catch for your goalie, if not for yourself.

It is just like Shane Battier stepping across the main opposition rebounder so that his teammate can gather possession unchallenged. If you don't do that and are ball watching, the forward is challenging in the air for the ball with your goalie. Wherever you have seen a forward flicking a ball to the net off a high delivery, a defender hasn't done his job.

As mentioned already, the stutter step facilitates that quick directional change, to lose a marker or react to an evolving situation, at either end of the field.

The drop step is invaluable for forwards looking to leverage defenders who have got really tight when they gather possession. You have to have your two feet planted before dropping your left foot back behind the marker's left foot and pivoting in one movement or doing likewise on the right.

This is a really effective way to beat a tight marker. Just remember that if you are moving left, you have the ball in your right hand. If you are moving right, you hold it in your left. This is to ensure maximum protection.

It is almost impossible for a defender to get at the ball without fouling you.

It is really important that you break the hip line when you pivot. If your foot gets behind your marker's foot, you have done that, causing him to become unbalanced. There is no way back for a defender if you execute this move properly.

PEOPLE USED TO talk about how strong I was when a referee decided to throw up a ball. It was assumed, not entirely incorrectly, that my basketball experience and size helped in this regard.

It didn't hurt but I really thought about my actions in that scenario.

It was all about getting my hip an inch in front of whoever was standing in with me. What's more, I would set up initially standing just behind, to give my rival the impression that he had grasped the initiative. Then, at just the right time, I would step across, get that half-inch as the ball was propelled upwards by the ref.

Once I did that, I had established dominance of the battleground; I had taken the space by breaking the hip line. Yes, I was a big, strong man but it wasn't that I was competing with Lilliputians.

It was the technical aspect that was most relevant to the end result.

The slide step is what you use to cut off angles when an opposition playmaker is looking to send a long kick into an inside forward. Or if you are closer to an opponent, you are making sure he doesn't get by you with good movement, side to side.

This is *coaxing* pressure, looking to turn an opponent into a particular channel, away from the danger zone. It is absolutely imperative that your feet are at a wide base and you are slightly squatting, to ensure good balance. The feet should never come into contact.

A half-step makes a difference to the centre of gravity, to the space, to the lines of running. Are your feet planted or are you standing at a 45-degree angle to shepherd a player in a direction.

Where do you want the player in possession to go? Send them that way.

Body shape is important and should not just be left to chance. In basketball, this is always coached. For some reason, it is not in GAA.

It's not always bad luck or execution when someone just misses a point – at least sometimes, it's the pressure they were under that makes the difference. These are the small margins that make a difference in close games.

Take 5 for 50, which is about running five metres to save yourself having to run 50. This is about recognising danger, taking up a position that requires you getting goal side of an opponent five metres away, getting a hand in the chest or blocking the run. You take your opponent's line of movement away from him.

Failure to make this decision and take up this position leads you to chasing that player down the field. Making that five-metre move may well prevent a score.

On occasion, you will see a player just miss making an interception and it might appear that he or she was unlucky. But I would wonder if it is a skill deficiency. Certainly, I would investigate whether it happens a lot. That would suggest a weakness in reading and decision-making. Was diving in the right move?

It wasn't if you have left your team exposed.

I am not against players committing to such an all-or-nothing move or putting a hard tackle on an opponent. That is far from the case. It is just like having a shot for a point, taking a player on or trying a kick pass. You have to pick your time and you have to have the right people doing it.

In county football, if you commit to the tackle, get it wrong and the man is in behind you, you're dead.

In the club game, tackles are considered a good measure of workrate but if you have 15 breaches and concede 3-6, that's a problem. It is the defensive equivalent of the forward winning a load of ball in non-threatening areas; only worse, because if you are isolated, you are leaving your team open.

You need support if you are going to dive in. If you are isolated, *standing* or *coaxing* pressure is far wiser, until reinforcements arrive.

SO, IT IS one thing teaching the steps, the pressures, how to take and make space. But you have to teach which pressure to use in each given situation that will put your opponent under the most pressure. What space to take and where to take it.

Ultimately, that sort of decision-making is learned over a long period of time from repetition in training, viewing video clips and encountering the variety of situations in games. You can't make them choose the right call but you keep ramming the message home.

As Will Durant wrote in *The Story of Philosophy*, though the line is often misattributed to Aristotle, 'We are what we repeatedly do. Excellence, then, is not an act but a habit'.

You have to be forensic about teaching these skills because they are very technical. My motto is… 'Think Big, Coach Small', so I use small spaces first to illustrate these skills to players. I did it with Sligo and Galway. It was easier as the years went on.

When I started with Sligo, I didn't have the ease of access to video clips. Now, players can constantly delve into a vision archive. With Growcoach, when we do our webinars or go to clubs, we'll always work in an indoor hall. You do it in small spaces before progressing it to the pitch.

Because it's technical, it must be slow. It isn't about fitness or intensity. It's purely about the acquisition of a skill. Being comprehensive in breaking it down and having patience with it, will pay off in the long term.

A screen is not a basic skill but footwork is, just like catching and kicking with either hand. When you have the basic skills, you have the foundations to advance. Those foundations should be laid at a young age. All the foundations.

CLEARLY, I AM only touching on a handful of the thousands of ways a player can impact proceedings for all his time on the pitch, almost all of which is without a ball. But hopefully the reader is getting some sense of what is possible, and of the recklessness of leaving so many skills uncoached, from the youngest ages.

Coaches are always learning.

It is my favourite part of it, picking up something new.

We have to review ourselves all the time. Sometimes you'll hear a coach say, 'I told him to do this'… 'I told him to do that'.

You have to show them. And you have to show them again.

And again. And again.

There is something like a 9:1 differential in the effectiveness of showing and telling.

I am aware of the irony of pointing that out in a chapter that is all tell, and no show. That's a book for you.

So let's try to do something about that.

CHAPTER 26

PROOF POSITIVE

A man with new ideas is a madman, until his ideas triumph.
– Marcelo Bielsa

There has been a lot of coaching under Kevin, whether in basketball gyms in the winter and then transferring that from the halls onto the pitch, (which) has been another task in its own right. It is great because you are always learning something new and improving on the small things – footwork, for instance. Having your feet in the right position if a man is running at you. Instead of diving in, you bring him down a line or whatever. Knowing how to tackle. It takes a long time. He is here four years and we are still learning. You do make mistakes along the way. But you also see the improvements as you go and that makes it easier.
– Johnny Heaney, The Irish Times, May 12, 2018

WHILE I HAVE had to deal in 'tell' rather than 'show' in a book, I think it's worthwhile addressing some incidents in the last few years and breaking them down with the use of footwork in the making and taking of space in mind.

So, here are a few case studies. Some of them are high profile and the clips are readily accessible online.

Others are from our own recordings or might be less available to the general public but are on the GrowCoach website (www.growcoach.ie) so that you can have vision to go with the detail.

DUBLIN V MAYO, 2017 ALL-IRELAND FINAL
Illustration of the triple threat

You have three choices as a forward when getting a ball such as the one Cillian O'Connor receives from about 25 metres out from the Dublin goal with 53.14 on the clock of this humdinger of a duel. You can keep running out looking for help, without ever causing chaos to your defender. If the defender is up your arse, you can stop suddenly so that he runs into you and fouls you, or you can leverage him.

If the defender is standing a little bit off you, as Johnny Cooper is here, the right thing to do is turn and be a *triple threat*.

Far too often, forwards are happy to take the first option and run out to lanes one and five, but O'Connor makes a substantive impact by turning the second he collects the ball from Aidan O'Shea's neat kick pass – a decision that results in a fantastic goal for Lee Keegan that restores Mayo's lead after Dublin had stormed out of the traps in the second half.

Once he can look Cooper straight in the eye and is facing the posts, O'Connor is a *triple threat*. He can take Cooper on if the Dublin defender moves in to make contact. If Cooper backs off, he can go for a score.

Alternatively, he can pass to someone making a run to lanes two, three or four. Unless he turns, he cannot do any of those things. If he has his back to goal, he is relying completely on a runner coming off his shoulder, which is difficult in packed defences, and Andy Moran doesn't even bother with his run.

There isn't an awful lot available to O'Connor but because there is a *triple threat*, he can get the ball to the man that is open. Moran does really well to offer the option and take O'Connor's kick pass. He turns inside and spots Keegan's well-timed run.

Keegan takes the hand-pass without breaking stride and finishes brilliantly, seven seconds after O'Connor gathers possession.

Moran and Keegan clearly play huge roles here but none of it happens if O'Connor takes the easy option. It happens because he turns and makes himself a *triple threat*.

DONEGAL V MAYO, 2012 ALL-IRELAND FINAL
Illustration of poor defensive pressure choice and footwork/good offensive space creation

Michael Murphy's goal arrives in the third minute and though there are thousands of significant events subsequently, it is the score that gives Donegal the foothold they thrive on and the difference between winning and losing an All-Ireland final.

There are just over two minutes elapsed when Eamon McGee intercepts Alan Dillon's attempt to find Cillian O'Connor. The ball is in the net at the opposite end of the field 23 seconds, four passes and one thunderbolt later.

McGee evades O'Connor's attempted tackle, hand passes to Neil Gallagher who quickly offloads to Rory Kavanagh. At 2.10, Aidan O'Shea has a decision to make. He has a ball carrier and a runner – Ryan Bradley – coming towards him. Karl Lacey is hugging the outside channel and Dillon has him.

A couple of things happen that cause a huge problem for Mayo.

Dillon points to Lacey, leaves him and is sucked in to make a challenge on Kavanagh. Even worse, O'Shea moves forward to engage as well and suddenly, there are two Mayo men closing in on Kavanagh without much likelihood of forcing a turnover.

The Donegal midfielder has a simple offload to Lacey, who has been left alone by Dillon and a misguided attempt at physical pressure has put the two Mayo players out of the game.

Whatever about Dillon committing, and not tracking back afterwards, O'Shea should be reversing off Gallagher. In other words, he should impose *nil* pressure, keeping the twin threats of the ball carrier and runner in his eyeline, defending both by being goal side. By reversing, you are blocking the passing lane and the running lane, holding up the play until help arrives.

When Murphy is bulleting his shot beyond David Clarke, there are three Mayo jerseys coming into the picture. They only needed another two seconds to be back. That is the significance of O'Shea's choice.

When I coach defending that kind of 2 vs 1 situation, I call that engagement of the carrier *cheating* on your team. To my mind, it is one of two things. Either O'Shea made a poor decision, hadn't been coached on it, doesn't understand it, or took the lazy option. This is not an uncommon trait in forwards, especially at club level, where replacements are not in such supply.

You would see it a lot in the county game too, however. Coaching fixes the poor choice. Cheating the team by copping out is a cultural problem. Both have to be addressed.

Bradley continues his selfless run, drawing defensive cover and also catching the attention of Barry Moran. It is a vital contribution. But when Bradley has a marker, Moran's entire focus should be on coaxing Lacey down lane one by the sideline. If he takes a *drop step* to his right, with the correct angle and body position of a high right shoulder on Lacey's left shoulder, that is where Lacey goes and his threat is reduced considerably.

Sent down lane one, Lacey has the use of one hand or one foot and has at best half-vision of what's ahead of him. His only other option is to turn back. But because Moran has two feet planted and if anything is leaning a little to the left to where Bradley has run, he is inviting Lacey into the danger zone of lanes two and three – where he has the use of both hands, both feet and full vision.

The kick pass is exquisite. Murphy is in pole position to win this battle, which he does. He then leverages Keane perfectly, transferring the ball to his outside hand to protect it, getting across the defender with his left to give himself that vital yard to unleash his shot to the roof of the net from the 13.

There are a lot of unseen acts and decisions both defensively and offensively that lead to just this one score alone. Eliminate just a few of the defensive mistakes and you have a better chance of coming out the right side of close games.

ROSCOMMON V GALWAY, 2017 CONNACHT FINAL
Illustration of poor angle defending

The footage we have here is from behind the Galway goal and it shows two defensive errors that lead to a goal for Cian Connolly. In it, you can see Eoghan Kerin picking up Diarmuid Murtagh, around the semi-circle, with Cathal Sweeney attending to Connolly behind them. Roscommon have a kickout and we have pushed right up, with only this quartet inhabiting our half of the pitch – so much for Galway always flooding the defence!

We had terms for this sort of situation and how you would mark an opponent in them. L1KA and M1KA, pronounced 'Lika' and 'Mika' though the second character is the number '1' rather than an 'I'. They refer to 'less than one kick away' and 'more than one kick away'. These are key criteria for *angle* defending.

When the ball is transferred to a position where it is less than one kick away, you have to mark the opponents. That doesn't mean automatically, that you stand behind them, but you must have contact, have your hand on their chest. If the ball goes high over your head in that situation around the 20 metre line, it's an easy one for the goalie or it runs out wide.

If it's a L1KA and the carrier is within 30 metres of your goal, you have no choice but to move behind or beside.

If the kicker is more than a kick away, there is absolutely no need to be touch tight. It is the old way of defending that is coached but it makes it far easier to feed your opponent as it only has to go to the space in front of him. As a defender, you are reacting and giving up that few metres of space if you are starting at level pegging or behind.

It is one of the most glaring deficiencies in traditionally coached GAA defences.

When the opposition have possession more than a kick away, you take away that space in front with *nil* or *standing* pressure. That means you can play in front, with a good body angle. The phrase that encapsulates *angle* defending is 'See man, See ball'.

A sweeper is the most commonly used tool to cut off a long kick pass but if *angle* defending is carried out properly, you can use that extra player to put the squeeze on higher up the field.

So the defender stands in front of the opponent, on the half-turn at about a 160-degree angle, facilitating vision of kicker and potential receiver, marking the space in front of the attacker, taking away the easy delivery. The *angle* will vary depending on where the ball is but it should never be 180 degrees, as you cannot see kicker and receiver, which is a recipe for trouble.

If you find yourself at 180 degrees, you have to move to resolve that.

When coaching *angle* defending, if there is a doubt about it, just get your longest kicker to prove it. That will give the defender confidence. They will not execute the skill if they don't believe in it.

Eoghan starts off with good standing pressure. He is in the right area in front of Murtagh but loses focus, loses his *angle* and as a result has to turn his head to look at the kicker. In that moment he loses sight of Murtagh, who smells blood and makes his break. That makes the delivery of the pass easy and

Eoghan is just reacting.

Cathal also starts in a reasonable position where he can see both man and ball, but also loses the *angle* and has to switch attention from one to the other. Crucially, as Murtagh collects possession, Cathal is looking at him and Connolly takes the opportunity to make a dart to his left.

Murtagh delivers a peach of a cross-field pass, ensuring that Cathal cannot recover. Like Eoghan, it is reactive defending at that point and reactive defending rarely puts pressure on an opponent. Connolly finishes brilliantly to the corner of the net, giving Ruairi Lavelle no chance.

Had Cathal had a good *angle*, he would have had a very good chance of intercepting Murtagh's delivery. At worst, he would have been in prime position to assert *coaxing* pressure on Connolly and shepherd him towards the outside lane, where the threat would be reduced significantly, and time bought for the cavalry to arrive in the form of covering defence.

The decision to adopt *standing* pressure for angled defending was the right one because there was no way that ball could go in behind Eoghan and Cathal, it was just that the execution was not what it should have been, and we paid a heavy price.

FERMANAGH V GALWAY, 2017 NATIONAL LEAGUE DIVISION 2
Illustration of good angle defending

Like the previous piece of vision, you can have a look at this clip on the GrowCoach site because we had our wide-angled camera behind the goal for that purpose. In it, Luke Burke gives an exhibition of angle defending.

Luke, who was very unlucky to suffer a cruciate knee ligament injury subsequently, displays outstanding strength of mind and focus, in addition to his complete understanding of the skill he is exhibiting so perfectly.

The first thing to point out is that Luke is isolated just outside the 20 metre line with Eddie Courtney, as once again, we are pushing up looking to force an error. So there is unmanned territory in front of the pair up to around the 45 metre line. This is a situation most forwards relish and Fermanagh would have been delighted with that.

But what unfolds is a minute and 11 seconds of Fermanagh being increasingly frustrated. They have the possession all this time but Luke has his *angles* covered perfectly. Courtney tries his best evasive techniques, with sudden changes of direction and pace, but Luke has him and the ball in his eyeline the whole time.

What is noticeable is how often Luke changes his body position as the situation demands and deliberately backs away from Courtney, to ensure the *angle* is maintained and he can see man and ball without having to swivel his head. His footwork is immaculate.

With good *angle* defending, you are giving the kicker and the receiver a problem. You are also just enticing the kicker to have a go at an ambitious kick pass, because they can see their teammates. The intended receiver is having to think, when he is programmed to make a run and have the ball delivered in front of him. If the ball is carried, you have plenty time to get back.

Exasperation prompts an attempt at finding Courtney with a diagonal kick pass. Some might construe it as an error but it is very much a forced one. Without laying a glove on Courtney, Luke has defended expertly. There may be space there but he takes it away. He intercepts the ball and immediately gets us going on the counter with a good kick pass of his own.

Fermanagh had scored 1-16 just eight days previously in Newry. We held them to 10 points – only three in the second-half – and we didn't do it by getting numbers back. We did it by defending smartly.

FERMANAGH V GALWAY, 2017 NATIONAL LEAGUE DIVISION 2
Illustration of the screen

This is from the same game as the last clip. It is no accident that this contest has such prominence. I always felt this was the most important tie in terms of us earning promotion, which we did as champions.

We had been held to a draw at Pearse Stadium by Cork in our opening tie and travelled to Enniskillen to face the cock-a-hoop Ernesiders after their nine-point drubbing of Down knowing if we lost, we could not afford to drop another point with five rounds still to go. That would have been a lot to ask for at that stage of our development.

It wasn't looking good at the end of a first-half in which we were far from inspiring, having scored just three points and trailed by four. So it was really pleasing that we got a goal within 12 seconds of Fergal Kelly getting proceedings back under way. To do it with a *screen* was a testament to the coaching we had been doing, first in indoor halls and then out on the pitch.

There are about 10 skills in a *screen* and this wasn't the perfect one but that is the beauty of the skill. It will create space for you if you even manage to implement it adequately. The fact of the matter is that it is very difficult to get it perfectly when you're introducing it to players over the age of 20, and in the time that we had together.

I would introduce the *screen* to the 12-14 age group in basketball. Many of the Killannin under-16 footballers who reached the semi-final of the A championship in 2020, including my own son Dara, would utilise screens regularly all over the pitch. Because it is second nature to them, its implementation is seamless, like clockwork.

This one, by Seán Armstrong for Damien Comer, isn't because Seán has to use his hands a little but it remains effective because it buys Damien valuable space. That it is Seán providing the *screen* is indicative of his buy-in to our coaching, the result of which was an increase in his all-round contribution to the team, with and without the ball.

One really important aspect of the *screen* is that the teammates are really close together. The other key ingredient is that the beneficiary of the *screen* has to have oodles of patience and must not run too early. He shouldn't be trying to get away from his marker. The closer you are to your marker, the easier it is to set up the screen.

In this instance, it is Damien who is staying quiet on the back post, waiting for Seán to make his run. It is Seán, the player providing the screen, who determines where Damien runs – it will always be in the direction the backside of the player providing the *screen* is turning. When Damien makes his run, he has to rub off Seán's shoulder, leaving no space for his marker.

You can see Seán watching the play, waiting to see if we have possession. Normally in GAA, the closest man runs towards the ball but we liked to come away from there, providing more space for someone else to utilise.

Séan moves towards Damien, who is doing his best to look disinterested. Damien makes his run just before Seán gets there and so Seán has to raise his hands a bit. The perfect *screen* would be where the guy creating the *screen* gets to within nine inches to his colleague's opponent before he takes off and blocks the run, 'accidentally', creating up to 10 yards of space.

But an imperfect *screen* is sufficient. Damien is away and before Fermanagh know it, they have conceded a goal and our tails are up.

It is important to emphasise that the *screen* can be utilised in any part of the field in any scenario, not just among the forwards. It is particularly useful from dead ball situations – free kicks, sidelines, kickouts – where the opposition might be pressing up on you and you need to create a few yards of space.

One other thing. In time, when *screens* are common, the defending players will read the situation and may just switch players, but if they do that, the player that came to set the *screen* is now, technically, in front of his new marker with his back to the ball; he can roll off into another angle and he'll get the pass.

KERRY V GALWAY, 2016 ALL-IRELAND MINOR FINAL
Illustration of poor blocking out

There's a funny story around this game. I asked for a ticket low down and around the 20 metre line specifically so that I could look closely at movement in this area. I had people asking me, 'What kind of county board do you have, to give ya that sort of a ticket?'

'Oh they're wicked divils alright', I'd reply with a grin, but I got the ticket I had looked for. Every day's a school day when you're a coach.

It just so happened that Kerry got two goals at this end of the field that gave them a 2-2 to 0-2 interval advantage. They won by eight points in the end but those goals could have been avoided and helped ease the pressure that had been building as Kerry, seeking a third consecutive title, had been frustrated by a very good game plan almost very well executed. That pressure would only have built if the teams had gone in level at half-time.

People seem to be slow to coach *blocking out* but it is not dirty and it is not cynical. It is good play. Of course it is not just about defending, being useful for kickouts or general breaking ball situations. It was a key element of my own game.

When a high ball is coming into the edge of your own square, you have to know what's around you, make a survey of the dangers and how you can impact the game, even though the ball might not be yours to fetch. If the ball is landing on the goalie, should you be going for it?

Will you get in the way? The goalie is facing the ball so make it a 2 v 1 rather than a 1 v 1.

Of course if it's not dropping on the 'keeper, the threat is different. These are the calculations you make as the ball is dropping but if it's dropping, it's a L1KA situation – less than one kick away – so you will already have contact with your opponent.

The important elements are to 'Find, Feel and Fetch'.

The *fetch* isn't necessarily you catching the ball though it might be. It might be the goalie. Sometimes, it's the ball bouncing harmlessly wide. But you have to find your opponent, then *feel* him – make physical contact, block his run by stepping across him. Take his ground away and make it yours.

This is Battier blocking the opposition's key rebounder again, ensuring a teammate picks up the possession. You don't' get the stat but your coach will see the impact of it and will ensure you get that credit within the group.

There is 17.58 on the clock as Seán O'Shea kicks for a point. Galway have done so much right, trailing by just a point to no score and should really be in front, having wasted a number of good opportunities.

Fionnán Harvey is caught ball-watching however and has either forgotten Diarmuid O'Connor is behind him or is just leaving him to his goalkeeper, Cormac Haslam to deal with. The running-in forward always has an advantage over the stationary goalie and O'Connor flicks it to the net.

If Fionnán finds his man, *feels* him, puts an arm on his chest and blocks him out, Haslam has an easy catch. A situation that ends ruinously with the concession of a goal is neutralised without any drama.

Three minutes later and some more poor defending leads to Kerry's second goal, this time for David Shaw. A diagonal ball is sent in by Dara Moynihan towards David Clifford, who has two Galway defenders for company. Because it's a L1KA situation, less than one kick away, Clifford's immediate marker, Seán Mulkerrin, has to have a hand on his chest first, then step across him and take his ground to either gather possession himself or give his supporting teammate an easy catch. But he has lost him and as the ball is in the air, you can see he's looking for him, but is too far away. As a result he can exert no pressure and Clifford has an easy catch.

Eoin McFadden is on the wrong side and is watching the ball as well. He should be coming around to get goalside and block Clifford out. If he is not doing that, he should be watching Shaw. By not coming around, he makes no impact. If he had come around, he would have been in the perfect position to attend to both threats and worst-case scenario, it was a point for Kerry instead of an easy goal.

In all these cases, we are talking about good footballers, county players of quality and in the case of the minors, such mistakes are inevitable and will be eradicated by good coaching and with intelligent players, by recognising the error and learning from it. Most of these skills fall, once again, into the *79:1*.

My commentary is not personal, it is just an example of the detailed breakdown I favour of incidents that occur within a game, and how the use of a variety of pressures and footwork would impact a game, often without ever touching a ball.

It is nothing anyone in my dressing-room would not be accustomed to. This is what I would have done with my own players.

This is how they improve.

PART FIVE

The End Game

CHAPTER 27

RULES, REFEREES AND THE SUNDAY GAME

Don't criticise what you don't understand, son.
– Elvis Presley

THE GAA RULE book needs a radical overhaul. There are too many grey areas, leaving too much to referees' interpretations. That isn't fair on them and leads to coaching staff preparing for games depending on who is officiating.

That isn't always a good idea however, because there is no guarantee of a consistency of application of the rules from the same official, not to mind different ones.

You are allowed two steps in basketball. If you take two and a half steps, it's travelling. In the GAA, you are allowed four or the equivalent time, but you could take 10 or 12 quite easily and not give away a free. It's crazy.

We see it mostly in goalscoring situations, when a forward goes around a goalkeeper or is leveraging around a defender using small steps. There is a skill in that, but a small step is a step the same as a big one. If you want to give leeway on them, change the limit to six and be done with it.

Allow coaches to teach for the rules that exist.

By not implementing the rule, you are punishing the team that has used a different set of skills to force an overcarry or some other technical foul, to win back possession for their team. That is unfair.

And yes, I know Pádraic Joyce took about 12 steps by the time he rounded Christy Byrne for our goal in the 1998 All-Ireland final against Kildare.

A lot of goals are scored in big matches by taking extra steps, not just a Galwayman in one All-Ireland final, but also Eoin Murchan for Dublin in the 2019 All-Ireland final, for example.

That's how the game was and is being refereed. It is as if you are allowed another handful of steps to get away from a situation, having used what is actually the allowed amount to evade the initial challenge. But that's not the rule.

IT IS NO secret that the tackle is a huge problem but despite that, it has remained unaddressed during the course of the constant tweaking and tampering that has gone on in football in recent years. It is one of the most integral elements of our game and nobody could tell you for sure what is legal.

It is another reason to place such store on non-physical pressures. You cannot give away a free blocking off a passing lane or turning a player backwards just with a good body position. That is as much a tackle as a physical one.

But plainly, you cannot go through a game without imposing physical pressure and a defined tackle would help coaches, players and referees.

There is not enough of a rule there that it can be policed so I have some sympathy with officials in terms of the tackle.

That said, too many games are decided or at least heavily influenced by poor refereeing. This is accepted, even as millions are being spent on preparing senior county teams in the GAA. Yet the amateur line is trotted out to make the referee a protected species. Where's the protection for the manager and the player, and the county board?

It is really hard when a player makes brilliant tackles, as you coached him, and he is pissed off because he has been blown for fouls. I left no doubt in my messaging in that instance. I recall a few instances with Declan Kyne and another with Damien Comer, where I told them not to change a thing and to make the same challenge again the next time.

I did that the other way too, where possession had been won by fouling an opponent. You aren't coaching if you are not pointing out bad practice and fixing it, even if bad officiating let them away with it on occasion.

WE ANALYSED REFEREES the same as we would the opposition.

Some were consistent in how they applied different rules and situations from game to game. That was fine. We could coach to what the rules would be that weekend.

There are far too many county referees that officiate the same situation differently, however. And when they are refereeing it differently depending on the team, that is the real killer.

It seemed to me that punditry had too much impact on the GAA at central level and that applied to referees too. Going way back to Pat Spillane and the 'puke football' comment, which illustrated a snobbery and lack of comprehension of football, an image was painted of three players surrounding another in possession as looking awful. As if ferocious workrate were a negative thing.

There is no consistency here by the way because in hurling, Kilkenny's appetite for hounding down the opposition in numbers was revered. Yet hurling was never deemed as negatively as football anyway, due to the mindsets of the analysts.

The fact you can score from 80 metres out in hurling is an advantage in scoreboard optics obviously.

Still in football, I see a player surrounded by three others who have the two hands visibly out and are using the hips to block the player in possession with good footwork and strong core. It is right out of the basketball playbook. There is no pulling, just strong bodywork. It's an overcarry all day.

There is no grey area. But time and again, the referee awards a free to the player in possession.

I began to feel that there was a bias against Galway. Maybe it wasn't that, maybe it was the perception that had been created by some sections of the media and especially pundits on *The Sunday Game*, that had permeated their sub-conscious – just as it did about numbers ganging up on a player in a legal tackle.

Perception becomes reality and that perception was a major contributor to me standing down as manager, for the overall benefit of the Galway players.

When we did our analysis, we unearthed occasions when we got the rub of the green. I'm not saying we never got a lucky decision. We did.

The first couple of years, I would have had no complaints and felt the officiating was balanced. The last two were dreadful but it started in 2017, when David Gough gave four points to Roscommon for so-called off-the-ball incidents involving our defenders. They are they kind of scores that suck the life out of a team, but they came at a time when we were fighting back and just kept stymying any attempt to build up momentum.

There was nothing in the incidents in question and the calls were all the more perplexing when compared with equivalent exchanges at the other end of the pitch.

There were plenty other games where it was horrendous. One incident was just ridiculous in the 2019 Qualifier against Mayo. After David Clarke had saved Liam Silke's penalty, we still kicked the next three points to bring the gap down to three.

Mayo ended a 17-minute scoreless run to increase that to four but we were still in contention when Mayo won a free around 50m out with three minutes of regulation time remaining. Instinctively, I understood the significance of this moment. A point here, and we would be unlikely to complete the comeback. So they would try and steal a few metres.

Aidan O'Shea brought it to the 45 but Joe McQuillan ushered him back. That was my cue to get onto the linesman, Conor Lane to make sure it didn't happen again when Cillian O'Connor took the ball from O'Shea.

Taking it from the hands, he stole four or five metres. I roared. And Lane said, 'Kevin, will you stop it. Twelve inches either way won't make a difference.' It was obvious from the cut of the grass that he took nearly five metres. O'Connor's kick just cleared the crossbar, Mayo were infused with energy and ours was drained away. They scored a point immediately after, as our energy levels dropped off and we lost two players to black cards due to the change in circumstances.

If Lane had reacted positively to my objection, the ball would have dropped short. Maybe Mayo would have scored a goal, but we should have been battling for that ball as it landed out of the sky, not feeling our hearts sink.

I would use the foam that has been introduced in soccer, especially for scorable frees, when a couple of feet may make all the difference. Mark where the free kick is to be taken from and how far back the opposition must stand from it. '45s' are taken on the '45' metres line, and there is a line there. It works. Frees should be treated in a similar manner to afford fairness to all teams.

Incidentally, Joe McQuillan also stumped me that day. It felt like he was nailing us for everything. The free he awarded against Damien when he absolutely buried Colm Boyle with a superb shoulder was confounding. Damien would have been through, with Boyle out of the game, but McQuillan blew for a free.

Instead of a definite point and a possible goal, we had our momentum halted again as we chipped away at Mayo, beginning to put doubt in their minds.

There were a few similar examples, where the boys pushed up and put massive pressure on Mayo but were not rewarded, and in a tight game, two-point swings of frees denied at one end and awarded at another are energy-sappers.

WE REALLY NEED referees to be assessed. I know someone is apparently doing it on match day and there may be meetings in Croke Park, but I never see any sense of accountability.

Habitually poor officials get more games, to offend once more against another team that has poured heart, soul and wallet into being competitive. Then we have the policy of Omerta, where referees are not allowed explain their decisions.

If it's the right decision, we should be educated on that. If it's the wrong one, they should be adult enough to take responsibility.

Referees need to be trained and coached in a more transparent manner. I would pay them too for the bigger games. The GAA cannot become professional because of the geographical loyalties at its heart and foundation, but nobody would argue with the officials getting paid a proper fee if the standards improved.

Perhaps then, the best people would get the biggest jobs.

If there was a proper wage for a smaller group of referees and a fella was removed from the panel for making repeated errors, maybe then not so many of them would leave a field smiling after a slew of egregious calls. Because that's what's happening now and there's too much at stake for that to be the case.

Now look, I do understand that being a referee is a horrible job. And mistakes are a part of their game just as they are for players and managers. Clearing up the rules would help the officials. So would taking timekeeping and other responsibilities away from them. I just think the standards should be higher and have not risen in the same way the playing and coaching has.

They should be held to those standards in the same way the rest of us are.

It amazes me that the GAA hasn't looked at increasing the number of on-field referees for county games. I know basketball is a quicker game, but the surface area is far smaller, as is the number of members you can draw from, and yet for all games over under-14 you have two referees and in the Super League you have three.

Football is gone so fast and physical now, it would be great to have the head referee following the play, and one each watching what's going on off the ball in either half.

You do actually have a lot of officials around the pitch already when you consider umpires and linesmen. If they were all better trained, were selected through a central high-performance system and given more defined powers, that would help the referee considerably.

◆◆◆◆◆

LEN SHACKLETON WAS an English soccer player from the 1940s and 50s before becoming a sports journalist. He had one chapter in his autobiography entitled, *The Average Director's Knowledge of Football*, that consisted of one blank page.

Having listened to a lot of guff in 10 years as a county manager and 17 as a player, I would nearly have been tempted to do them same, replacing the word 'director' with 'TV pundit'.

What is astounding is that the likes of Colm O'Rourke and Pat Spillane are still doing analysis on games now, when they were already showing their lack of knowledge in my days as a player.

In 1998, Seán Ó Domhnaill and I were being criticised as too slow, too immobile. Every team was going to take us to school. We took on the cream of the midfield crop and got the upper hand.

They were at it again after I suffered a bad injury in the 2000 All-Ireland final replay, having had a huge impact in the drawn game as a sub and started well before breaking my kneecap. *Time now for him to pack it in.* I was an All Star 12 months later.

It is the end of 2021 and while there have been some changes in personnel, the most prominent individuals are still there apart from Joe Brolly, who was thankfully replaced but is still gainfully employed as a pundit with other media organisations. Week after week, they display a complete absence of understanding of what county teams are doing. Their analysis is basic and while I understand that they are strapped for time, they have access to all the same software county managements have and could at least have some information on which to base their pronouncements.

There is an onus on analysis to evolve along with the game and while *The Sunday Game* has fancy graphics and technology, they have too many of the same people talking about the game. The sad aspect of it is that their ill-informed analysis of a game they knew about 30 and 40 years ago but not in its evolved iteration continues to set agendas in the GAA, be it with disciplinary incidents or the constant introduction of new rules.

You would think the elite coaches would be consulted in these matters, but they are viewed as the enemy threatening the fabric of the ancient game. You rarely see much manager approval when the latest hare-brained alteration is made. It is Croke Park reacting to the perception that the game needs to be more of a spectacle, because the lads in the comfy seats are saying it was better in their day.

Yet even the vaguest perusals of history show how scoring rates have increased. Coaching innovation and improved game understanding have increased the ability of teams with less resources than the powerhouses to compete.

It's fine to think these TV panels are good fun and that they prompt debate, but the absence of balance has been notable. They pick on a team and never let up. Galway were just one of those teams.

And the problem with that, is that the commentary seeps into the minds of referees. It also seeps into the minds of supporters and the general public outside of the county. Maybe they don't recognise their influence. If not, it's time they took it on board.

They don't analyse the refereeing properly either, though they might be under orders in that regard. But I see no reason why the referee and his team of officials are not subject to the same rigours of commentary that players and management are. It has yet to be explained well enough to me.

How do I know about TV commentary? I always tried to get a look at it, because my managerial style was to listen to everyone. I have no ego in that regard. If I could pick up something that might make me a better coach and manager, and improve the team as a result, I didn't care where it came from. Somebody might pick something up that I missed.

There wasn't much value in the analysis on *The Sunday Game* though. Just unbalanced, playing-to-the-gallery tripe.

I always said I wanted players dealing in facts, not hope.

A lot of these so-called analysts in particular dealt in headlines and didn't seem to want to put in the work to gather the information that was out there.

There is a real void in terms of deep analysis of games that isn't so infatuated with entertainment over substance. Put on a programme on Monday or Tuesday of an hour or 90 minutes, breaking down the games in a professional manner, to at least offer people some insight, and an accurate portrayal of the events as they occurred rather than some gut instinct or commentary founded on 'how things were in my day'.

You would find a true picture of what is occurring in a team and individual sense, with players not being granted superstar status solely for being flashy or fortunate to be on the end of things. Proper analysis would ensure the spotlight landed in the correct areas.

The popularity of what Gary Neville and Jamie Carragher do on *Sky Sports Soccer* on a Monday night is proof that you can get that balance right, breaking down how a corner kick routine is coached, why so much of the play is down one flank, how a defender's stance is all wrong when faced with a striker running at him. All done in an entertaining manner.

THE ALL-IRELAND semi-final in 2018 is a standout case of completely inaccurate analysis. It was as if Dublin had sauntered to victory, a triumph for creativity and expression over the evil forces of destruction and doom.

Yet the tally of when both teams had 15 men behind the ball in that game was 15-14, almost identical – but with Dublin protecting their goals in that fashion on one more occasion.

In attacking terms, Galway created 18 scoring chances in the first-half compared to Dublin's 12. Galway scored 1-7 and missed 2-8, including a penalty. Dublin scored 1-9.

None of these facts support the commentary that Dublin were the team doing all the attacking, Galway only interested in holding a defensive pattern and hoping for the best. We didn't get an ounce of credit for our game plan, the success of the tactics and the creativity it promoted.

You see it often, when a goalkeeper is being criticised for kicking a ball down the one wing all the time, despite his team not winning possession. How some of these pundits cannot understand that he is playing to instruction is beyond me.

What is assuredly beyond them is that you might be purposely overloading on one side, with one or two other options for the kickout and the overload used if the other options cannot be hit safely. And that you might have set up in such a way so as to ensure that despite losing seven out of nine of those kickouts, you will win back four or five of those.

And by winning them back, you have sucked in the opposition and can expose them on the counter by moving the ball very quickly. Something we did often.

That won't show well in the kickout stats, but you have to know what stats are important. When Leicester won the Premier League, they had the second lowest possession figures and conceded the highest number of turnovers. Neither inhibited their ability to win games though.

They conceded turnovers in parts of the pitch that didn't matter, and with the defensive shield provided by N'Golo Kanté, the passing of Danny Drinkwater and the pace and finishing prowess of Jamie Vardy and Riyad Mahrez, they murdered teams on the counter.

Their success rate from chances created was almost double what the second team in that particular table managed.

Trying to force turnovers high up the pitch would be madness against Dublin in Croke Park, unless you have 15 players on the pitch who are consistently hard workers. They would destroy you in behind and that was what happened at the end as we had to try get the ball back once we were in arrears. You brought their players into channels they weren't comfortable in. You slowed the pace.

There were other teams you felt you could outshoot, and we would concede more against them than we would against stronger teams. It was convenient to ignore the big tallies we constantly racked up and the kick passing we deployed in those games, when the narrative was that we were the most defensive team in Ireland, shovelling hand passes around because we hadn't the skills or ambition to do anything else.

We would kick the ball if there was somewhere to kick it to, but we weren't going to give it away cheaply. Just as Dublin don't.

Educated analysis would lift the lid on the countless different systems being deployed in a game. Instead, we get a comedy show where even the rudiments of the game escape most of the analysts. It is hard for them to provide insight and education when they don't have the technical or tactical experience. It's just the same old story.

We see it now with Galway, where the narrative is that Pádraic Joyce has completely dispensed with his predecessor's systems and freed the poor Galway forwards from oppression. Yet it was Shane Walsh giving away a penalty in the very first National League game against Monaghan in 2020. Conor Gleeson saved Conor McManus' kick and Galway won by a point.

Now I understand, it's a new manager, a new story but in actual fact, the old narrative continues. The big bad wolf has been replaced and Joyce will have Galway zipping it around without a care for defensive solidity and structure.

Pádraic is not a foolish man. He will bring his own strengths and philosophies to the mix of course, rightly so. But he knows that to win an All-Ireland you have to set up well and I wasn't surprised that he didn't throw the baby out with the bathwater; that the arc defence, for example, was still in use to a large degree.

And we saw him revert to setting up well for the championship outing against Mayo last November - after a gung-ho approach in the first game of resumed activity in the league the previous month had concluded with a 15-point defeat and the concession of 3-23 to James Horan's crew. That kept the heavy-scoring Mayo to just 14 points in the championship, though Galway did not create enough and missed a few scoring opportunities, and fell agonisingly short by one point.

Yet, seeing Shane continue to work hard for the team in all aspects of the game confirmed how he embraced our coaching.

Don't expect to hear that said on *The Sunday Game* anytime soon.

CHAPTER 28

THE NEXT EPISODE

We have a powerful potential in our youth, and we must have the courage to change old ideas and practices so that we may direct their power toward good ends.
– Mary McLeod Bethune

I am a beginner only once, but a student forever.
– Wladimir Klitschko

LIFE IS ABOUT reinvention and innovation, without ever losing track of your core principles. Injury forced progression on me in my playing days, as I developed a style conducive to using the capabilities I still had as much as I could.

I could only jump for a certain amount of kickouts and running at defences was a thing of the past on most occasions. But I learned to look around, to see a bigger picture and recognise far more was going on than I had considered as a 20 year-old.

That made me a better player for the team. I contributed far more winning possession, laying it off and getting back in the hole to close off the channels available to the opposition, than I ever did looking flash tearing up and down the field. I would always make sure to be in a position to help my team-mates.

That gives me a lot of satisfaction, that I rolled with the punches and finished my career with a couple of All-Irelands and three All Stars, because I was a team player rather than an individual.

The way I'm wired though, for all the successes, I think of the ones that got away. And there were a few. We could have gone down as among the all-time greats. That sort of legacy was there for the taking.

You don't want to be greedy when you have two All-Irelands but never being satisfied was probably a constant driver. You could always do better.

That ethos of the collective would be at the epicentre of my coaching and I gathered as much professionalism as I could around me to supply it. Technology advanced through my 10 years, making the 'Show me, Don't tell me' aspect of teaching easier. I developed better methods of breaking down so many of the skills I took for granted having used them myself.

All the time, I learned about leadership and other key aspects of culture creation, but I never strayed from caring for players, a policy that went all the way back to my childhood and upbringing. You thought of others and looked after people.

I MADE AN awful lot of friends along the way, in Sligo and Galway. I value those highly.

Doon, Rosscahill and Killannin is where I am rooted however. The club and the locals were staunch in their support in bad times and good.

Family will always be my anchor and whatever there has been worth writing about, wouldn't have existed without Mary. While Galway became successful in the latter end of my playing career, we were both in the guards, often on night shifts, while our family was expanding rapidly.

When it came to the annual consideration about what to do in the future, it always came back to what I felt I could offer and if I was wanted, as long as I was willing to put in the effort and could handle everything else. Mary's backing was unflinching. Total.

We often passed each other at the door or did handovers with the kids on the side of the road from one car to another. It can't have been easy, but Mary brought a gaggle of infants with her to the games. She and I are cut from the same cloth. We espouse the same values and I am proud that the kids have the same standards now too.

They needed them as they had to put up with a lot in the course of my management career. So did my mother. They could separate themselves from the bile, even if it cannot have been easy to see their husband, father and son be subjected to it a lot. They knew I was able for it and my concern was always the impact it might have on them.

It certainly had an impact on the players in the end, mentally and in actuality in terms of how they were being treated on the pitch.

IT IS IMPORTANT to emphasise that the vast majority of Galway supporters have always expressed complete kindness towards me. The amount of goodwill after I stood down as manager was incredible. Sligo was the same.

The number of people that rang, sent cards and texts, or came up to me at games was a mighty lift.

The real supporter backed me as a dyed-in-the-wool Galwegian who wanted only what was best for the team and gave my all to that end for most of my adult life.

Every tribe has its loudmouths and I would never let the actions of a few tar my opinion of the many. My relationship with the Sligo supporters was just as good and there were many messages of thanks from people I didn't know after I finished there in 2013. They were all deeply appreciated.

I may return to county management one day, and I may not. I would view myself as a coach first and foremost, in both Gaelic games and basketball.

Brian, Seán and I are excited, enthusiastic and passionate about GrowCoach (www.growcoach.ie). We feel we have a lot in the locker that we can share and our success in the county environment over a sustained period tells us we can empower coaches and impact players, at every level.

It is not about being dogmatic and saying, 'This is the only way'.

I believe, fervently, that we in the GAA are missing the boat. That there is a whole spectrum that hasn't been explored, that we remain focussed too much on when we have the ball.

The traditionalists are blanching even as they read those words. They think there is too much running, too much emphasis on defence and that the players aren't as skilful as they were.

That's rubbish.

During the Covid-19 lockdown through 2020, I looked at some of the old games I had never watched before. A lot of them were poor. I knew Galway were more direct - all teams were in that era - but I was genuinely surprised by how much ball was hoofed away without the head ever being lifted.

With GrowCoach, we want to offer a deeper level of coaching while breaking it down simply. Not all of it is for everyone. But I hope some of it will be eye-opening and people might dip in and out.

Because we know as a fact now, that for an 80-minute county game, allowing for injury time, the most a player will spend on the ball, on average, is a minute. So you need to coach for the players to make an impact, offensively and defensively, during the 79 minutes they do not have possession.

Doesn't that make sense?

To coach the invisible game, rather than viewing the action entirely through the prism of the supporter, only ever seeing the player with the ball?

Anyone interested in being a high-level coach will trawl every resource possible to improve themselves. Some of our television analysts would get a serious fright if they looked up the UEFA coaching manual for soccer. The detail just on midfield defence as an individual and a unit is mind-blowing. There is so much that isn't happening in GAA.

Certainly, the feedback we have received from our workshops around the country, and since putting on webinars online has been extremely positive.

JUST BEFORE I finished up with Galway, I met up with Damien Comer, the team captain, for an hour and a half. My message to him was that he and the rest of the lads in their mid-twenties would determine where the squad would go from here. The likes of Gareth Bradshaw and Gary O'Donnell were at their maximum, giving everything they have already in that regard.

You need Damien, Shane Walsh, Ian Burke, Tom Flynn and others to become proper leaders now, not just players with ability, because the newcomers and lads that were introduced last year will need that

Pádraic Joyce has come in and been kind in acknowledging the strength of what he has inherited, compared to when I got the job.

That strength is there in experience, in skill, in game understanding, in hardness, in physicality, in expression, in creativity. Pádraic is putting his own style into that and with luck in terms of injuries, the odd bounce of the ball, referees' decisions and taking the chances when they are created, they are well placed to go all the way.

The priority now must be to win Connacht and not allow Galway endure another lengthy famine with regard to provincial primacy. While a few players have made themselves unavailable, our greatest opponent, Mayo lost the majority of their stalwarts to retirement after the 2020 All-Ireland defeat to Dublin. It is never easy in our province, with Roscommon, Sligo, Leitrim and New York to contend with also, but winning is a habit and so is losing. We only have to look at where we were when I became manager, when Mayo were the *Dublin* of Connacht.

But I believe the players and the expertise are there, and if Pádraic gets the resources he needs from the county board, Galway will become No.1 in Connacht again. From there, they can then turn their sights on winning the All-Ireland.

No-one would be happier than me.

Meanwhile, I will help out with Killannin, particularly in setting up processes and structures that will really flourish given the remarkable volunteer work and community spirit of Rosscahill.

The way I think about football has clearly developed over the years. Like everything, it has been a journey.

And it all started at home.

With my mother and father.

On the hillside holding.

In Doon.

MORE
GREAT
SPORTS BOOKS
FROM
HEROBOOKS

www.**HERO**BOOKS.digital

GALWAY
GAME OF MY LIFE

TWENTY-FIVE OF Galway's greatest hurlers remember the one game that will live with them forever ...

including Jimmy Hegarty, Ned Dervan, Andy Fenton, Iggy Clarke, Sean Silke, Joe Connolly, PJ Molloy, Noel Lane, John Connolly, Mike Conneely, Anthony Cunningham, Pete Finnerty, Eanna Ryan, Gerry McInerney, John Commins, Michael Coleman, Micheál Donoghue, Padraig Kelly, Kevin Broderick, Ger Farragher, David Collins, Ollie Canning, Alan Kerins, Fergal Moore and Gearoid McInerney

... the day that defined their lives.

Author: Ollie Turner
Print Price: €20.00
Ebook: €9.99
ISBN: 9781910827284

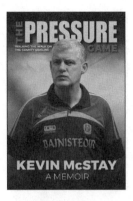

The Pressure Game
Kevin McStay: An Autobiography

FOR THE FIRST time one of the top GAA managers in the country has revealed the inside story of what it's like to 'Walk the Walk on a County Sideline'. Former Mayo Allstar footballer Kevin McStay gave up 20 years of working as a commentator and analyst on RTE's Sunday Game to take up the position of Roscommon team manager in 2016.

The whole country watched to see how he would survive on the sideline – and how he would face up to the pressures of facing Jim's Gavin's Dublin, Mayo and Kerry and Tyrone, on the toughest stage in Gaelic football.

In his three years in charge, McStay led Roscommon to a Connacht title in 2017 and a prized place in the Super 8s in 2018 before quitting the job. He has now returned to the RTE broadcasting booth.

This is the amazing inside story of the *The Pressure Game*.

Authors: Kevin McStay with Liam Hayes
Print Price: €20.00
Ebook: €10.00
ISBN: 9781910827086

Available on
Amazon
Apple Books
Kobo
And all good online stores

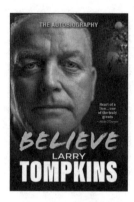

BELIEVE

Larry Tompkins: An Autobiography

HIS SELF-BELIEF WAS unbreakable.

His iron will inspirational.

Nothing could stop Larry Tompkins. No man, no team, as he made his football life the greatest story ever told in the long and brilliant history of the GAA.

Six years with his native Kildare left him empty-handed and heartbroken. He emigrated to New York to find a job and find a team he could lead to championship glory. In the United States, Tompkins' belief in himself never dimmed. He led Donegal to four New York championships in the Big Apple. He also found a new home for himself in Ireland and led Castlehaven to two Cork and Munster titles. In between, he also became the most valuable and feared footballer in Ireland.

BELIEVE is the story of a man who defied all the odds. In Cork's magnificent red shirt, he led his adopted county to two All-Ireland titles in 1989 and 90, one National League and six Munster titles, and he also was honoured with three Allstar awards.

Upon his retirement, Larry Tompkins continued to lead and inspire, and make others believe too. He managed Cork for seven years, winning Munster glory again, and drove Cork to the 1999 All-Ireland final where they agonisingly came up short.

BELIEVE is a story which proves to everyone, in every sport, that anything is possible and everything is there to be won!

Authors: Larry Tompkins with Denis Hurley
Print Price: €20.00
Ebook: €10.00
ISBN: 9781910827123

Available on

Amazon
Apple Books
Kobo
And all good online stores

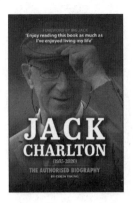

Jack Charlton
The Authorised Biography

AS ONE OF the true legends of Irish and English football, Jack Charlton was a man both loved and feared, but now the people who have lived with him all of his life introduce the real 'Big Jack' in this brilliant authorised biography which is presented in a foreword by Jack himself.

For the first time Jack's wife and family, his teammates as a World Cup winner with England in 1966, and his players during his management years with Middlesbrough, Sheffield Wednesday, Newcastle, and Ireland tell their stories of the man who dominated their lives.

Graeme Souness, Chris Waddle, and Peter Beardsley amongst others, are joined by Mick McCarthy, Niall Quinn and the greatest footballers who played under Big Jack for 10 years as Ireland team boss.

This is the most personable, inviting and intimate account of Jack Charlton's life, and the book contains photographs published for the first time from Jack and Pat Charlton's personal collection.

Jack Charlton: The Authorised Biography is written by former Daily Mail Northern Football Correspondent, Colin Young.

Author: Colin Young
Print Price: €20.00
Ebook: €10.00
ISBN: 9781910827017

Available on
Amazon

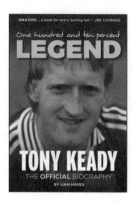

One Hundred and Ten Percent Legend
Tony Keady: The Official Biography

WHEN TONY KEADY died suddenly in August of 2017, at just 53 years of age, a whole county mourned and the rest of the country stopped in its tracks to say goodbye to a legend of the game of hurling.

Except Tony Keady was more than a legend.

In 1988, after leading Galway to a second All-Ireland title in succession, he was crowned the greatest hurler in Ireland. He was 25 years of age and there was nobody like him, nobody to touch him in the maroon No.6 shirt.

But, four years later, and still not 30, after being wrongly banned for 12 months by the GAA, he was also discarded by his own county and refused a maroon jersey the very last time he walked out onto Croke Park behind the Galway team.

A few months before his death, Tony Keady visited Liam Hayes and told him he wished to tell his own story. He felt it was time, but tragically time was not on Tony's side. One month after he died Galway won the All-Ireland title for the first time since 1988, and 80,000 people rose from their seats in the sixth minute of the game to applaud and remember a man who was more than a legend

Tony's wife, Margaret and his daughter, Shannon and his three boys, Anthony, Harry and Jake, decided to finish telling the story of a father and a hurler who always asked those around him for '110%'.

Author: Liam Hayes
Price: €20.00
ISBN: 9781910827048

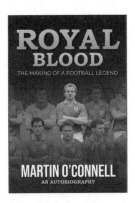

Royal Blood
Martin O'Connell: An Autobiography

THREE TIMES ALL-IRELAND winner, Martin O'Connell was crowned the prince of wing backs in 2000 when he was selected on the GAA's Team of the Millennium, and had a postage stamp issued in his honour.

This honour also stamped O'Connell's name down in Meath football history as the greatest of the greats.

As a Meath footballer, O'Connell truly had Royal Blood. He was a central player on Sean Boylan's 1987 and 88 All-Ireland winning teams, and then remained with Boylan to win a third All-Ireland in 1996 in an infamous replayed final against Mayo.

Now, O'Connell reveals the inside story of those battling years, and explains how it might never have happened after he quit the Meath team in the mid 80s. But his love of the game brought him back.

In addition to his three All-Irelands, Martin O'Connell won six Leinster titles and three National league titles and in 1996 was named Footballer of the Year. After retiring from the Meath team he continued playing football with St Michael's, his club and his first love in football, until he was 42 years old.

Authors: Martin O'Connell and David Sheehan
Print Price: €20.00
Ebook: €10.00
ISBN: 9781910827109